# Beyond Book Sales

Neal-Schuman purchases fund advocacy, awareness, and
accreditation programs for library professionals worldwide.

# Beyond Book Sales

The Complete Guide
to **Raising Real Money**
for Your Library

## EDITED BY SUSAN DOWD

for Library Strategies
*A Consulting Group of*
*The Friends of the Saint Paul Public Library*

**Consultants who contributed to this book:**

LIZ BOYD

SUSAN DOWD

SUE HALL

ANN McKINNON

WENDY MOYLAN

PETER PEARSON

Neal-Schuman

An imprint of the American Library Association

Chicago   2014

**Susan Dowd** is a staff member of The Friends of the Saint Paul Public Library, where she serves as Capital Campaign Coordinator and Special Projects Coordinator. She is also a consultant for Library Strategies. She holds a master's degree in librarianship from Emory University and is certified in fund-raising and fund development from the University of Saint Thomas. She has authored a number of advocacy and fund-raising toolkits for ALA's Advocacy University and coauthored a how-to book on mergers for Minnesota nonprofits. She collaborated on *Beyond Book Sales: The Complete Guide to Raising Real Money for Your Library* with fellow Friends' staff members and Library Strategies' consultants Liz Boyd, Sue Hall, Ann McKinnon, Wendy Moylan, and Peter Pearson.

© 2014 by the American Library Association.

Printed in the United States of America

18  17  16  15  14      5  4  3  2  1

Extensive effort has gone into ensuring the reliability of the information in this book; however, the publisher makes no warranty, express or implied, with respect to the material contained herein.

ISBNs: 978-1-55570-912-9 (paper); 978-1-55570-892-7 (PDF).

**Library of Congress Cataloging-in-Publication Data**

Beyond book sales : the complete guide to raising real money for your library / edited by Susan
    Dowd for Library Strategies, a consulting group of The Friends of the Saint Paul Public
    Library; consultants who contributed to this book: Liz Boyd, Susan Dowd, Sue Hall,
    McKinnon, Wendy Moylan, Peter Pearson.
        pages   cm
    Includes bibliographical references and index.
    ISBN 978-1-55570-912-9 (alk. paper)
    1. Library fund raising—United States.   I. Dowd, Susan.  II. Library Strategies.
  III. Saint Paul Public Library. Friends.
    Z683.2.U6B49 2014
    025.1'1—dc23                                                  2013017139

Cover design by Kimberly Thornton. Illustration © Ufuk ZIVANA / Shutterstock, Inc.
Text design in the Chapparal, Interstate, and Popular typefaces.

♾ This paper meets the requirements of ANSI/NISO Z39.48–1992 (Permanence of Paper).

# contents

Chapter 6    **Ready, Set, Go!**    **43**

Chapter 7    **Thanking, Honoring, and Nurturing Your Donors . . . and Keeping Track of Them**    **51**

Chapter 8    **The Role of Marketing and Public Relations in Library Fund-Raising**    **61**

# foreword

**IKE MOST SUCCESSFUL WRITERS, I HAVE PERSONALLY** experienced the transformative power of the public library. Several years ago, I became aware of the tragic lack of funding for libraries. I found it shocking that states and municipalities were cutting into the very backbone of our educational infrastructure. I have made it my personal mission to do as much as I can for libraries, whether supporting them through my trust, Save the Libraries, or speaking to the Georgia State House on the importance of a well-read citizenry. I think my experience represents a microcosm of the greater tragedy that has struck library systems all over the world.

In the United States, it is a fact that every dollar spent on public libraries returns $5 to the community. Eighty percent of our incarcerated juveniles are functionally illiterate. Adults who are unable to read are twice as likely to end up in prison as those who can. The math is simple: a child who reads does well in school. A student who does well in school goes to college. A college graduate earns a better living and not only pays more taxes, but has more disposable income to spend on services. They are also more likely to raise children who value education and reading and will in turn follow the education path of their parents. Contrast that with the millions of dollars spent every year on truants and in the juvenile justice system and you'll find an exponential gain in investment by simply keeping the doors of our local libraries open.

This is but one argument I've found helpful in persuading politicians and local businesses to get on board with library fund-raising: by investing in libraries, they are making a fiscally sound choice for their communities. This message is catching on. In the past few years, there has been a great deal of national media attention given to the plight of today's libraries, and this attention has stimulated an uptick in citizens' public support of their libraries. It's difficult to predict, however, whether this attention and goodwill will convert into financial support; and, frankly, simply hoping that it will happen is not a good strategy.

It's time for libraries large and small to mobilize and focus on serious fund-raising. The consequences of leaving future library budgets in the hands of local public decision-makers alone will sound the death knell for many beloved libraries. It is an unfortunate reality that very few librarians are prepared to be fund-raisers. Even many of those with a master's degree in library science are woefully inexperienced (and often intimidated) by the idea of asking for money. To make matters worse, the day-to-day challenges facing any library director leave precious little time for taking on the additional task of mounting a comprehensive fund-raising effort.

That is why practical, achievable help is at hand in the pages of this book. This new resource will go a long way toward helping every librarian, trustee, Friend of the Library, and library lover avoid the pitfalls of fund-raising. In it you'll find great ideas and specific suggestions for conducting all types of fund-raising activities. You'll learn how to create a plan and identify partners to help you realize your goals. Outlined within this book are clear, concrete tools for implementing the activities you will include in your fund-raising plan. The authors have even included a gallery of examples of fund-raising materials created by libraries that are leading the way in the brave new world of library fund-raising. However you choose to approach this book, do it with the knowledge that whatever plan you implement, you are moving in an essential direction for your library's future.

I can think of no other warriors who are better prepared for battle than the men and women who have historically been on the front lines of literacy. Good luck!

*Karin Slaughter*

# preface

## Welcome to Library Fund-Raising

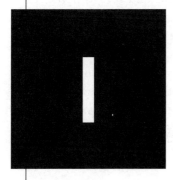**N THIS NEW MILLENNIUM, PUBLIC LIBRARIANS, STAFF,** and library supporters have reached an overwhelming conclusion: *If public libraries are going to remain strong, people must get creative about funding them.* The old model of banking on public revenues and occasional special funds—and hoping for the best—has gone the way of the card catalog. It has been replaced by purposeful library fund-raising designed to keep existing programs and services strong and provide opportunities for innovation.

Library fund-raising is beautiful in its flexibility. It can be adapted to meet the needs and resources of public libraries and communities of any size, ranging from the smallest library's book or bake sale to huge urban library galas and generous corporate underwriting. It can be simple or sophisticated. It can involve the efforts of a few people or hundreds of people. And the best news of all? It can be sized to fit *your library* perfectly. Regardless of the size or complexity of library fund-raising, it is always about forging and strengthening relationships with the stakeholders in a library's community.

The American Library Association (ALA) believes that private fund-raising is essential for U.S. libraries' future survival. Under the leadership of President Roberta Stevens in 2010–2011, the ALA deepened its resources for private fund-raising, developing the association's first online fund-raising toolkit. The toolkit was added to the ALA website's "Advocacy University" as part of its wide array of online help for libraries seeking advocacy and fund-raising assistance.

Whether your library undertakes only occasional fund-raising projects, or is well along in this effort and wants to become more successful, the chapters that follow are designed to guide you through proven methods of effective library fund-raising. They will help you think about raising dollars in new ways, about going beyond your traditional fund-raising activities. In fact, because so many libraries already know how to do book sales (and other kinds of sales) successfully, this book will not include that topic, except to offer one piece of advice: when selling books or other merchandise, determine how you can connect your sale to the other fund-raising that you do. For example, take advantage of the interest in your sale to promote membership in your Friends organization, as well as annual, special, tribute, and memorial giving. Whenever possible, gather names of customers at your sale and add them to your database for future fund-raising solicitation.

Instead of reading more about sales, however, you will learn the importance of developing a strong case for supporting your library, nurturing relationships, employing a broad range of fund-raising techniques (including the Internet), and moving your library's fund-raising from hit-or-miss to solid and successful. Part I, "Focus on Fund-Raising," will help you think through your fund-raising needs and position your library to be a strong partner for private supporters. You'll be guided through the process of assessing your library's strengths and challenges, developing a fund-raising plan, building an effective fund-raising team (perhaps through your current board, Friends group, or Foundation), identifying potential funding partners, and building relationships that benefit both your library *and* its funders. You'll learn to understand what motivates donors to give generously and why thanks and recognition are important. Throughout Part I, you will find paths to the "Fund-Raising Toolkit" where there are easy-to-use tools that break down new challenges into manageable tasks.

In Part II, "Roll Up Your Sleeves," you will find a wealth of good advice and more practical tools for a wide range of fund-raising activities, from the simplest annual fund to the grandest gala. If you have a small annual fund effort that needs improvement, or want to begin an annual Fund-Raising campaign, start here. If you have ever considered soliciting memorial, tribute, or major gifts—or if you know that planned giving (such as gifts made through a will) is important but don't know where to begin—there are several chapters that cover these in detail. If you want to identify opportunities to partner with businesses (as library sponsors or underwriters) and to apply for grants from corporations and foundations, this book can make both of these feel easy and natural. If your library is in serious need of capital improvements, but you find the thought of raising large sums of money through a capital campaign terrifying, *Beyond Book Sales: The Complete Guide to Raising Real Money for Your Library* will hold your hand through every step of that multi-year process. If you feel daunted by online fund-raising, you can learn how to adapt your website and utilize social networks to use the Web effectively for library fund-raising. If you believe that everyone loves a party, library fund-raising events can run the gamut from punch and cookies to black-tie galas with best-selling authors. Your library's special event "sweet spot" is somewhere along that spectrum, and this book will help you find it for maximum results.

Regardless of your level of experience in library fund-raising, you will finish this book with fresh ideas and an eagerness to roll up your sleeves and start raising dollars for your library.

*Library Strategies is a consulting group of The Friends of The Saint Paul Public Library, created in response to increasing requests for services from libraries and library organizations. The mission of Library Strategies is to provide the highest-quality consulting services to support libraries and all library organizations. Our consultants are both leaders in the library community and outstanding specialists in other fields who offer a wide range of practical skills and decades of successful experience.*

PART ONE

# Focus on Fund-Raising— Fund-amentals for Libraries

# 1

# Libraries Need
# Fund-Raising More Than Ever

**THIS CHAPTER COULD JUST BE THE SHORTEST IN HISTORY, IN FACT, JUST** one word: crisis.

"Budget Cuts Force Charlotte Libraries to Shut Down," "Library Cuts Threaten Research," "Residents Protest Library Cutbacks" are just a few of the many headlines we see with increasing frequency. As cities, counties, and other government branches face budget deficits and struggle with service cutbacks and employee layoffs, libraries (particularly public and school libraries) struggle too. Temporary downturns in funding used to be just that: temporary—something people simply weathered. That old adage, "This too shall pass" was the mantra. That is no longer the case because the foreseeable future appears to be one of permanent fiscal challenge, even crisis, for libraries of all kinds. But this book is not about doom and gloom; it's about what you can do to lift up your library when circumstances combine to bring it down.

The challenges libraries face are not unique. All nonprofit institutions are readjusting their practices and seeking new revenue streams. Creativity and persistence are the buzzwords of today, and there are more opportunities for creativity than ever before. Later chapters of this book will tell you why and how.

## Library Use Is Increasing

How much time do you spend thinking about the ways your library matters to your community? Have you ever counted all the hats library staff are asked to wear? Try listing them. You might be surprised at how long the list is. In many communities, library use is at an all-time high. It's a well-known fact that library use increases in times of economic stress, and these challenging times confirm that fact just about everywhere. Door counts are up, computers have waiting lists, and people want their libraries to be open longer hours. They're also demanding a broader range of services than ever before. Gone are the days when people went to their library solely to check out books and music. Today, they want their libraries to offer multi-language resources and programs, skill-building classes, help with resumes and job searches, and more. They want libraries to be kids' places, teen places, and meeting places. Today's library staffers are teachers and counselors too.

A report released in 2011 by the Online Computer Library Center (OCLC) found that, in 2010, over three-fourths of Americans used the Internet. Researchers called this group "information consumers." The authors state, "In 2010, 68% of information consumers had a library card. For those Americans economically impacted, that rate was even higher—81%. Information consumers who have experienced a job impact were not just getting library cards at greater rates; they were using the library for more services and more often in 2010. And their perception of library value was significantly [higher] than those not impacted" (OCLC 2011, 5).

In 2009, the American Library Association published a report titled *The Condition of U.S. Libraries: Trends 1999–2009*. It chronicles library use, comparing 2006 and 2009 data. Researchers found that library use has increased between 2006 and 2009.

In 2011, a Harris telephone survey of 1,012 adults over age 18 found that nearly *two-thirds of Americans reported using their public library, either in person, by telephone, or computer in the past year.*

A similar Harris Poll was conducted in 2010. Comparing the results between 2010 and 2011, Harris Polls revealed that:

> Americans continue to value the importance of services provided by public libraries. In fact, when considering a list of eleven library services, two-thirds or more of the American public consider every factor to be very or somewhat important to them personally, surpassing the proportions in the 2010 study. The most highly valued services pertain to the provision of free information and services that promote education and lifelong learning.

---

25.4 million Americans in 2009 reported using their public library more than 20 times in the last year, up *25 percent* (from 20.3 million households) in 2006.

The average number of in-person public library visits *rose 40 percent* from 9.1 per year in 2006 to 12.7 per year in 2009.

Use of the public library by computer (from home, work, or school) *doubled* from 2006 to 2009 (6 times per year, *up* from 2.9 times in 2006).

(ALA Office for Research and Statistics, *The Condition of U.S. Libraries: Trends 1999-2009, 2009*)

---

Twenty-nine percent (29%) of respondents said their library use *increased* during the past six months.

Among those who have visited the library by computer, one third report *increasing* their public library access by computer over the past six months.

Seventy percent (70%) reported feeling *extremely/very satisfied* with their public library.

When comparing the public library to other tax-supported services, almost one-third of adults (31%) ranked the library *at the top* of the list.

(ALA Report, "January 2011 Harris Poll Quorum Results," 2011)

More than nine in ten Americans (93%) believe that it is very important
or somewhat important that library services are free, representing an
increase of two percentage points from 2010.

Similar proportions place great value in the library's provision of information for school and work (91%, up five percentage points), as well as the
fact that the library provides a place for lifelong learning (90%, up three
percentage points), and that the library enhances one's education (89%,
up five percentage points).

Eighty-four percent of adults consider it very or somewhat important that
the library serves as a community center, is a source of cultural programs
and activities (83%, up four percentage points from a year earlier), and
provides computer access, training, and support (83%, up seven percentage points).

Three-quarters of Americans consider it very or somewhat important that
the library provides health information (75%, up two percentage points)
and financial information (75%, up six percentage points) that is accurate
and up-to-date.

(ALA News and Press Center, *The State of America's Libraries, 2011*.
www.ala.org/news/mediapresscenter/americaslibraries/publiclibraries.)

# Libraries Matter

It's clear that, as the gap between rich and poor and the resulting "digital divide"
continues to widen, more people than ever before must rely on the library for important resources—particularly computers. State and local governments continue to
cut costs by requiring individuals to access their services *online,* and people flock to
their libraries for this purpose. Without a computer, it's nearly impossible to apply
for government assistance, register for school, or look for work.

Computers are essential for social contact today. E-mail and social networking are
two of the most important ways we connect to one another in our modern world.

> **Words to Know**
>
> *Digital divide* refers to the gap
> between people who have access to
> computers and digital information
> and those with limited or no access.

If you don't own a computer, or if you can't access one from
work or school, the library is the place you go to use one. Even
if you do have access to a computer, if it doesn't offer high-
speed Internet service, you're not likely to use it if you have
another alternative.

All this technology, however, can also isolate us. When
everyone is in his or her own private world—chatting, tex-
ting, e-mailing, tweeting, and posting on others' Facebook walls—face-to-face
social interaction becomes less frequent. The library provides "people space" where
individuals can interact with others in story times, book clubs, classes, teen groups,
and senior activities. The library has been described as "the community's living
room," and that is a very good description of the function it serves for many people.

Libraries also matter to the economic health of their communities. They are partners in economic development, providing resources to small businesses and other community organizations and serving as the go-to place for employment searches. Many of the individuals walking into the library to look for work have never before sought employment using a computer. Many have limited English skills or have never written a resume. Many are people who haven't looked for work in decades because they thought their jobs were secure. Without the library—and librarians who can provide personal assistance—the community would face huge challenges in serving this population of job seekers, and local businesses would face longer periods of time with unfilled jobs.

A study published in March 2009 by Library Research Service looked at eight public libraries representing geographically, economically, and demographically diverse regions of Colorado. Using these libraries, researchers quantified the return on investment (ROI) to taxpayers for monies invested in public libraries. For most of the libraries participating in the study *the ROI was five to one—that is, for every $1.00 spent on public libraries, $5.00 of value was realized by taxpayers* (Steffen et al. 2009, v). An ROI study published in a February 2011 issue of *Library Leadership & Management* found similar results. Its author states, "The use of Return on Investment studies in a library setting have produced ROI numbers that are quite variable, although many seem to group in the *$4 to $6* of benefits for each dollar spent by the library" (Matthews 2011, 11).

> ## Words to Know
>
> *Return on investment* (or *ROI*) is a cost analysis process that measures the cost of a program or service versus the financial return realized by that program or service.

As school library services are cut back and even eliminated in some school systems (an action once thought incomprehensible), parents, teachers, and students rely more heavily on public libraries than ever before. Libraries are the lifeblood of learning. They are essential for students at *all* levels, and they're the only place where many preschoolers can obtain the skills they need for school readiness. The library provides young children with opportunities to build literacy abilities they'll carry with them into school—and into life.

The conclusion is clear: libraries of all kinds are more utilized and more important than ever today. For libraries to survive, alternate means of funding must be sought, and the clock is ticking.

## REFERENCES

ALA News and Press Center, *The State of America's Libraries, 2011.* www.ala.org/news/mediapresscenter/americaslibraries/publiclibraries.

ALA Office for Research and Statistics. 2009. *The Condition of U.S. Libraries: Trends 1999–2009.* http://ala.org/ala/research/initiatives/Condition_of_Libraries_1999.20.pdf.

ALA Report. 2011. "January 2011 Harris Poll Quorum Results." January 26, 2011, www.ala.org/research/sites/ala.org.research/files/content/librarystats/2011harrispoll.pdf.

Matthews, Joseph R. 2011. "What's the Return on ROI? The Benefits and Challenges of Calculating Your Library's Return on Investment." *Library Leadership & Management* 25, no. 1:1–14. http://journals.tdl.org/llm/issue/current.

Online Computer Library Center. 2011. *Perceptions of Libraries, 2010: Context and Community.* Dublin, Ohio: OCLC.

Steffen, Nicole, Zeth Lietzau, Keith Curry Lance, Amanda Rybin, and Carla Molliconi. 2009. *Public Libraries—A Wise Investment: A Return on Investment Study of Colorado Libraries.* Library Research Service. www.lrs.org/documents/closer_look/roi.pdf.

# 2

# Four Reasons Why
# Now Is a Good Time for
# Library Fund-Raising

**WISDOM SAYS THERE'S NO TIME LIKE THE PRESENT. THIS IS ESPECIALLY** true for library fund-raising, and it's true for four reasons:

## 1. There Are More Ways Than Ever to Connect with Donors

It wasn't long ago that the library's options for reaching advocates and donors were limited to handing out materials at library locations, using the U.S. mail, making phone calls, and hoping for media publicity. All of those methods are still valid and valuable, but today, thanks to the Internet, you have many more options. It is important to remember that, whatever online sites you choose (your library's website, Facebook, Twitter, etc.), be sure that your presence in each digital format connects to that in others. You should also be sure you have done a good job in one area—allowing for online donations on your website, for example—before moving on to another—such as Facebook. There is little point in having a Facebook page to assist with fund-raising if it directs readers to your library's website, and that web-site *doesn't* have a DONATE button.

A 2010 report on the charitable giving habits of our four current generations (Mature/Traditionalists, Baby Boomers, Gen X, and Gen Y/Millennials) found that, while the traditional method of direct mail works well for Traditionalists and Baby Boomers, Gen X and Y respond better to a multichannel approach consisting of e-mail, social networking, text message campaigns, word-of-mouth, and fund-raising events (Bhagat et al. 2010, 6). Members of all generations use some of the same channels for making contributions—and all respond well when asked for donations by friends—but the younger generations are far more likely to use technology as part of their donation process. That's why it's important for your library to feel comfortable with each of these communication tools and donation methods because the sharper your proficiency with them, the better your fund-raising results. In many cases, a donor may hear about your library through direct mail or a social networking site, then visit your library's website for more information and an opportunity to donate.

## YOUR LIBRARY'S WEBSITE

Don't underestimate the importance of your library's website. The American Library Association's 2009 *Conditions of U.S. Libraries* report found that remote use of the public library (by computer from home, work, or school) *more than doubled* from 2006 to 2009 (ALA Office for Research and Statistics, *The Condition of U.S. Libraries: Trends 1999–2009, 2009*). This is a trend that can only increase. Think of your library's website as a virtual branch and its home page as the front door of that branch. All of the people who visit your library's website will start out on its home page. Make sure your fund-raising group's link is there in the form of a DONATE button, so people know immediately where they can go if they want to make a donation to support the library. Your DONATE button should be obvious and located in a permanent place on your home page so visitors don't have to search for it.

To keep donors and other users actively engaged, websites must be regularly updated. A stale or static site loses followers fast. When you update your website, keep the format the same, but vary the content so that it always feels fresh. Be sure to highlight your library's special events with graphics and links from your home page, and use those event or program pages to remind visitors that *your library needs their support* to continue offer-

### Words to Know

*Search engine optimization (SEO)* is the process by which you can increase the visibility of a website or web page in search engines, such as Google, Bing, or Yahoo. SEO is what you do to ensure that people find your website, and sharing links between your library and its fund-raising organization's site will improve SEO. Internal links within your site will also help. SEO is a technique, and tuning your site to appear in search results can be tricky. Getting Google and other search engines to properly read and index the content of your web pages requires a lot of work. (As much as possible, follow Google's search engine optimization guidelines, which you can find by Googling "search engine optimization.") Seeking out a company that specializes in SEO may give you the best results, but there are some basics anyone can do:

- Create unique, accurate page titles
- Use words in the structure of your URL
- Use descriptive file names and alt text for images
- Make your site easy to navigate
- Offer quality content and services
- Build backlinks from other websites that point back to your site

SEO is about putting your site's best foot forward when it comes to visibility in search engines; but your ultimate consumers are your users, not the search engines. Users know good content when they see it and will likely want to direct other users to it. This might be done through blog posts, social media service, e-mail, forums, and other means. If you want to learn more about SEO, you'll find a wealth of information on the Web, with tips such as "Nine Ways to Improve the SEO of Every Website You Design" at http://sixrevisions.com/web_design/improve-seo-website-design.

ing these enhanced services. Provide a DONATE link there to the site where they can donate online. These links are an important tool for search engine optimization, or SEO.

## BLOGGING

A blog is today's online journal or bulletin board. It can be anything from a personal diary to a carefully crafted corporate communication. The content you write on your blog is called a "post," and it can consist of written text as well as messages and links to your library's website. You can use a blog to talk about your library, about opportunities to support it, and to direct people to the DONATE button on the library's home page. Make your blog interesting and lively, but remember that everything you write is available for anyone to read. There are a number of free, easy-to-use blog hosts that can guide you through the process of setting up your blog. A few options are Blogger, Posterous, Tumblr, LiveJournal, WordPress, xanga, Blog.com, and digg.

## E-MAIL BLASTS

E-mail is really an amazing communication tool when you think about it. The ability to send written communication, graphics, and documents over long distances instantaneously has transformed the way we communicate. It affords immediate communication with many people at once. An e-mail blast is not the same as a personal e-mail sent to a large number of people, however. An e-mail blast is a form of direct marketing that uses e-mail as a means of communicating a message. Think of it as a mega-blog, a fund-raising eruption that can reach a large number of people with the press of a single button. It can be designed to look almost like your website, with graphics, video, and live links to your library or fund-raising website or other complimentary sites. You'll want to use an e-mail marketing service such as iContact, Constant Contact, MailChimp, Emma, or Vertical Response because they can manage your address lists, help you comply with anti-spam laws, and let you easily create dynamic e-mails that will drive people to donate to your cause. There are many e-mail marketing service options out there, and most are very affordable and easy to use, thanks to the tutorials provided on their sites. The small cost of using these services will bring you a far better return on your investment than if you saved your money and tried to send the e-mail blasts on your own. You don't need permission from recipients to send them e-mail blasts, but the law requires that you include an "unsubscribe" option for individuals who do not wish to receive periodic e-mail messages.

## SOCIAL NETWORKS

Simply put, social networks help you see and connect with people. These connections may be hidden in the real world, but they help you get things done online. It's important for your library and fund-raising group to have a presence on social networks that are built around commonly shared interests. The effectiveness of social networks as a fund-raising tool is still being evaluated, but they are a great conduit for communicating your library's message beyond your circle of influence.

With well over one billion users worldwide, Facebook is the largest social network on the Internet, and the second most utilized site (after Google). For many people it's the place they connect with all their favorite organizations and friends. If you want to reach these one billion people, you'll need to create a Facebook presence for your library or its fund-raising group. With Facebook, you can connect to people via pages, groups, and ads.

Another highly ranked network is Twitter, with more than 500 million users. Twitter describes itself as "a real-time information network that connects you to the latest information about what you find interesting. Simply find the public streams you find most compelling and follow the conversations. At the heart of Twitter are small bursts of information called Tweets. Each Tweet is 140 characters in length, but don't let the small size fool you—you can share a lot with a "little space." You don't have to tweet to get value from Twitter—you can just follow others and get up-to-date information, but if you want to build relationships that support your library, you'll want to post tweets about the programs and services you offer and activities you're engaged in. You can link your Twitter profile to your Facebook page, website, and blog.

Another kind of social network that is not directly related to fund-raising, but can connect you with people who might eventually become interested in your library, is LibraryThing. It is used by individuals, authors, libraries, and publishers as a place to meet and talk about books. Its community of 1.6 million users connects with others who read what they do. It's a much more single-focused social network than Facebook or Twitter, but you may make some good connections to book lovers who can be converted to donors.

There are hundreds of social networks out there, many focused on common areas of interest. Whatever social networks you choose for your library's fund-raising efforts, it's important to fill out your library's profile completely. The more information you provide, the easier it will be for search engines to locate you. This will raise your profile and increase your search engine optimization. It's also important to prioritize which digital formats are the most important to you. Once there, find your voice. Keep in mind your objective of inciting a response to donate. If you can, post messages on your Facebook wall or send tweets on your Twitter feed daily. (Eventually you may not have to do this daily because your followers will find one another and begin conversing about your library on their own.) Be sure to interact with your followers. Social networks are not a one-way street. They can be a lot of fun, but to successfully promote your profile and build relationships requires a time commitment, too. Have a designated person who handles your communication on each site, and plan to spend at least 3–5 hours per week on social media marketing—more, if you're in a larger market or network.

## 2. The Media Has Taken an Interest in Libraries

Awareness of libraries and their myriad roles in the community is on the rise. In the twenty-four-hour news cycle, libraries are frequently the topic of coverage, both good and bad. News stories focus on the library's growing role as a resource for job seekers and its importance to students as school library services are cut back, as well as on the distress of communities facing library closures. Fortunately, even what could be perceived as "bad press" can be used to help potential donors understand why their support is needed. The onus is on you to encourage positive coverage through media contacts, and leverage *any* coverage (positive or negative) to your benefit.

One reason for all this media interest is that more and more media forms and forums are accessed via the Internet. Newspapers, periodicals, television stations, and radio stations are all dedicated to engaging their audience with additional content via their websites. But that access is constrained by the digital divide, which itself has become a news story. Because owning a computer and purchasing high-speed Internet service remain financial impossibilities for many—effectively blocking access to digital information—both the media sources *and* their audiences depend on the public library and its computers for access to this critical information.

Interest in library stories comes from a wide variety of perspectives. With 2008's Great Recession came a corresponding surge in library use, typical of economic times when individuals cut back on their discretionary expenses. Those increases continue in most places, so mainstream media like network and cable news, the *New York Times, Newsweek,* and many other national and local news sources still write and talk about the increase in public library visits, computer use, and job searches, among other stories.

In fact, the library's role in workforce development has been an increasingly important news item. With government cutbacks, Small Business Administration centers are closing, and entrepreneurs are turning to libraries to become the new workforce centers. Unemployment is of high interest to the majority of people, especially those who are in decision-making positions in government and business. When these people see your library as "part of the solution," financial support (public and private) is easier to secure. Likewise, when your library's budget becomes a target for major cutbacks and savings, media coverage can help you rally supporters to defend your hours, as well as to make gifts to support the collection.

Changes in the publishing industry are also frequent news stories. We all have heard someone comment on the imminent demise of the printed book. When this is news, libraries must be at the microphone to talk about both the positives and negatives of this change, while reiterating they will continue to be a critical access point—regardless of format. If you are offering innovative products or services, such as e-book readers or self-publishing workshops, the media and potential donors in your community should hear about it.

Your library reflects the community it serves, and census data can be a powerful tool to highlight your library's value to the community. As changes occur in your community, the media is making note of it. You can too. Use census data to encourage more media coverage and financial support. Use your research resources to point out the relationship between your community's demographic profile, achievement in local schools, and the services and resources you provide such as homework help or GED equivalency study guides. This kind of information is not only valuable as a public relations tool to highlight the library, it also tells a powerful story as you build relationships with individual donors, businesses, and foundations. Sharing this kind of coverage is a great opportunity to inform people of your library's crucial role without asking anyone for anything at the time.

Finally, don't forget celebrities! Authors and other celebrities are using the media to speak up on behalf of libraries more frequently, demonstrating their personal support. Reach out to local notables and engage them to support your library. Some high-profile individuals in your community, as well as on the national stage, receive media coverage regardless of the topic, and that coverage is noticed by more people than many other news stories. Take advantage of opportunities to repeat positive things celebrities have said about libraries to your potential donors. ALA's website has resources to help you identify and partner with local notables, including media personalities, to promote your library and its programs and services. Check out the ALA website under "Advocacy University" to access its "Cultivating Your Local Notables Toolkit" (www.ala.org/advocacy/advleg/advocacyuniversity/localnotables).

# 3. Fund-Raising Has Become Part of Today's Library Landscape

Not that many years ago, only a handful of libraries were actively engaged in ongoing fund-raising. Many held book sales or read-a-thons, but these were usually one-time annual events. Why was that adequate? One reason is that library budgets were far less strained a decade ago than they are today. In addition, demand for libraries is up today—just as budgets are falling precipitously—and libraries are under increased pressure to supplement dwindling public dollars. As a result, fund-raising has become part of the everyday public library landscape today, despite the fact that most librarians and library staff do not think of themselves as fund-raisers, nor do many feel competent in this role.

There's an abundance of resources and tools to help library staff, volunteers, and other supporters overcome their reluctance (or fear) when it comes to library fund-raising. The American Library Association's website is a good place to start. That website contains helpful fund-raising information, as well as a number of excellent online toolkits to help you design and implement advocacy campaigns that will complement your private fund-raising capability. Check out ALA's website at www.ala.org. There is also a great deal of free fund-raising information on the Internet, although those sources are not specifically about library fund-raising.

# 4. Libraries Have a Strong Pool of Volunteers to Help Raise Funds

Volunteerism is alive and well in America today. A Corporation for National and Community Service report released in 2010 had this to say about individuals' willingness to give their time in service to their communities:

> During this economic recession, as individuals across the country grappled with financial instability, one might predict that the volunteer rate should decrease between 2008 and 2009. This expectation comes from the assumption that during hard times, individuals turn inward to focus on their current plight or on the issues most central to their families. The data, however, tell a different story. In 2009, 63.4 million Americans volunteered to help their communities. This is an additional 1.6 million volunteers compared to 2008, *making 2009 the largest single-year increase in the number of volunteers since 2003.* (Corporation for National and Community Service, 1)

What's even more important for you to know as a library fund-raiser is that, in terms of activities, volunteers most often participated in *fund-raising/selling items to raise money* (Corporation for National and Community Service, 3).

Because libraries are so beloved in their communities, it is often easy to develop a troupe of educated, well-connected, and successful individuals who can be tapped as volunteers to assist with your library's fund-raising. Furthermore, Baby Boomers, those born between 1946 and 1964 and often lifelong library users, are reaching retirement age now and can provide a rich pool of energy, education, experience, and wealth that can be invaluable as you seek private support for your library. In 2011 Baby Boomers made up one-fourth of the U.S. population, according to the 2010 U.S. Census.

Once you've identified an engaged group of fund-raising volunteers, how can you use them most effectively?

> **As members of a fund-raising committee or board.** You'll read more about this in chapter 5, but the basic idea is that your strongest volunteers should form the nucleus of a group of individuals whose sole function is to facilitate fund-raising for your library. These individuals can also serve as effective advocates to help persuade decision makers (public and private) to support your library.

> **As links between the library and potential funding sources.** There is no substitute for someone who can open a door for you. Volunteers can connect your library to their places of employment (or former employers, in the case of retirees) and sometimes even to foundations. They might also be able to interest wealthy individuals in helping your library be great.

**As grant writers.** If you know someone who has experience as a grant writer, by all means elicit their help. Grant writing is a specialized skill, and a well-written grant proposal shines in the face of weaker ones.

**As promoters.** You can't have too many cheerleaders. People who are willing to speak up on your library's behalf are worth their weight in gold. Do you know anyone with media connections who would be willing to give you a few hours of their time? Even the simple act of handing out library fund-raising information at a community event counts as promotion.

**As advocates for your library's most pressing needs.** Advocacy means the active support of an idea or cause, and its goal is usually to influence public policy and resource allocation. Volunteers can champion the library's cause to elected officials—writing letters, attending town council meetings, anything that's needed to grab the attention of those who determine resource allocation.

In summary, what can we say about today's library fund-raising environment? *Opportunities abound.* Taking advantage of new ways of reaching and engaging donors, leveraging the media's interest in libraries, and dipping into the deep pool of capable volunteers your community offers can bring your library the rewards of new relationships and creative new support.

## REFERENCES

Bhagat, Vinay, Pa, Loeb, Mark Rovner. 2010. *The Next Generation of American Giving: A Study on the Contrasting Charitable Habits Generation Y, Generation X, Baby Boomers, and Matures,* Arlington, VA: Edge Research. www.edgeresearch.com/Edge%20Research%20Case%20Study%20-%20Next-Gen-Whitepaper.pdf.

Corporation for National and Community Service, Office of Research and Policy Development. 2010. *Volunteering in America 2010: National, State, and City Information,* Washington, DC. www.volunteeringinamerica.gov/assets/resources/IssueBriefFINALJune15.pdf.

# 3

# Private Fund-Raising Is a Natural for Libraries

**FOR MANY PEOPLE, THEIR FIRST EXPOSURE TO THE WORLD OF IMAGINA-**
tion and learning happened when they walked through the front doors of their public libraries. That fact is no less true today than it was a century ago. The reason their communities had public libraries to welcome them can be summed up in two words: Andrew Carnegie.

Carnegie was an iconic figure who altered the public library landscape of the Western world. He was born in the small village of Dunfermline, Scotland, in 1835, the son of a dirt-poor linen weaver. Attending school from only the ages of eight to twelve, Carnegie learned to love books and learning, and he read voraciously on the rare opportunities that he could borrow a book from a friend. He was first exposed to a library when a wealthy colonel in Allegheny, Pennsylvania (where the Carnegies, out of work and desperate, emigrated in 1848) allowed working boys to borrow books from his personal library. There was only one catch: the library wasn't free. It cost two dollars a year for the privilege. Young Andrew thought this was unfair, and he successfully lobbied the colonel to drop the two dollar annual fee and make the library free. Hindsight reveals this moment to have been a momentous one in history.

Library of Congress Prints and Photographs Division, Washington, D.C.

**Andrew Carnegie**

Andrew Carnegie made his fortune in the steel industry, founding the Carnegie Steel Company, which later became U.S. Steel. In the nineteenth century and beyond, steel was the building block of this nation and many others, contributing to the explosion of railways and industry. Ultimately, it became the building block of libraries too.

At the beginning of the twentieth century, Andrew Carnegie was considered to be the richest man in the world. Not satisfied with this distinction, he vowed to become the most generous man as well. Carnegie possessed an almost unquenchable desire to return to society some of the riches he had amassed. His own words say it best. "This, then, is held to be the duty of the man of wealth: To consider all surplus revenues which come to him simply as trust funds, which he is called upon to administer . . . in the manner which, in his judgment, is best calculated to produce the most beneficial results for society" (Nasaw, 2006, 348–49).

> ## Words to Know
>
> *Philanthropy* comes from the Greek word *philanthropos,* meaning "loving people." The purpose of philanthropy is to use one's own wealth to promote the common good and to enrich and improve the lives of others.

In short, philanthropy became Carnegie's passion.

"I am in the library manufacturing business," said Andrew Carnegie (Nasaw 2006, 607). True to his devotion to books and learning, Carnegie decided that one of the main beneficiaries of his generosity would be libraries—*free* public libraries—and he set about developing a system by which communities could themselves be enriched by reading and learning. His plan included the use of both private money (his personal wealth) and public funds. It was simple: Carnegie would provide the money to build a structure to house a library, but the community receiving the building had to agree to stock it with books, pay staff, and maintain the library on an ongoing basis. It was his way of saying, "I'll help you, but you have to do your part too."

> "Rich men have it in their power . . . benefactions from which the masses of their fellows will derive lasting advantage, and thus dignify their own lives."
>
> Andrew Carnegie (Nasaw 2006, 349)

It worked. In his lifetime, he provided $41 million to build over 1,600 libraries in the United States (Nasaw 2006, 607). Consider this: prior to 1880, there were hardly any public libraries in the United States, in fact, only 188 in 1876. By 1923, that number had jumped to 3,873 and nearly 57 million people, over half of the U.S. population, had access to a public library (Bobinski 1969, 192–93). Many of those people were—and still are—immigrants like Carnegie himself.

What does this mean for modern libraries? It means that the linkage of public and private funding was foundational to creating the public library system we enjoy today. It means that public libraries in the United States *can trace their very beginnings* to the public/private partnership that Andrew Carnegie set in motion. Without this innovative partnership, the public library landscape in this nation would look far different today.

# The Value of Libraries

There are few institutions as revered in this country as the library, particularly the public library. If you don't believe that, try closing one. Recent years have seen numerous rallies and other demonstrations of support by citizens who are fiercely loyal to libraries they know to be under threat. In some of these instances, public outcry has successfully prevented library closures.

While the reasons for this affection and appreciation are as numerous as the individuals who use them, here are six qualities of libraries that make them matter to their communities:

1. **Libraries anchor communities.** They are learning places, gathering places, meeting places. In some communities, the public library is a physical focal point as well as an intellectual one. Some of the most striking and beautiful buildings in urban and rural communities are their libraries. People are drawn to their public library because it welcomes all who enter its doors.

2. **Libraries serve a large cross-section of their communities.** No one could accuse the public library of being exclusive; it's not a niche institution in any way. The public library is open to everyone, regardless of demographics or economics. There are no admission fees, no requirements to enter its portals. It's free in every sense of the word. What's more, the library champions the privacy of its users, not caring about income, race, educational level, or any other demographic identifiers of the individuals who access its resources.

> Nearly two-thirds of Americans polled in 2011 said they used their public library.
> (ALA Report, "January 2011 Harris Poll Quorum Results," 2011)

3. **Libraries serve the underserved.** It's easy for the underserved population of any community to become invisible. Libraries ensure that everyone has equal access to information and resources. They do this without neglecting the needs of the more prosperous members of their communities, too. How many organizations even attempt this feat, much less accomplish it?

4. **Libraries strive to be all things to all people.** American libraries wear more hats than ever before. In keeping with their traditional role, they are centers for reading and learning at all ages and stages of life, but today's libraries go far beyond that. They are the go-to places for finding employment, accessing government services, learning a language (especially English), and taking skill-building classes. They're centers for out-of-school enrichment and entertainment, and for preschool readiness. Libraries do more now than ever before.

5. Libraries connect people to ideas. "Man's mind, once stretched by a new idea, never regains its original dimensions," is a quote that has been attributed to poet and essayist Oliver Wendell Holmes. Libraries are, and will continue to be, the places where minds come in contact with—and are expanded by—new ideas.

6. Libraries allow free expression of ideas. One of the hallmarks of our free society (and part of the mission of public libraries) is the freedom to express ideas, opinions, and viewpoints. Libraries are one of the guardians of this freedom. In addition, because public libraries are non-politicized public institutions—that is, they are bipartisan in their scope, service, and support—they are places where all ideas matter.

The American Library Association report cited in chapter 2 that quantified the increase in library use also quantified *the value* of libraries.

> More than 222 million Americans agree or strongly agree that because it provides free access to materials and resources, *the public library plays an important role in giving everyone a chance to succeed.* (This is an increase from 216.6 million reported in 2006.)
>
> More than 217 million Americans agree or strongly agree that *the public library improves the quality of life in their community.* (This is an increase from 209.8 million reported in 2006.)
>
> (ALA Office for Research and Statistics, *The Condition of U.S. Libraries: Trends 1999-2009*)

Likewise, a 2011 Harris Poll attempted to measure the *value of libraries*. It found results that paralleled those of the ALA report.

> 94 percent of respondents agreed that [libraries] provide free access to materials and resources . . . [and] play an important role in giving everyone a chance to succeed.
>
> 91 percent of respondents agreed that the library improves the quality of life in their community.
>
> (ALA Report, "January 2011 Harris Poll Quorum Results")

Clearly, the library is one of the most important public institutions our nation has ever known, shaping communities and individuals in important, sometimes profound, ways.

# Library Donors Understand the Value of Libraries to Their Communities

People give for many reasons. We know that they must first personally value an institution or an ideal before they decide to support it financially. Second, they give because they are able to give. Third, they give because giving feels good. Because so

"The value of libraries to American households is unquestioned."
(ALA Office for Research and Statistics, *The Condition of U.S. Libraries: Trends 1999–2009*)

many individuals value—even cherish—the library, it's an institution toward which many people feel a natural inclination to support in a personal way.

Library donors who demonstrate with their personal gifts the value they place on the library also care about *how* their money is used. Most donors don't want to donate just to keep the lights on and the copier running. In fact, in a perfect world, private dollars would fund library *enhancements*. Recognizing the importance and value of public-private partnerships in funding libraries, in 1989, the Chicago City Council passed a cooperation agreement declaring that private funding for the library should *complement and augment* public funds, not replace them. The council further agreed that it would not reduce public funds to city libraries because of the successful acquisition of private funding (*Journal of the Proceedings of the City Council of the City of Chicago, Illinois 1989*, 24298–99).

Library donors are often attracted to funding enhancements because they want to make their library—your library—*great*. That's why, when you think about whom you want to approach for private support, whether individuals, institutions, or both, it's important to be able to present potential donors with clear, rational funding opportunities that they will feel are innovative, essential, and will move your library toward greatness. The need to develop such funding opportunities may cause you to think more creatively about what constitute "core services" for your library, which can be a very good thing.

**Words to Know**

*Core services* are those library services considered to be basic and essential.

We usually think of core services as material circulation, reference help, children/youth/adult programming, computer access, and so on, but core services can be interpreted even more broadly. Here are two examples:

1. When the Phoenix Public Library faced a 30 percent budget cutback and drastically reduced hours in 2009, it feared losing after-hours English language classes, something its director considered a core service. The solution was finding private funding to pay for a security guard so the library could continue to be open later hours for these classes.

2. In Chicago, a corporation provided funding for 50,000 Chicago Public Library Summer Reading Program T-shirts. The T-shirts were considered core (i.e., basic and essential) to the program and could not have been secured any other way. Mary Dempsey, Chicago Public Library director, called those T-shirts "50,000 walking billboards for the Chicago Public Library" (Miller 2010, 49).

While most of the people and organizations that value and support your library will not give exceptionally large gifts, such as 50,000 T-shirts, some will. These are your major donors, and they demonstrate with their extraordinary generosity the value they place on the library. While comprising only 10 or 20 percent of givers, major donors will provide most of your private funding. (The 80–20 Rule states that 80 percent of your total private funding is likely to come from 20 percent of your total donors.) Major donors often possess two additional characteristics in addition to the facts that they value the library and they are able to give. First, they are usually well educated; and second, they are usually successful in some capacity. You will read more about major donors in chapter 13. The reason they are mentioned here is because, for these individuals in particular, the library's two missions—*to foster lifelong learning and improve their users' chances of success in life*—dovetail nicely with major donors' own values and personal stories.

# Closing the Circle

What does this mean for library fund-raising today? It means that we have come full circle and are back to the public/private model that worked so well a hundred years ago. To say it another way, keeping strong public libraries in the twenty-first century means going back to the roots that nourished them in the nineteenth, *creating a solid partnership between public and private resources.*

Our century has witnessed individuals and organizations whose philanthropy toward libraries equals, and even exceeds, Andrew Carnegie's. Bill and Melinda Gates and their Foundation is the most obvious example. Their contributions to libraries and learning in this country and abroad continue to make a huge difference in the capacity of libraries to serve their communities and, ultimately, to the quality of life in those communities. The Gates Foundation's website states:

> Libraries are safe, central spaces. Their services are free and available to all. Unfortunately, many libraries face shrinking budgets even as their use grows. Staff receive less training in technology skills, computers are becoming outdated, and Internet connections can't handle the high-speed streaming audio and video requirements for distance education, research, and other activities. Libraries are struggling to stay up to speed in the face of too many library patrons and too little Internet bandwidth. We're helping U.S. libraries provide the free, reliable computer and Internet access that will allow patrons to make meaningful contributions to society.

Libraries have evolved in amazing ways in the hundred years that separate Andrew Carnegie from Bill and Melinda Gates. In those intervening years, millions of benefactors have made large and small gifts to support public libraries. They have helped build new buildings, expand collections, enhance resources, and provide programming and education. Some of these benefactors have lived—or currently live—in your community. Your job as a library fund-raiser is to identify them and others like them, then to persuade, thank, and nurture them, creating library supporters for a lifetime and into the future.

**REFERENCES**

ALA Office for Research and Statistics. 2009. *The Condition of U.S. Libraries: Trends 1999–2009, December 2009.* http://ala.org/ala/research/initiatives/Condition _of_Libraries_1999.20.pdf.

ALA Report. 2011. "January 2010 Harris Poll Quorum Results." January 262011. www.ala .org/research/sites/ala.org.research/files/content/librarystats/2011harrispoll.pdf.

Bobinski, George S. 1969. *Carnegie Libraries: Their History and Impact on American Public Library Development.* American Library Association.

"Chicago Public Library Foundation Contributions Committed as Additional Rather than Alternative Source of Revenue for Chicago Public Library." 1989. *Journal of the Proceedings of the City Council of The City of Chicago, Illinois.* Regular Meeting, Wednesday, February 1, 1989, 24297–99. www.chicityclerk.com/journals/1989/TOC_feb1 _1989.pdf.

Meltzer, Milton. 1997. *The Many Lives of Andrew Carnegie.* Franklin Watts.

Miller, Rebecca. 2010. "Fund-Raising in the Downturn." *Library Journal* 135, no. 1 (January 1): 48–50. www.libraryjournal.com/lj/communitymanaginglibraries/849935–273/ story.csp.

Nasaw, David. 2006. *Andrew Carnegie,* Penguin.

*Webster's New College Dictionary,* 3rd ed., s.v. "philanthropy."

4

# Twelve Must-Know Facts about Library Fund-Raising

**LIBRARY FUND-RAISING IS A DYNAMIC ACTIVITY. IT'S ABOUT EFFORT,** energy, and results. The essence of library fund-raising is captured in the "Twelve Must-Know Facts" below. These will give you a snapshot of where your fund-raising energy should be applied in order to see maximum results.

## Fact 1: Effective Fund-Raising Is about Relationships First, Money Second

"Fund-raising" is any organized activity that's intended to raise money. Some fund-raising efforts are one-time projects—a book sale, for example, where people walk in, buy books, and walk out. Grant writing is sometimes a one-time activity. A library may submit a grant application and receive a check for a specific purpose, such as purchasing materials or equipment. While these are valuable and proven methods of raising money, the most important point to remember is that effective fund-raising is about much more than one-time efforts. *It's about people and building relationships.*

What qualities characterize a strong relationship? Respect, trust, and communication are central to any meaningful relationship. These are qualities the library must cultivate to foster strong relationships with its stakeholders because library stakeholders are potential library supporters. Individuals and institutions are often motivated to support your library because of the relationships they have with those who represent or speak for your library. They give, not just because they value your library, but also because they value the people who represent your library to them. In other words, *people give to people*.

A donor may give once, but if he or she doesn't feel a personal connection to your library or its fund-raising organization, it's unlikely you'll see repeat giving. A primary goal of effective fund-raising, then, is to create a connection between the library and its supporters. This connection should communicate sincere appreciation for a book buyer's or donor's support. It communicates *the value of the donor to the library*, not just the other way around. Effective fund-raising also seeks out and nurtures the next generation of library supporters and donors. The end result is a win-win situation

> **Words to Know**
>
> *Fund-raising* is any organized activity that's intended to raise money.

for everyone. If your library has a Friends organization or a Foundation, its mission is all about relationship building, bringing individuals into the fold, then making them feel glad to be there. Library Friends and foundations constantly seek new members, supporters, and donors, and they carefully nurture the relationships with those they already have. Every library should do this too.

# Fact 2: A Clear Case for Support and Strong, Consistent Messages Are Crucial

You know why your library is critical to your community. Do others? If you fail to persuasively communicate why your library matters, don't expect people to understand why they should support it. Unfortunately, libraries don't have a strong track record when it comes to marketing themselves, but this is an omission that they— and you—have the power to change.

Libraries don't simply have a story. They have many stories, and this is the reason why people feel an emotional connection to libraries as well as a practical one. These stories can foster pride in your library in the hearts of those who hear them. That's why everyone who uses your library has the potential to speak to its value and the importance in their lives.

Think about the things your community cares about. For example, if it's economic prosperity, show that your library is the go-to place for job seekers and people who want to start small businesses. If your community cares about literacy, point out that you offer language classes, reading materials, and literacy support for all ages. Does your community value a safe place for children and teens? Let others know how full your library is after school and in the evening. Gather those examples, and use them to craft a message that tells people why your library matters and why it deserves their support.

Make sure your library's message is clear and strong. Be direct. Tell it often and in as many ways as you can. Look for fresh opportunities to speak it, write it, publish it. After a while, you might get a little tired of your library's message and be tempted to start over and come up with a new message. *Resist the urge!* Remember that repetition is not a negative thing and that many potential library supporters may still be hearing it for the first time. Winston Churchill, one of the greatest orators of his century, advised making your point three times, the last time with "a tremendous whack."

# Fact 3: To Value the Library Is Not Enough

Let's assume you've crafted a powerful message that communicates the value of your library. Now what? The next step may sound daunting to some people, but it doesn't have to be. That step can be summed up in one word: *ask.*

Notice that the word isn't "suggest"; it's "ask." You can't expect people to support your library if they're not directly asked to do so. How do you do that?

**Have the right person do the asking.** People give to what they value, and that's particularly true when the right person asks. Think about it. If a friend supports a cause and asks you to help too, you're far more likely to say "yes" than if you receive a cold call or are part of a large unknown pool of individuals who are being solicited. The right person is someone the listener knows and respects. Remember that people give to people.

**Make giving easy.** Don't underestimate the importance of taking the hassle factor out of giving. There are so many new ways of giving today that there's no reason anyone should have to go to any trouble to support your library. Here are a few suggestions:

Make sure your library's website accepts online donations.

Be specific. Spell it out. When you communicate with people, let them know all the actual ways they can give.

Whenever you put the message out there that your library is seeking private funds, include the means by which individuals can reply. For example, if you mail a fund-raising request to a potential donor, include a self-addressed return envelope.

# Fact 4: Libraries Have Both an Intellectual and Emotional Appeal to Donors

This dual appeal is a very good thing. Not all nonprofits can make this claim. Public libraries are about lifelong learning. They're about preschool readiness, literacy, reading and knowledge, technology, and classes. That's the intellectual part, but it's not all. Libraries are neighborhood anchors, community meeting spaces, arts places, teen hangouts. New moms gather there. Kids have fun there. Seniors expand their horizons there. That's the emotional part.

Most people have positive personal feelings about public libraries. Interestingly, people's positive feelings about the public library may not even be a result of their experiences at *your* library. They might feel happy and nostalgic when they think about walking to the library with their mother in their childhood. They may fondly remember taking their own children to get books during summer breaks from school. This dual appeal gives you, a library fund-raiser, a two-pronged approach to fund-raising. Your fund-raising messages can speak to both the intellectual and emotional qualities that your library offers.

# Fact 5: Everyone on Your Staff Plays a Role in Fund-Raising

Yes, you read that right. Fund-raising is not solely the job of the library director or manager, your Friends group, or fund-raising organization. *Every* staff member can take an active role at his or her own comfort level.

Before this can happen, however, library leadership must be absolutely committed to growing library support through fund-raising. Without that commitment, staff at other levels can't be expected to buy into the effort. Library leaders really have two jobs. They communicate the library's needs and achievements to government officials and other decision makers who determine the library's budget. They must also take the lead in fostering pride in the library among its staff and empowering library workers to speak out on the library's behalf.

Pride in the library means using every point of contact to demonstrate great customer service and practice effective public relations. Business owners and managers know that outstanding customer service at all levels impacts customers' opinions about that business. The person who welcomes you with a smile at your coffee shop and the restaurant server who remembers that you don't like pickles are two simple examples. For libraries, outstanding customer service is a foundation of effective fund-raising, but it's not enough; you need effective public relations too. *Everyone*— even those library staffers who never come in direct contact with library users— plays an important role in shaping others' feelings about the library and, hence, their likeliness to support it. Here's why.

It's easy to understand how the reference librarian and circulation desk clerk can do this. They interact directly with library users. But what about the person who works behind the scenes, processing materials, updating the website, handling communication, even sweeping up after the library closes? They can contribute to the library's positive public image because they live in the community with people who know they work for the library. They are the face of the library to those who know them. What they say to others directly impacts listeners' feelings (good or bad) about the library. Behind-the-scenes staff members play as important a role in communicating the library's great work and its value to the community as the reference librarian and circulation clerk do. They can also communicate the personal satisfaction they derive from being part of the library's staff.

> **Words to Know**
>
> In fund-raising, *ask* is both a noun and a verb. An *ask* (noun) is the act of requesting monetary support from an individual or institution, for example, "She is the best person to make the ask."

Thus, *everyone* on a library's staff can function as a library promoter—and indirectly as a fund-raiser at his or her own comfort level—without ever directly asking anyone for a dime. (Important note: Library staff should *never* have to ask anyone for money. In fund-raising, it's important to identify the right person to make an ask, and that is almost never library staff in non-leadership positions.)

# Fact 6: A Strong Fund-Raising Committee or Board Makes Strong Connections

Your library probably has a Board of Trustees connected with it. That board is made up of volunteers, or elected/appointed officials, who oversee the governance of the library. However, this board is *not* a fund-raising board and should not be asked to perform this role. Instead, effective library fund-raising requires a distinct fund-raising committee or board, one that is made up of volunteers whose main job is to help raise private dollars for the library. Don't underestimate what a strong committee or board of this kind can do for you. In fact, their importance can be summarized in one sentence: *The effectiveness of your fund-raising is directly linked to the quality of your fund-raising committee or board.*

Committees and boards are sometimes built by happenstance. Someone knows someone with enthusiasm and time, and voila! That person is invited to be a board or committee member. The new member may have a friend with enthusiasm and time, and they, too, join the group. But high-quality fund-raising groups are made up of individuals with more than just enthusiasm and time.

A well-known library fund-raiser is known to say, "The last person you want on your library fund-raising board is a book lover." That's a catchy way of saying don't confuse book lovers, who may seek a kind of "book club" or other social experience with individuals who bring valuable knowledge and networks to your board. Effective fund-raising committees and boards are carefully, even methodically, constructed to include individuals with the specific skills that the organization requires (such as fund-raising, legal, marketing, or financial expertise), as well as the connections to other organizations and individuals that an organization like your library needs. For example, a foundation or Friends board member with personal wealth, or one who holds a position of influence in a corporation, or one whose network extends to philanthropy or the media will enhance the capacity of your library or your Friends group or foundation to raise dollars. These individuals open doors to resources—including private funders—that would be difficult to open without these personal and professional connections.

One last fact about your fund-raising committee or board is that, in order for fund-raising to be effective, these individuals must be 100 percent committed to fund-raising. They must be willing to use their influence and connections to help raise money for the library, and they should all be willing to contribute personally (in any amount) to your library's fund-raising efforts.

# Fact 7: Most Donors Are People, Not Institutions

Here's a little word association quiz. When you hear the word *fund-raising,* what word pops into your head? If it's *grants,* try again.

You may be tempted by the idea that grants and sponsorships are easy to understand because they represent a finite process: they have a beginning, middle, and end. But your library's best investment of its time and resources is unquestionably identifying and soliciting *individual donors.* While grants and business underwriting are very, very important facets of effective fund-raising, the fact is that *75 percent of philanthropic giving in the United States comes from individuals, not institutions.* The remaining 25 percent comprises gifts from Foundations (13%), bequests (8%), and corporations (4%) ("Giving USA 2010 Executive Summary"). This is another reason why effective library fund-raising means developing strong personal relationships with *individuals* in your library's community.

# Fact 8: Your Largest Donors May Not Be Library Users

What? It sounds counterintuitive, but the people who walk through your library's doors every day may not be your best prospects as major donors. Conversely, your best prospects as major donors may be people who rarely or never enter a public library.

In the early twentieth century, an Italian economist, Vilfredo Pareto, observed that 80 percent of Italy's land was owned by 20 percent of the people, and he realized that this 80/20 relationship was true in other areas of the world he knew. That notion has expanded into many disciplines and is now widely known as "the 80–20 Rule." The rule is commonly applied to everything from management to the physical world. For example, in general, 80 percent of the time you wear 20 percent of the possible items of clothing in your closet; and in your library, it's likely that 20 percent of your journals account for 80 percent of journal use. It works in fund-raising too; and it says that, as a rule, *20 percent of your donors will provide 80 percent of your dollars raised.*

> ### Words to Know
>
> A *major donor* is an individual or institution who is in your top tier of givers. The level of giving required to become a major donor varies from one nonprofit organization to another.

Who are the people who make up your top 20 percent? They are your "major donors," and every organization that raises money needs them. The definition of a major donor varies widely from organization to organization. In small organizations or libraries, a major donor might be someone who gives $100 or $500. In a large organization, such as a symphony orchestra or art museum, you may have to give $10,000 to be considered a major donor. Regardless of the level of giving required to be a major donor, one fact is always certain: *a major donor will be someone you already know.* He or she may not be a library user, but you can be certain they will be someone with a relationship to your library or, most likely, to someone associated with your library—with a staff or board member, for example.

Identifying, cultivating and soliciting major donors will be taken up in chapter 13 of this book, but major donors generally possess three attributes:

1. **They are capable.** They have a personal ability to give.

2. **They are philanthropic.** They are generous in other areas of their lives.

3. **They are connected.** They have a relationship of some kind that connects them to your library.

Once again, *the relationship* is critical. Capacity and a history of giving alone will not bring your library a major gift.

# Fact 9: Corporate Philanthropy Is about More Than Altruism

Name a business or corporation, and chances are good that some part of that business—its employees, marketing/PR department or Foundation—gives to charity. The business may write checks, or it could donate products, offer discounts, or provide volunteers. This kind of giving undoubtedly helps the organization receiving the gift, but, equally significantly, *it also benefits the business or corporation.*

> **Words to Know**
>
> *Philanthropy* is the act of giving to a specific cause or organization to affect social change or for the common good. The word is often used interchangeably with *charitable giving.*

Charitable giving attracts customers who appreciate the connection between the business and the charitable organization it supports. It raises awareness of the business's brand. It creates opportunities to cooperate or partner with community organizations, and it may even boost the business's support in local or state government. How? The answer is simple: *association.* Today, many businesses and corporations focus their giving on institutions with missions that align with their own, and they want their name visibly associated with those institutions. It's how they get something back for their support. This practice does not in any way undermine the generosity of corporate giving, but it does recognize that corporate motives are not just about altruism. They are about marketing, public relations, and, ultimately, about convincing people to purchase their product or service.

> **Words to Know**
>
> A *brand* refers to a business's name, logo, product, or service, as well as to the emotional response an individual has to that name, logo, product, or service. By symbolizing certain values and benefits, brand positioning helps harried consumers make decisions in a crowded marketplace.

Today's business and corporate giving culture can work to your library's advantage. Keep in mind that the library is a long-standing, cherished institution, well-loved by the public and potentially serving everyone. These attributes make it attractive to businesses and corporations. As you broaden your methods of library fund-raising, there are ways in which you can position your library as a beneficial place for businesses and corporations to direct their dollars and connect their brand.

# Fact 10: Advocacy and Fund-Raising Go Hand-in-Hand

Advocacy means actively supporting an idea or cause. It means building support for your library through relationships with community members, decision makers, and organizations that are in a position to provide the financial resources your library needs. Advocacy requires making a strong case for public funding of your library—its value and its needs—and communicating that message to the right people, particularly those in decision-making positions, such as elected officials. Effective advocacy yields supporters ("advocates"), and relationships built on that support can lead to the conversion of these advocates

> **Words to Know**
>
> *Advocacy* is the active support of an idea or cause. Its goal is usually to influence public policy and resource allocation.

to donors. Additionally, when your library is successful at raising *private* dollars through successful fund-raising, those funds can sometimes be leveraged to help you gain support for *public* funding. You'll read more about how to engage your community in effective advocacy in chapter 9 of this book.

# Fact 11: Fund-Raising Is a Year-Round Activity

Once you've deposited a few checks, if you think you can delete "raise money" from your to-do list, think again.

Fund-raising should be high on your library's list of *ongoing* strategic activities. Remember that effective fund-raising is about relationship development, and the best relationships are built on regular points of contact. An annual event or occasional sale of a product with your library's name on it does not cultivate a relationship with a library user or donor, nor does it attract potential donors. Ongoing fund-raising ensures that your library's strong message about its value and needs is heard over and over, and in many different ways.

Remember, fund-raising is *dynamic*, not static. It looks for opportunities and responds to them. It involves everyone on the library's staff, every day of the year. Even those staff members who are reluctant to mention library fund-raising directly can play a role by providing outstanding customer service *year-round*, offering brochures about giving opportunities (such as gifts to honor or remember someone) *year-round*, sending e-mail blasts with library news *year-round*, and taking advantage of every chance to say something good about the library *year-round*.

Once you start thinking about fund-raising as an ongoing activity with contact points to all the resources, programs, and services your library provides, you'll find it easy to keep it front and center throughout the year.

# Fact 12: Saying "Thank You" Matters

Thanking your donors can boil down to this: *You can't say "thank you" too often.* Chapter 7 of this book contains a crash course on "appreciation"—thanking, honoring, and nurturing your donors.

We live in a world where thanks, if expressed at all, is often done hurriedly, off-handedly, or electronically. Sometimes it's just "thx!" Appreciation is one of the hallmarks of a strong relationship, and if your donors don't feel appreciated, don't look for their continued involvement and support. Most institutions that ask for and receive donations thank their donors by letter—form letter, that is. Do yours differently and get noticed. Occasional handwritten notes, a phone call, or even an in-person thank you are far better than a form letter, and certainly better than an e-mail. Take time to do it right. Be personal and sincere. Say thanks in more than one way—a handwritten note *and* a phone call, for example. It will make a difference and get your library noticed.

Finally, think of some ways to make contact with your supporters that don't ask them for money. Send them a library newsletter or hold a recognition and appreciation event just for them. If you have a Friends group or a Foundation, this will be their job. If you do not, it's the library's job. Sincere thanks and recognition will go a long way. It will build good will, good relationships, and bring increased opportunities to receive individual and organizational support. Most importantly, it's the right thing to do.

## REFERENCE

"Giving USA 2010 Executive Summary." 2011. Giving USA Foundation.
    www.pursuantmedia.com/givingusa/0510/export/GivingUSA_2010
    _ExecSummary_Print.pdf.

# 5

# Who Can Help with Fund-Raising?

**IF YOUR LIBRARY DOES LITTLE TO NO FUND-RAISING, OR ONLY SMALL-**
scale fund-raising, it may be time to think bigger. It's getting increasingly difficult to meet community needs with small fund-raising efforts.

What do you need in order to ramp up your library's fund-raising efforts? First, you need the guidance of the library director and approval from your library's Board of Trustees. Next, you need the help of volunteers with fund-raising and other skills. Third, if your library is embarking on a really large fund-raising effort, such as a capital campaign, you will want the guidance of outside consultants who specialize in this.

(Note: An important point to remember is that your library's Board of Trustees is *not* a fund-raising board. Most library boards are governing and oversight boards that are elected or appointed. While trustees can—and should—be asked to support your library with personal giving, they usually cannot be expected to go out and raise funds.)

## Finding Fund-Raising Volunteers

Your best prospects for help when raising private money are influential community *volunteers*. These are individuals who are not on the library's staff, nor are they on the library's Board of Trustees. They have nothing to gain by the library's fund-raising success, except a great deal of personal satisfaction.

When choosing volunteers to help with fund-raising, a very important rule is: resist recruiting "book lovers" to do your fund-raising. Book lovers probably frequent your library, but they may not bring the kind of influence that makes a difference when it comes to raising serious dollars.

Instead, look for community and civic leaders who understand the importance of your library and are willing to give their time to make it the best it can be. Seek people who bring a belief in the library's importance *and* a willingness to share their personal experience, connections, and networks in order to help the library raise private dollars. The community and civic leaders you'll want for your fund-raising committee or fund-raising board should possess two important attributes—*influence and affluence*. They should be able to use their personal and professional networks to assist with fund-raising efforts, and they should be willing and able to make a personal gift as well. The purpose of their personal gifts is to set an example for others. In fact, your goal should be 100 percent giving from your fund-raising committee or board. That means that *every* member of your fund-raising committee or board should become a donor, regardless of the size of his or her gift.

When you think about how individuals with connections in the business community can help with fund-raising, don't limit yourself to thinking solely about monetary support. There are other things that well-connected people can do for your library's fund-raising efforts in addition to seeking checks. For example, a person associated with the media can help get your library's fund-raising message out. An advertising or marketing business can help you with design expertise, and a business owner such as a printer can donate flyers or brochures. This is called "in-kind giving," and it can provide valuable assistance by saving the library fund-raising costs (overhead).

> **Words to Know**
>
> An *in-kind donation* is a gift that is given in the form of goods or services, rather than as cash.

There are many people who you already know who can help with your library fund-raising.

# Library Friends

Who makes up your library's Friends group? What purpose do they serve currently? Do they do any fund-raising now? Do you think they will want to move to a higher level of fund-raising activities? If the answer to this last question is "yes" (and you hope it will be), and your Friends group has the skills needed to become an effective fund-raising committee or board, by all means put them to work (and recruit some additional influential community members) to lead your fund-raising efforts. If the answer is "no," and the group has reached its fund-raising comfort level, let them know they are sincerely appreciated. However, at the same time, start recruiting a fund-raising committee or board that can bring some higher-octane fund-raising activities to life.

# Library Foundation

Library Friends groups and Library Foundations have some activities in common. Both exist to carry out the library's mission and enhance the library's presence in the community. Both probably engage in some fund-raising.

But there are important differences too. The biggest one is that a Library Foundation will usually have paid staff; a Friends group may not. Another difference is scale. Friends groups generally carry out small-scale activities such as book sales, while foundations engage in higher-level fund-raising, such as corporate underwriting and grant writing. Library Foundations are always 501(c)(3) nonprofit organizations; Friends groups should be, but often they are not. A Library Foundation will have its own board of directors, distinct from the library's governing Board of Trustees. Ideally, this board should be comprised of people with some influence and professional standing in the library's community. A Friends group, on the other hand, may have a board that is more "grassroots" in nature.

The table below summarizes the similarities and differences between Friends groups and Foundations:

|  | *Library Friends* | *Library Foundation* |
|---|---|---|
| *Engages in fund-raising* | Yes | Yes |
| *Has paid staff* | Not usually | Almost always |
| *Engages in small fund-raising projects* | Yes | Yes |
| *Engages in high-level fund-raising* | No | Yes |
| *Is a 501(c)(3) nonprofit organization* | Not always | Yes |
| *Has a Board of Directors* | Yes, grassroots | Yes, more influential |

## Words to Know

The word *foundation* itself can be confusing in this fund-raising context. One simple definition is "an organization that gives money away by awarding grants." The amount a foundation gives away and the means by which it does so are governed by specific IRS regulations. There are corporate foundations, private foundations, family foundations, community foundations, and more. Often, their revenues come from endowments, investments, and corporate profits. These kinds of foundations frequently have multiple priority areas that they support.

A Library Foundation is a 501(c)(3) nonprofit organization that is governed by IRS regulations that differ from the kinds of foundations mentioned above. Most of its revenue is raised from within the library's community, although the most fortunate Library Foundations also have access to revenue from endowments as well. (A goal for many Library Foundations is to create such endowments for sustained long-term funding.) *A Library Foundation has only one priority: the library.* A Library Foundation takes *all* the funds it raises from a variety of fund-raising sources and activities and uses those for one purpose—to advance the library's mission.

The best model for library fund-raising is a *merged* Library Friends and Foundation organization. In this model, a single organization combines the traditional fund-raising activities carried out by Friends groups—book sales, annual funds, author events—with higher-level fund-raising enterprises more typical of Library Foundations, such as maintaining relationships with philanthropic organizations and grant writing, for example. A merged Friends and Foundation will always be a 501(c)(3) nonprofit organization, and it will usually employ paid staff. Paying people to conduct fund-raising activities may seem like a luxury in today's fiscal environment, but the old expression about having to spend money to make money is often true.

If your library does not have a Foundation, establishing one isn't difficult, but the process takes several months. It requires registering a name, filing articles of incorporation, establishing a board of directors, and filing forms pertaining to nonprofit and tax-exempt status. You will have to file forms with both the Internal Revenue Service and your state. Check out the website of your secretary of state's office and navigate that site until you find instructions for forming a nonprofit corporation. See "How to Start a Nonprofit 501(c)(3)Library Foundation" (page 169) for a general guide to the process.

## RECRUITING LIBRARY FOUNDATION BOARD MEMBERS

It is essential to populate your Library Foundation board with individuals who possess the skills, energy, influence, and networks to help with library fund-raising. When recruiting for such a board, look for

- Fund-raising experience
- Legal expertise
- Financial expertise
- Advertising/marketing/PR expertise, or media connections
- Individuals with connections to philanthropic organizations
- Individuals with personal wealth and/or connections to wealthy persons
- People who already support your library with substantial donations

See the "Fund-Raising Board or Committee Recruitment Worksheet" (page 174) to help you start this process.

Once you have recruited an effective Library Foundation board, it will need building and replenishing when members leave or rotate off. Unfortunately, board recruitment in our busy world often works this way: board members realize that they need to recruit some new people, and often they need to do so quickly. What happens? The board members contact friends and colleagues and invite them to join the board. If the invitees feel favorable about the organization, honored to be asked, eager to work with their friends, or feel they have the time to serve on the board, they usually say "yes." The result? There may be enough "bodies" on boards built in this fashion, but critical skill sets are often woefully lacking.

Board recruitment should be a careful, deliberate process. It should not be left to chance or convenience. The method that will guarantee you the strongest members is a formalized one. First, develop a written job description for a board member. See "Board Member Job Description Template" (page 175). Next, establish a small standing committee that meets throughout the year. It should be made up of influential people who appreciate the library's value and will recruit like-minded individuals. Call it the Recruitment Committee or the Nominating Committee. This committee's job will be to (1) identify skill sets and community connections your board needs, then (2) through its members' own networks, identify individuals with those skills and connections.

The committee must then prioritize its list of individuals and determine who it will invite to join your Library Foundation board. Ideally, the best people will be individuals who are known to others already serving on your Library Foundation board. Prospective board members should be *personally* invited to join the board (by a phone call or in person, not through a note or e-mail). If the invitation is issued by someone they know—a friend, business colleague, or neighbor—it will be harder to say no than if it's issued by a stranger. Another effective strategy to persuade someone to say "yes" to your invitation to join your library foundation board is to bring a second individual with you when you issue an in-person invitation. The second person should likewise be someone who is well-known to the invitee and who values the library and understands the importance of private fund-raising for its sustenance.

After your carefully chosen individuals have agreed to join the Library Foundation board, it's imperative to develop an orientation process to familiarize them with the library, as well as with the roles and responsibilities of Foundation board members. At this time, you will also want to be sure they become familiar with the Foundation's meeting schedules, committees, and staff.

## Library Fund-Raising Committee

What if your Friends group isn't willing or able to become higher-level fund-raisers, and you have chosen not to establish a 501(c)(3) Library Foundation? The best strategy under these circumstances is to form a volunteer Library Fund-Raising Committee.

Recruit for this committee in the same way you would recruit for a Library Foundation board; that is, look for energetic *leaders* within your Friends group and your greater community to form the nucleus of your Library Fund-Raising Committee. They should bring enthusiasm, experience, and connections if they're going to be effective at raising private dollars. The goal of a volunteer Library Fund-Raising Committee is the same for that of a Friends group and of a Library Foundation board: to raise the maximum amount of private funding for your library. For help identifying Library Fund-Raising Committee members, see the "Fund-Raising Board or Committee Recruitment Worksheet" (page 174).

Whether your library accomplishes its fund-raising goals through a Friends group, a Library Foundation, or a Library Fund-Raising Committee, give everyone involved opportunities to help on multiple levels. For example, your volunteer fund-raisers can

**Become visible library advocates.** Individuals who are willing to attend city or town council meetings and other gatherings where decision makers hear from their constituents are valuable assets to your library fund-raising efforts. If any of your fund-raising volunteers are retired or former elected officials or holders of influential positions, their visible support brings power and influence, and their advice will prove invaluable. You will read more about the relationship between advocacy and fund-raising in chapter 9.

**Help promote your fund-raising efforts.** They can write letters to the editor of your local paper and help develop stories for your local media outlets. They can make phone calls and send e-mails when it's time to vote on the library's budget or when your fund-raising campaign reaches a critical phase.

**Share valuable fund-raising experience.** A fund-raising volunteer who has been a successful school, church, or other organization's fund-raiser will have much wisdom to share. Experienced fund-raisers can help you avoid common mistakes and make the best use of your library's fund-raising resources.

**Provide hands-on help.** Staffing a fund-raising event, such as a "meet and greet" for potential donors or an author appearance in connection with your fund-raising campaign, is a great way to use fund-raising volunteers. Likewise, when you want personal notes of encouragement on your fund-raising solicitation letters, or when envelopes for solicitation letters need hand-addressing, your fund-raising volunteers can perform these duties.

**Become donors.** Your fund-raising volunteers should all be asked to give. Their personal gifts will not only help provide critical private dollars for your library's resources and services, they will set examples for others who are undecided about giving.

# Library Staff

Don't underestimate the power of library staff when your library is fund-raising! While your non-administrative staff should never ask anyone for a dime—that's your Library Friends, Foundation, or Library Fund-Raising Committee's job—they are your front line when it comes to public opinion.

In today's competitive struggle for private dollars, *a staff that delivers great customer service is your library's best asset.*

## Words to Know

*Front line* refers to any employee who interacts with library users and with individuals in your library's community. In reality, *every* library staff member, regardless of whether he or she has direct contact with library users, is on the front line because *every* staff member is the face of your library to community members who associate that individual with your library.

Their outstanding attitude, energy, and willingness to go the extra mile can turn library users into library lovers, and library lovers into potential library supporters and donors. In fact, poor customer service that generates a negative opinion of your library can seriously damage your fund-raising capacity.

When rallying your staff to help with fund-raising, be sure they understand that they are part of a team. It's imperative that all library staff understand why and how your library is raising money and what the fund-raising message is, so that your community hears a consistent, unified message, not a mixed one.

# Library Trustees

Your library's Board of Trustees was *not recruited*, appointed, or elected to be a fund-raising board. Its job is governance. Its members may be volunteers, but they are not fund-raising volunteers. How can these individuals, then, help with your library's fund-raising?

> **They can be asked to give.** Presumably, their participation on your library's Board of Trustees indicates a personal interest in the library and its well-being. Asking them for personal gifts is entirely appropriate.

> **They can be asked to use their personal and professional connections to advance your library's fund-raising efforts.** Do any of your trustees know persons of influence in your business community? Do they know people who your fund-raising team can solicit for a gift to the library? Ask them!

> **They can assist with communication during a fund-raising effort or campaign.** They can serve as liaisons between the library's governance structure and its Friends or Foundation.

# Consultants

Sometimes it really does take money to make money. You may not need a professional's advice for a book sale, annual fund, or a small fund-raising project, but some kinds of fund-raising activities can benefit from professional assistance. Capital campaigns, for example, can be very difficult to complete successfully without this expertise.

How do you evaluate whether your library can go it alone, or if you need outside help?

---

**Words to Know**

A *consultant* is an expert hired to give advice or guide a client through a project or process.

## Ten Ways Consultants Can Help You

1. **Just starting?** A consultant can help you organize, plan, and set goals, helping you avoid problems down the road.

2. **Can't afford another staff member?** A consultant works on a limited contract, thus you only pay for what you need and for the duration of time that professional help is useful.

3. **Confused?** A consultant can share experiences, both good and bad, to assist you as you make choices along your fund-raising path.

4. **Is your head spinning with fund-raising details?** A consultant can redirect your thinking to the big picture when you get bogged down.

5. **At a loss for ideas?** Consultants have connections to many kinds of resources you may need.

6. **Concerned about coordination?** A consultant can facilitate processes by which your Friends, Foundation, and trustees can act together to strengthen your library's fund-raising efforts.

7. **Worried about board fund-raising fatigue?** A good consultant can energize your board.

8. **Need the truth?** A consultant will provide objectivity, telling you things that library insiders won't—maybe things that are hard to hear.

9. **Feeling doubtful?** A consultant can keep you feeling strong and confident by problem solving and helping you maintain forward momentum.

10. **Losing sight of the end?** Consultants will hold you to your stated goal.

Hiring a consultant doesn't have to be scary or expensive. Good consultants are more than willing to negotiate fees to fit your budget or to work within your budget, whether it's $1,000 or $75,000. Remember: all consultants are not equal. If you want to be successful at raising private funds for your library, it's important to hire a consultant with fund-raising experience.

Begin by talking to others who have used a consultant for fund-raising. Ask questions. How did they find this consultant? What made them think this consultant was a good fit for their fund-raising efforts? Was the consultant easy to work with? Did he or she meet expectations? Was the price for the services a good value? Was the fund-raising effort or campaign successful?

After you select a consultant, be sure to draw up a memo or letter of agreement. That document is a two-way agreement that spells out expectations, deliverables, responsibilities, fees, timelines, and terms of payment. A "Sample Consultant Memorandum of Agreement" is included (page 177).

> ### Words to Know
>
> A *capital campaign* is a fund-raising effort attached to the construction of a new, renovated, or expanded building, or, occasionally, to start or increase an endowment.

Library fund-raising is a team effort in every sense of the word. Raising private dollars successfully requires energy, along with a wide variety of skills, experience, and connections. Tapping into every group associated with your library and its community will bring you a rich bounty of talent and, ultimately, the rewards of fund-raising success.

# 6

# Ready, Set, Go!

**BY NOW, YOU MAY FEEL CONVINCED THAT PRIVATE FUND-RAISING FOR** your library is something worth beginning or expanding. You might have assembled a fund-raising team as outlined in chapter 5, whether that's your Friends group, Foundation, or fund-raising committee. Where's the starting line? The best place to start is with an honest assessment of your library's strengths and challenges. After that, you should assess your library's current fund-raising activities, then develop an implementable future fund-raising plan and a simple means of evaluating success.

## Your Library's Strengths and Challenges

Assessing the library's strengths and challenges is the job of the librarian and the fund-raising team. The insight your team learns from this seven-step process will help it develop a realistic fund-raising plan. See the "Assessing Your Library Worksheet" (page 179) for help with all seven steps of this process.

1. **Understand your library's community.** Begin by looking at your library's community. How is your community changing? What constituency groups does your library serve? List them in *column one* of this worksheet. When you consider constituency groups, think beyond age groups to other kinds of demographic or characteristic identifiers, such as people accessing government services, individuals who want to build language or technology skills, or your local arts community. You may also want to

identify some subgroups, for example, non-English-speaking preschoolers or immigrant-owned local businesses.

2. **Understand what the community needs from your library.** Each of the constituency groups you've identified has specific resources, programs, and services it needs or wants your library to provide, and these will differ from group to group. Job seekers will want computers to access employment sites. They may also want classes in resume writing or creating spreadsheets. Parents of young children will want story times and picture books to check out. Book clubs will want ample copies of their reading selections. Sometimes the needs of one group may conflict with those of another. For example, teens will want the library to be a fun place where they can go after school to study, use computers, and hang out with their friends, while a book club may want your library to be a quiet oasis for adult discussions. These are perennial problems that all public libraries face, and it will take creativity to work them out.

Don't limit yourself to your community's current needs. Look to the future and imagine your library five years from now. What resources, programs, and services will people want more (or less) of then? Use column two of the worksheet to list the kinds of library services each of your community's constituent groups need/will need or want/ will want.

3. **List the ways your library currently seeks to address your community's needs.** Your library provides wonderful resources, programs, and services for most of the constituent groups you've identified, so you're already satisfying many of their needs. These are your library's *strengths.* Use *column three* of the worksheet to list all the ways your library is trying its best to provide appropriate resources and services to various constituent groups in your community. While you're thinking about your library's strengths, what other things can you add that may not be tied directly to a service? For example, your library may be one of your community's most respected organizations, or it may enjoy a strong network of community partnerships. Remember to consider these qualities when you're thinking about your library's strengths.

4. **Identify unmet service and resource needs.** These are your library's *challenges,* and they may have been increased by budget cuts in recent years. Here's where the librarian and fund-raising team must be honest about identifying what your library is *not* able to provide in its current funding environment, and why. When thinking about unmet needs, it's important to remember that many library services are the responsibility of your public officials—not your private funders—and that you may have to advocate actively for these (more on the connection between advocacy and fund-raising in chapter 9).

Your unmet service and resource needs can present you with exciting opportunities too. What innovative services or programs would you like to offer that you currently do not? These may be attractive to private funders. Use *column four* to identify unmet needs and opportunities for enhancement, as well as any other challenges your library faces. (For example, have your private donations or your Friends membership gone down in the past year? Have there been disruptive changes in library staffing? Include these in this column.)

5. **Prioritize your needs.** You can't raise private funds right away for all the unmet needs you've identified, so you should begin by planning to address the needs that are the most compelling and for which a strong case for support can be made. Your fund-raising team should look at all the needs and opportunities you have identified and determine which are the most critical. Choose your top five to ten fund-raising priorities this way. Use *column five* to number your priorities, with number one representing your most urgently needed resource, program, or service.

6. **Estimate costs.** Now, try to put a price tag on each priority. Approximately how much would you have to spend to offer English language classes at your library? To develop a homework help center? To offer workstations for students and adults using laptops? Apply this kind of thinking to each of the highest priorities you identified. Investigate the cost of goods and services for each of your priorities. For example, what's the hourly rate to hire someone fluent in a non-English language to teach English to library users? What will it cost to double the number of electrical outlets in your library? What will it cost to add two extra computers and desks for a homework corner in your youth area? Use *column six* to list approximate costs.

7. **Public or private funds?** The library is a public institution, and it's important that public dollars support it to the fullest extent possible. Private fund-raising should be used to *enhance* library services, not to replace public funds. Take a hard look at each of your priorities and decide which ones should be publicly supported, and which might be attractive to private donors. Remember that donors don't want to pay for the basics. They want their funds used to make your library *great*. Use *column seven* for this purpose.

# Your Library's Current Fund-Raising Activities

If your library doesn't do any private fund-raising at this time, you may want to start with a simple activity that can lay the groundwork that will lead to fund-raising. That activity is "friend-raising."

Friend-raising activities are often entry points—"on ramps"—to an organization such as your library. These activities introduce people to your library's mission, with the purpose of encouraging deeper levels of interest and support. A few examples of friend-raising activities are free community programs and events at the library, your kids' summer reading program, and services to book clubs. They're valuable because they can introduce people to your library when it's at its best. Chances are, your library already does a lot of friend-raising, but you may not have thought of it as a partner to fund-raising.

> **Words to Know**
>
> *Friend-raising activities* are those which expose your organization to different groups of people, but do not include requests for donations to the organization.

Once your library moves beyond friend-raising to actual fund-raising, it must decide whether it will raise money for general needs, also known as unrestricted funds, or for specific purposes (restricted funds). You may decide you must raise money for both purposes.

Use the "Current Library Fund-Raising Activities Worksheet," on page 180 of the Fund-Raising Toolkit to list all the fund-raising efforts you typically undertake in a year. In each of the four columns provided, list (1) the type of fund-raising effort or solicitation, (2) the time of year when you normally do it, (3) the dollars you raised through the activity last year, and (4) "yes," "no," or "maybe" to describe whether it's worth continuing. When considering if an activity is worth continuing, take into account resources

> **Words to Know**
>
> *Restricted funds* are funds tied to a particular use and not available for an organization's general purposes. The party that establishes the restrictions is usually the donor. On the other hand, *unrestricted funds* can be used for general operations or to respond to needs and opportunities that arise. Practically speaking, the most desirable funding to acquire is *unrestricted* because of its flexibility.

such as costs, staff time, volunteers, and space required to do it; and decide whether the activity earns enough to make it worth the effort. In other words, conduct an informal return on investment (ROI) analysis on each of your current fund-raising activities.

# Your Library's Fund-Raising Plan

At this point, you and your fund-raising cohorts have compiled some very valuable information. You've looked at your library's resources, programs, and services to the community, and you've identified unmet needs and opportunities for enhancements. You have prioritized those needs, and thus, you have some idea which ones require immediate attention. You have also taken a hard look at your current fund-raising activities and determined which ones are worth continuing—or possibly starting or expanding—and which ones you might even discontinue. It's time to put a fund-raising plan on paper.

> **Note:** It's not a good idea to raise money for your current budget year. You may not raise enough to cover your expenses, and this can bring on serious budget challenges. Your best plan is to raise money this year that will be spent in your next budget year. That way, you will know exactly how much to count on when planning next year's programs and services.

You want to plan for the upcoming year, of course, but you should consider planning beyond one year. In fact, penciling in a three-year plan will give you a better idea of your future activities and will put year one into perspective. See page 181 in the Fund-Raising Toolkit, "Your Library's Fund-Raising Plan." Use the worksheet to list each of the activities you are going to continue or expand, when you will do it (month or season), what you will do, and your goals for years one, two, and three. Determine who will be responsible for each strategy. Here's an example. Let's say your Friends group conducts an annual fund drive at the end of the year. It consists of a form letter and a response card. Last year you received 100 individual gifts totaling $4,000. How will you improve this effort in the future? What do you want to strive for as dollar goals? Using this example, your worksheet might look like this:

| Fund-Raising Activity | When? | Strategies to Expand | Person(s) Responsible | Goal Year 1 | Goal Year 2 | Goal Year 3 |
|---|---|---|---|---|---|---|
| Annual Fund | Nov./ Dec. | Increase size of mailing by asking all Fund-Raising Committee members for names of individuals they feel should be added to the mailing list. | Ellen, Amy to ask | $6,000 | $8,000 | $10,000 |
| | | Consider purchasing a mailing list. | Ellen to investigate | | | |
| | | Personalize solicitation letters with handwritten notes from Fund-Raising Committee members. | All | | | |
| | | Have Fund-Raising Committee members who know solicitation letter recipients make personal phone calls of encouragement. | All | | | |
| | | Personalize thanks with as many phone calls as possible (by Fund-Raising Committee members). | All | | | |

What if you want to initiate a new activity? For example, assume your Library Fund-Raising Committee had a successful annual fund drive last year, and your mailing list has grown nicely. You think it might be time to see if people would like to purchase bookplates for tribute and memorial gifts. These are gifts given to honor a living person (tributes) or to remember someone who is deceased (memorials). One way libraries do this is to create a permanent book endowment and put all tribute and memorial gifts into this endowment. The drawdown (income) from the endowment purchases books in perpetuity. Here's what your worksheet for initiating a tributes and memorials program might look like:

| Fund-Raising Activity | When? | Strategies to Expand | Person(s) Responsible | Goal Year 1 | Goal Year 2 | Goal Year 3 |
|---|---|---|---|---|---|---|
| Soliciting Tribute and Memorial Gifts | Feb. | Create and print attractive bookplates that have a space for someone's name. | Denise | Total of 10 tribute and memorial gifts | Total of 25 tribute and memorial gifts | Total of 50 tribute and memorial gifts |
| | April | Develop a brochure that explains this giving op-portunity. | Denise | | | |
| | May | Display these brochures in the library. | Ellen to coordinate | | | |
| | June | Mail brochures to Friends, current donors, and other commu-nity members (mail annually). | Amy to coordinate | | | |
| | Every issue | Write an article about tribute and memorial gifts in your library's news-letter. | Charles | | | |
| | Every issue | List tribute and memorial gifts in your newsletter or annual report. | Charles | | | |

All of the fund-raising activities you undertake should have two purposes: to raise private dollars for programmatic and service enhancements, *and* to add names to your donor database and build your prospective donor mailing list.

As you gaze into your fund-raising future, always remember to look for ways to grow your base of support. Use the "Checklist of Sources of Private Support," on page 182 to help you identify many of your library's potential private donors, some of which you might not have considered. Use it to help create a picture of your library's private funding possibilities as you work with your fund-raising plan. The

## Words to Know

A *donor database* is your system for tracking donations and monitoring your donor relationships. While there is an abundance of sophisticated fund-raising database software on the market, a small library can manage its donor information using a simple spreadsheet program such as Excel. Your donor database should contain, minimally, donor contact information, a listing of solicitations he or she has received (with dates), and the amounts and dates of donations. Many organizations also find it helpful to track events that donors attend, note whether donors bring friends to events, and so on. All of this information can help strengthen the relationship between the library and its donors.

more people and organizations you can solicit for private funding, the better chance you have of raising the dollars you'll need to move your library from good to great.

# Evaluating Your Fund-Raising Activities

As you move forward with your fund-raising plan and activities, it's important to take time to assess which activities are worthwhile. After you hold a fund-raising event, pull the organizers together for an hour to discuss and debrief. Do it soon after the event, while memories are fresh. They should ask themselves: How time-consuming was this event? Did it raise enough to meet its goal? Is it worth doing again? If yes, what will we do the same or differently? What should our goal be for next year?

For *every* fund-raising activity you undertake, whether it's a book sale, an annual fund, a grant-writing effort, or any other effort designed to bring in private dollars, your fund-raising team should evaluate its effectiveness by asking questions such as:

- Did this fund-raising activity achieve its goal? (If not, why not?)
- Was this a friend-raising effort as well as a fund-raising activity?
- Did it strengthen individual or community relationships?
- Did it require excessive staff hours or volunteer help?
- Was it labor-intensive for the return it yielded?
- Is it worth continuing?
- Was it successful enough to warrant hiring help next time?

The "Evaluating Your Fund-Raising Activities," worksheet on page 183 will help you accomplish this. The better job you do with evaluation today, the more effectively you will use your fund-raising resources in the future. It's a learning process, and it takes years of experimentation to determine what activities work best for your library and your community. But a combination of careful planning and critical evaluation will go a long way to help ensure *fund-raising success*.

# 7

# Thanking, Honoring, and Nurturing Your Donors ... and Keeping Track of Them

**EFFECTIVE FUND-RAISING IS ABOUT RELATIONSHIPS FIRST, MONEY SEC-**
ond. It's important to remember that *every* point of contact you have with your library's donors affects their relationship with the library. That's why thanking, honoring, and nurturing your library's supporters are essential activities for growing and deepening those relationships. In fact, you can think of these activities as a cycle: (1) You ask for a gift; (2) You thank the donor; (3) You recognize or honor the donor in some fashion; (4) You nurture your relationship with the donor. Then the cycle continues: (1) You ask for a gift . . . and so on. (See figure 7.1.)

## Thanking Your Donors

An attitude of gratitude can carry a lot of weight in today's hurried world. Taking the time to *say thank you in a personal way* can distinguish your library from other organizations that receive donations. You can't say thank you too often. Thanking donors sincerely, promptly, and personally isn't just good business practice, it's the right thing to do. There is also a measure of dollars-and-cents efficiency in thanking supporters in this way because it costs a lot less to retain a current contributor than it does to get a first-time gift. The best way to retain contributors is by providing assurance that their gifts are truly appreciated and will be used to make your library the best it can be. In addition, how you treat each gift—and its giver—will determine whether other gifts follow.

Saying thank you isn't just about acknowledging a current gift; it can have consequences far into the future. When an individual makes a gift to your library—particularly a first-time gift—it might be a spur-of-the-moment decision. Maybe the donor was momentarily compelled by one of your library's fund-raising efforts or by a feeling that he or she wished to pay the library back for all the free services enjoyed. When you acknowledge the gift, you have the opportunity to confer on the donor a sense of personal identification with your library and its mission. As time goes on, that feeling of personal identification can turn into one of being truly invested in and having a sense of belonging to your library. When this happens, people not only continue donating, they usually increase their levels of giving.

*figure 7.1*

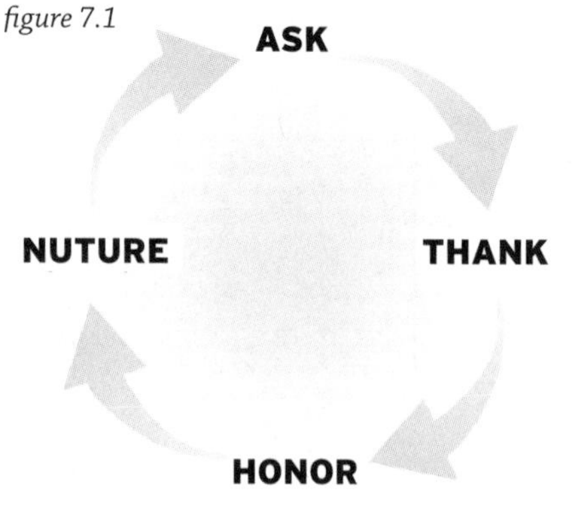

Regardless of whether you are acknowledging a supporter's first gift or hundredth, you should pay careful attention to how you thank your donors. Best strategies include:

- Thanking immediately (within forty-eight hours after receipt of the gift, if possible)
- Making sure donors know about the great work your library does
- Letting donors know about other ways they can support your library

## HOW TO SAY "THANK YOU"

*Thank-you letter*—The most common way of communicating thanks for a donation is to send a thank you letter. This letter—usually a form letter—actually serves two purposes: it tells the supporter that you appreciate his or her gift, *and* it provides a written tax receipt for IRS records. (The IRS requires written acknowledgment for cash donations of $250 or more and for in-kind donations valued at $250 or more.) Remember that while a form letter is the most common method of acknowledging a donation, it's also the least personal.

If you prefer handling your donation acknowledgments using a standard form letter, there are some things you can do to make the letter more personal. Tell the donor how his or her gift will benefit your library. If possible, tell the donor something compelling and newsy, such as how many people have donated so far, how a program to which people are donating is developing, or how gifts will benefit future library programs and services. A "(Standard) Thank-You Letter Template" is included in the Fund-Raising Toolkit (page 184).

In general, your thank-you letter should minimally contain the following elements:

- Name of your library, Friends group, or Foundation to which the gift was given
- Amount of the donation
- Date the donation was made

- Statement confirming that "no goods or services were provided in exchange for this donation." NOTE: If the donor received a thank-you gift or other token of appreciation, such as a meal at a fund-raising event or a complimentary copy of an author's latest book, the fair market value of those goods should be stated in your letter, so the donor knows to subtract that amount from the tax-deductible value of the gift. To see IRS guidelines on this topic, visit its website at: www.irs.gov/pub/irs-pdf/p526.pdf

*Every* gift you receive merits a thank-you letter, but some gifts call for additional thanks. The donor, the size of the gift, and your relationship with the donor all determine whether you should employ more than one method of saying thank you. When you decide that a thank-you letter is not enough, here are a few ideas for additional ways to say thank you in a meaningful way.

**E-mail.** If e-mail feels appropriate for the donor and the size of the gift, an easy option is to send a personal e-mail in addition to your standard thank-you letter. An e-mail message is quick, informal, and the recipient can open and read it at his or her convenience.

**Phone call.** You can also make a personal phone call. This gesture of thanks might be a welcome surprise. Few nonprofit organizations take the time

---

## A Few Financial Facts about Thank-You Letters

**Date of a gift.** Donors are allowed to deduct contributions only in the year the contributions are actually made. This applies whether the donor uses the cash or an accrual method of accounting. The difficulty of determining the "gift date" generally only arises at the end of December and beginning of January. It is the donor's responsibility to determine or assign the gift date, *not* the charitable organization. It is recommended that the receipt from the organization notes the date of the gift (i.e., check date) and the date the gift is processed. This leaves the final determination to the donor and his or her tax advisor.

**Time of making contribution.** Typically, a contribution is made at the time of its *unconditional delivery.* A check that is mailed to a charity is considered delivered on the date it is mailed. Contributions charged on a bank credit card are deductible in the year the charge is made. For stock certificates, the gift of a properly endorsed stock certificate is completed on the date of mailing or other delivery to the charity or to the charity's agent. However, if a donor transfers a stock certificate to the name of the charity, the gift is not completed until the date the stock is transferred to the corporation's financial records.

**Receipts.** It is good practice to receipt for every gift received. Donors must have an acknowledgment, in writing, for every gift of $250 or more. Organizations are required to receipt for any gift of $75 or more if the contribution exceeds the fair market value of the goods and services the donor receives in return for the contribution.

For further information, please review Publications 526 (Charitable Contributions) and 1771 (Charitable Contributions–Substantiation and Disclosure Requirement), which can be found at the Internal Revenue Service's website at www.irs.gov/formspubs.

to phone donors; and when they do call, the caller is usually *asking* for a gift, not thanking someone for one. For larger donations, a thank-you phone call (in addition to the thank-you letter) is always a good practice. The president of one Midwestern library's Friends organization always personally phones individuals who give $100 or more. "It's a great way to nurture donor relationships," he said. "People are happy to hear from us and often say, 'No one else ever calls me to say thank you!'" The best person to make the call is usually a peer—one of your fund-raising volunteers—not a library, Friends, or Foundation staff member (although a call from the head of the fund-raising organization always carries weight). Members of your fund-raising team are the perfect people to make personal phone calls to thank donors.

**Handwritten note.** Another personal and much-appreciated method of saying thank you is to send a handwritten note in addition to your standard thank-you letter. Many nonprofit organizations have developed the practice of scribbling a handwritten *"Thanks!"* or *"We appreciate your contribution!"* on the bottom of their (form) thank-you letter, but this is not the same as a handwritten note. A handwritten, personal note on nice stationery doesn't have to be long, nor does it need to contain any qualifiers about tax donations because that's in the thank-you letter. Its purpose is to convey the message, "Your gift meant so much to us that we took the time to write this note to tell you so." Hand-address and stamp it too. Don't run it through a postage meter. Like the phone call suggested above, a personal note from a *volunteer* on your fund-raising team or perhaps the head of your Friends or Foundation will be more meaningful than one from a paid staff member.

**Visit.** Lastly, probably the most gracious way to thank someone is to do it in person. Making this kind of effort to express your appreciation will really make your library stand out. Again, a member of your volunteer fund-raising team, particularly one who is acquainted with the donor, is the perfect person to do this.

# Recognizing and Honoring Your Donors

It's natural to want to feel appreciated and valued, and one of the hallmarks of appreciation is recognition—honoring your supporters. Here are a few ways your fund-raising team can honor donors:

**Create donor recognition groups.** One common method is by creating donor recognition groups. Nonprofit organizations create categories of donor recognition as a strategy to encourage donors to upgrade their gifts, to give annually, or to commit to special gifts. For example, if you

> **Words to Know**
>
> A *donor recognition group* is a category to which you can assign donors who meet certain giving criteria.

want to recognize *levels of giving*, your library's fund-raising team might determine "platinum," "gold," "silver," or "bronze" giving levels, depending on the size of gifts. A donor of $100 or less might be a bronze donor, while one who gives over $10,000 is a platinum donor. It's not unusual for a donor who has been giving at a certain level to decide to increase his or her gift in order to move up to a higher giving category.

Another way to use donor recognition groups is to name categories for *years of giving*, and/or *kinds of giving* rather than gift amounts. Individuals who have given to your library for ten successive years or longer, for example, might belong to your "Loyalty Circle," and those who have included your library in their wills might be part of your "Legacy Circle."

You can create donor recognition groups as part of your library's fund-raising efforts. How you designate these categories and what you call them are up to you. Remember that you can personalize them for your library and community.

**Recognize your donors in print.** You can do this through your library's newsletter, its annual report, or other publications. Media recognition (such as taking out a newspaper ad) is also a great way to recognize and thank corporate sponsors, table hosts, and so on after your library has held a successful event. Recognizing your donors in print will help in three ways: it demonstrates the existence (and popularity) of private support; it shines a light on those who have given; and it inspires others to follow their example. *Note: Do not publish donor recognition in Web-based social media such as Facebook, however, because donors may not want this information on the Internet in this way.*

**Offer a meaningful gift.** A donor recognition gift is another way you can honor your donors. This is not the same as a free gift or "premium" that you send out with annual memberships or in return for a general donation. It is a gift that recognizes extraordinary giving. It may be something of value, and it may be intended for display. For example, a library Friends organization consulted for this book gives a gift of marble bookends to individuals who have included the Friends group in their wills. These bookends are made from marble that was salvaged from the library's last physical renovation. The bookends are engraved with the planned givers' names. These are real keepsakes that recognize an extremely generous promise of perpetual library support.

**Display donors' names.** Some libraries like to display the names of their donors in a physically public location. Donor name displays, such as plaques or other signage, work best for special fund-raising campaigns such as capital campaigns, but if your community likes to know who supports its library, there's no reason why you can't display your library's supporters' names year-round.

**Hold donor recognition events.** A fun way to honor and celebrate your donors is through donor recognition events. These allow you to say thank you in a public way, and they also give donors a chance to connect with one another. Consider holding donor recognition events annually for individuals in designated donor recognition groups, such as those who give $500 or more per year, or those who have given for ten or more consecutive years. You can plan a simple "Cookies and Cocoa" gathering, an elegant luncheon or dinner, or anything in between. Use the event's program time to express your gratitude for those individuals who support your library and for their dedication to the library's future. Share news about new library resources, programs, and services. Make them feel like *valued insiders*. You might also invite a popular local author or other local notable to speak or to sign books. Before you do this, however, check around and determine whether or not he or she is an engaging public speaker to whom people will enjoy listening. (For help with this, go to the American Library Association's website and check out their "Cultivating Your Local Notables Toolkit" at www.ala.org/advocacy/advleg/advocacyuniversity/localnotables. You don't have to spend a lot of money to send the message "The library appreciates you!" Keep it simple, but make it special at the same time.

# Nurturing Your Donors

After you've thanked and honored your donors, you hope they will feel valued and appreciated. What more do you need to do? To nurture means to care for, and caring for your donors goes beyond thanking and honoring. It means demonstrating that their relationships with your library matter as much as their financial support. The process of nurturing donors is a kind of stewardship, the responsible management of something entrusted to one's care. Inherent in nurturing and stewardship is the goal of moving your donors into a deeper relationship with your library and, consequently, into deeper levels of support. Effective nurturing and stewardship help motivate your faithful donors to give annual gifts, tribute and memorial gifts, major gifts, and planned gifts. (Each of these topics will be discussed later in chapters 10, 12, 13, and 14 of this book.)

The key to nurturing your donors—and to moving them to deeper relationships and greater levels of giving—is to look for ways to have ongoing contact with them *that does not involve asking for support.* In other words, create opportunities for "non-ask contacts." Here are three easy suggestions:

> **Newsletter.** If your library or its fund-raising entity has a newsletter, be sure all donors receive it. If you don't have a newsletter, consider starting one. It's a great communication tool that can make your donors feel connected to your library year-round. The last thing you want is for your donors to hear from you only when you are asking for a donation.

**Personal touches.** Did your library just receive the latest title by an author who is one of your donors' favorites? Call him or her and offer to reserve a copy. Is there a donor with a special interest in a topic such as gardening, financial planning, or travel? If you have an upcoming library program on that topic call, write, or e-mail the donor and say, "Here's something I thought you might be interested in." This kind of above-and-beyond service conveys the donor's value to you in a personal way. You can capture personal information about donors on a simple "Donor Database Checklist," which you can find on page 185 in the Fund-Raising Toolkit.

**Invitations to special donor-only events.** These not the same as donor recognition events, but rather are events planned exclusively for your donors. The purposes are to show appreciation to your donors, to convey the idea that they really *are* special, and to provide them with an opportunity for social engagement with library fund-raisers, staff, and one another. An easy idea for a donor event is to invite an author in for an after-hours meet and greet. Serve refreshments and give people time to mingle. Update them on the library's news and thank them for their support, but *do not* ask for donations at this event. Have something for every attendee to take home, such as a special bookmark that you create for the occasion.

## Ten Great Ways to Thank, Honor, and Nurture Your Donors

1. Send thank-you letters promptly (within forty-eight hours after receipt of a gift).
2. Send personal e-mails to individuals, conveying additional thanks for their gifts.
3. Take the time to make personal phone calls or to send handwritten, personal notes to your larger donors.
4. Get others involved in thanking people—your volunteer fund-raising team or your Friends or Foundation board members, for example.
5. Create donor recognition groups by giving level and by kinds of giving.
6. Recognize your donors in print—in your newsletter, annual report, or other publications.
7. Hold donor recognition events annually, and consider holding special donor-only events too.
8. Develop an idea for a special, meaningful gift you can present to your truly extraordinary donors.
9. Communicate with your donors on an ongoing basis. Don't let your only communication with them be a letter requesting a donation!
10. Be consistently on the lookout for creative, new ways to thank, honor, and recognize your donors.

# Keeping Track of Your Donors

What is your fund-raising team's most important resource, after people? *It's data.* Thanking, honoring, and nurturing your donors are time-wasters if you don't do a good job of keeping track of your supporters, their gifts, and their evolving relationships with the library. As a library staff member or user, you've doubtless come to appreciate the value of databases in organizing important information of all kinds. It's important to capture all of your donors' essential information in a user-friendly donor management system, that is, a database. It will help you manage information about your donors and their gifts, so you know as much as possible about your donors. You can keep track of how much you've raised. You can manage mailings or online fund-raising, and you can print reports. Look at the "Donor Database Checklist" on page 185 for suggestions of donor information you should capture if you want detailed, well-rounded profiles of your supporters.

Your donor database will be your most valuable tool as you broaden your library fund-raising activities, serving as your library and fund-raising team's long-term memory. Effective record keeping and donor tracking will help grow your donor relationships; conversely, a poor or spotty system will ultimately result in weak relationships and fewer gifts. Set up a good, solid system right from the beginning. Don't do it hurriedly or carelessly, with the intention of going back and adding to it or cleaning it up because you may never get around to that.

There is quite a range of choices if you want to purchase software to help you record donations and profile your donors. Microsoft Access offers a database for tracking charitable contributions, and it can be downloaded from Microsoft's website (http://office.microsoft.com). Access has the advantage of easy, intuitive use because it works like other Microsoft applications, such as Word and Excel, and it can interface with those applications for functions such as spreadsheets and mail merges.

Access has limitations, however, so you may also want to consider purchasing a donor database system. These can be acquired for as little as a few hundred dollars or less, and you may find the extra dollars you bring in due to this efficiency pays for the investment. The simplest systems track donors and donations, while more sophisticated (and more expensive) ones have functionalities to support events, memberships, volunteers, and so on. To determine what kind of donor management database your library's fund-raising team needs, talk to others in your nonprofit community and learn what systems they use and how they like them. If your library has a tech staff member, bring him or her into the conversation. You can also find helpful consumer information on Idealware's website at www.idealware .org. Idealware is a 501(c)(3) nonprofit that provides thoroughly researched, impartial, and accessible resources about software to help nonprofits make wise software decisions. (In 2011, for example, Idealware published a free downloadable report, *A Consumers Guide to Low Cost Donor Management Systems*, that compared 29 donor management systems costing $4,000 or less for the first year.) You should also visit the website of TechSoup, a resource for donated or discounted technology products and services. TechSoup is a nonprofit that helps other nonprofits and libraries by providing technology that empowers them to fulfill their missions and serve their communities. Their resources are available for a small administrative fee. Visit their website at http://home.techsoup.org, and check out GiftWorks Standard and other software developed for small nonprofits.

If you choose to keep track of your donors another way, such as a card system or other tracking method, be sure to capture the same kind of information for each donor so you have standardized data in case you want to create specialized fund-raising appeals and to make the system easy and consistent for a variety of users.

However you choose to manage your donor data, do it with thought and care. It is just as important in keeping your relationships with your donors healthy as your newsletter, fund-raising events, and other points of contact are. In fact, if you manage your database well, you'll do a better job with your communication, newsletter, special events, and so on. Maintaining accurate and detailed donor information will serve you well as you grow your donors into lifetime supporters who truly view their library in a personal way.

# 8

# The Role of Marketing and Public Relations in Library Fund-Raising

**IN RECENT YEARS, THE GROWTH RATE IN THE NUMBER OF NONPROFITS** attempting to capture the hearts and dollars of the same people you want to reach has made competition fiercer than ever. At the same time, the weakened economy has reduced the number of discretionary dollars people have to spend on charitable donations. To remain viable and competitive, smart library leaders know that marketing is a process that can turn around a weak fund-raising effort—and it can make your library a friendlier place, too.

You might have an ideal vision of how your library will survive in a challenging economy and even thrive in the years ahead. You might not know that the decision to strive for that growth and success was a *marketing* decision. If you are the director of your library or play a leadership role in its fund-raising efforts, you're probably already engaging in marketing; yet few in your position know that marketing is not simply a promotions program. Everything you do—including fund-raising—has an aspect that supports or affects marketing. In a library, marketing is everyone's job, but someone must take the lead and coordinate the messages, programs, and strategies to build a solid brand, mobilize volunteers, and conduct effective fund-raising. Take charge now, so you can make your library the strongest it can be.

Libraries are great at providing high-quality services, but notoriously bad at bragging about their successes. Marketing, public relations, and advocacy are all about letting more people know about the library's services and value. If you're successful at these, you'll influence others, expand awareness, increase volunteer recruitment, and raise more money. It's important to approach fund-raising with a marketing perspective because people must feel compelled to open your messages and act on them. Use your success stories as the tipping point that turns those who hear your message into library supporters. People want to give, do good, and change their communities for the better. They just need the nudge and the opportunity to give.

# What Is the Difference between Marketing and Public Relations?

Many people use the terms *marketing* and *public relations* interchangeably, assuming they mean the same thing. They do not, although they do have some important aspects in common. Both build a strong foundation for good feelings about your library, and both help attract supporters to your library. Both have the potential to change the way people think, feel, and act.

The American Marketing Association (AMA) defines marketing as a set of processes for creating, communicating, and delivering value to customers and for managing customer relationships in ways that benefit the organization and its stakeholders. Traditional successful marketing comprises a mix of "the Four Ps":

- The right product
- Sold at the right price
- In the right place
- Using the most suitable promotion.

Marketing is about all those things, but marketing is especially about *people*. It's taking what's true and making it interesting and attractive to your audience. Good marketing takes time. To be successful, you must have a plan and the patience and persistence to pull it off.

Library marketing and marketing for fund-raising are different from traditional marketing because your product is not something tangible. Your product is a strong library and a better community because of it. Thus, the "Four Ps" of traditional marketing—product, price, place, and promotion—are turned somewhat inside out.

"Products" can include the programs, services, and resources your library provides, as well as more subtle things like understanding, knowledge, and belief in the role libraries have in improving lives.

"Price," in the case of public libraries, is what the public contributes to the library's resources through their tax dollars, but often public funding covers only the "bare bones." That is why libraries need private charitable donations. There are also other costs to library users, for example, transportation costs associated with getting there to access materials, and returning borrowed items on time.

"Place" refers to not only your location(s), but also public access to your library via its website, social media channels, mobile app, bookmobile, drive-through book drops, satellite community bookshelves, and so on.

"Promotion" can include free media placement and paid advertising; a vigorous social media program using multiple channels; strong, permanent signage; word-of-mouth endorsements and direct mail, just to name a few.

Public relations (PR) is about enhancing your image. It is the practice of managing communication between your library and the stakeholders and audience it serves. Good PR exposes your audiences to stories and news items that illustrate endorsement of your library by community members, business leaders, and elected officials. PR specialists are *advocates* who help create and protect an organization's image. They spread good news about their library, or they manage crisis communications by putting a positive "spin" on unfavorable news that may already be circulating. They accomplish this by working with the media, sending out press/media releases, and setting up photo opportunities to show the public that their library is doing great things in the community. They might also speak at conferences and civic events, engage in social media, and conduct employee communications.

> **Words to Know**
>
> Public relations specialists are sometimes referred to as "spin doctors." This nickname originated in the 1980s when people used it to describe public affairs specialists and press secretaries. Today, people use the phrase to describe anyone in public relations.

There are two prime messages you can use to promote your services, and both are about the value of libraries to your community:

**Statistics about volume, and positive outcomes.** Your library keeps track of many statistics, and people like to see information boiled down to understandable data. How can these be used to illustrate the importance of your library to its community? For example, talk about the number of hours that teens use your library for homework help. Students who do so often report improved grades as a result. (This is anecdotal support but can still convey an honest, powerful message.) The fact that the students keep coming back to the library for help with their homework illustrates the value it adds to their lives.

**Stories with emotional impact.** Your job is to explain how what you do *impacts people's lives.* Don't be afraid to ask the people who use the library to tell their own stories. Make those whom you've helped the voice of your library and its chief outreach ambassadors. You can tell a story that begins with a challenge, but focus on the positive outcome the library helped make possible.

Repetition, repetition, repetition. No matter which messages and themes you choose to use, it's important to be consistent and repeat them again and again. Most people need to see your message at least *three times* before they're going to respond.

# Online Marketing

You've read in an earlier chapter that *75 percent of all charitable giving in the United States comes from individuals, not institutions*. When you focus on individual givers, you need to remember that, today, more and more of those people are donating and taking action online. You'll read about online fund-raising in chapter 16, but it's important at this point to keep one thing in mind: *you should be collecting donations on your website with a compelling, library-branded and secure donation page*.

The World Wide Web offers an infinite number of ways to spend time and unlimited means of marketing your message and mission. With individuals spending more and more time online every day, your website must offer a virtual education, as well as a compelling experience that consistently engages users to visit the site. You also want them to click through on an e-mail campaign or follow up on a social message—ultimately making a donation—rather than an infinite number of other options that take them off your site. With that in mind, every option and design element presented to a user should be meaningful and relevant to your brand, mission, and desired outcomes for that user's visit.

Your online and offline outreach should be seamlessly and visually integrated. When you take the time to create beautiful and inspiring print materials for your latest fund-raising campaign, use those images and stories on your website and in your e-mail campaigns. You can use QR codes (for "Quick Response"—those little black and white digital squares you sometimes see in magazine ads and on posters) to allow constituents with smartphones the option to visit your website the moment they're inspired to do so. People will respond emotionally to your story and, when they scan the code that takes them to your online donation page, they'll recognize the look and contribute with confidence.

## E-MAIL—HTML "BLASTS"

The CAN-SPAM Act of 2003 authorizes a penalty per violation for spamming each individual recipient. Just as detrimental, your IP address or domain name can easily be blacklisted as a spam source, causing *all* your organization's e-mail—not just marketing messages—to be blocked. Therefore, if you want to engage in e-mail marketing, use a provider or software designed for bulk e-mail marketing, such as Emma, MailChimp, VerticalResponse, iContact, or Constant Contact—not Outlook—to communicate with your community of supporters and ensure compliance with the Act. The contact list that is used must be an "opt-in" (or permission-based) e-mail list. Services typically require users to authenticate their return address and include a valid physical address, provide a one-click unsubscribe feature, and prohibit importing lists of purchased addresses that may not have given valid permission. E-mail marketing campaigns targeting a specific demographic group can be tracked by capturing open and click rates to see how the campaign is doing.

## SOCIAL MEDIA

Not everyone who uses social media is young. According to insidefacebook.com, the largest group of users (43 percent) is 18–25 years old, but other segments are rapidly growing. One-quarter of users are over 35, and those 55 and older are increasing too. Women are the fastest-growing gender on the network, making up 56 percent of all users. When you combine that with the fact that women volunteer more and engage more in philanthropic giving, you'll see that social media are an important channel for reaching potential supporters. There are countless other organizations working right now to attract the attention of the people in your community. Your competition is using social media and you should too! Develop a social media strategy and commit the resources necessary to achieve your clearly articulated, measurable goals. Continually compare how your efforts are performing against your targets.

There hasn't been overwhelming evidence of a direct link between social media and effective fund-raising, but nonprofits are starting to realize how social networks can provide the ability to spread their missions to the masses. Insideface book.com reports that 17 percent of all time spent online via personal computers in the United States is on Facebook. Your relationship with your donors and volunteers can also be cultivated and nurtured through social media. Not only can you deliver updates and announcements, you can leverage those who join your network and ask them to pass on the word—the key to "the network effect."

> **Words to Know**
>
> The *network effect* is the effect that the user of a good or service (like your library) has on the value of that product to others.

Keep in mind that the rules on social networking are completely different from traditional marketing communications. In some ways you're dealing with a different breed of constituent—not necessarily a donor or even a prospect in the traditional sense—and your opportunity to engage is shorter and more ephemeral than ever. That said, the fundamentals familiar to any fund-raiser still apply: people engage with those recommended by friends and others they trust, and—as both veteran fund-raisers and social media strategists can agree—relationships begin with conversations based on listening and meaningful engagement rather than one-way dialogue.

## TEN TOP SOCIAL NETWORKS

The following list is not intended to be comprehensive, nor is it a list of all the activities that you need to engage in. It is merely an overview of some of the most popular and effective social networks for any library that's trying to raise private dollars. Don't try to do them all, but select a few that you can commit the time and resources to, and keep pushing your message and building relationships.

1. **Blogging.** Raise awareness of your library by blogging. A blog post doesn't have to be long; make it the length of an e-mail message. Update regularly to build a following and increase traffic to your website.

Hosting your blog on your library's domain and using keywords and tags will increase traffic to your site through search engine optimization.

2. **Delicious.** A network for sharing Internet bookmarks. Use it to research the most popular and powerful sites, improve your search engine optimization by linking to your own website and blogs, and connect with others by sharing links. Build relationships by visiting blogs and commenting on them.

3. **Digg.** Another social bookmarking site; members vote on their favorite links and the more popular the link, the more website traffic gained.

4. **Facebook.** Increase the frequency of your exposure by participating regularly. Deepen relationships, share photos, messages, likes and dislikes. Start discussions and create fan pages for library programs, and link to other social networking sites through Facebook. With more than 150 million users in the United States, you'll find many friends on the network.

5. **LinkedIn.** This is a business-focused network that will help you connect with professionals and entrepreneurs. It's a great place to ask questions and get answers from qualified experts, find new staff referrals and program partners, and get introduced to powerful people. Connect with more people by asking for introductions and recommendations from your contacts.

6. **MySpace.** Once a very popular social network, MySpace has lost some of its share but remains a good channel for reaching a culturally diverse audience with an especially strong emphasis on music and the arts.

7. **Podcasting.** Think of a podcast as an audio blog, and create one just as you would a written blog. Saving it in MP3 format allows people to choose how they want to access and listen to your content. It's not necessary to have high production values or long episodes. Make it available through RSS feeds and post it on iTunes and other podcast distribution sites. With permission, recorded author visits in your library make great content people want to hear.

8. **Twitter.** Posting 140-character updates throughout the day increases followers and expands awareness of your activities. Include links to your website and to news or other sites where followers can go for more information. Use a link-shortening service like bit.ly or TinyURL to make your links as short as possible so you can fit your message in that 140-character limit. Retweet others' posts, use hashtags (# followed by the topic) in ongoing conversations. Follow people who follow you, and people will generally follow you if you follow them.

9. **Wikipedia.** A comprehensive encyclopedia about everything, edited by its users. Don't try to market on the site because you'll be kicked off as a user, but make sure the information about your organization is accurate and up-to-date.

10. **YouTube.** Early in 2013, YouTube hit one billion monthly users. If the service was a country, its population would be the third largest in the world, after China and India. Get your message onto the largest network of video viewers by creating a video blog. Posting videos is easy, and engaging with others on the network through "favoriting" and commenting will help create relationships and increase awareness. Don't leave the info sections about your library blank. Use keywords, good copy, and include links.

# Branding and Identity

Branding is important for fund-raising because it is about helping people know how to remember you. It's not just about putting your logo on everything! Good branding fills people's minds with meaning and positive associations about your organization. If people don't have an idea about you already, don't leave it up to chance that they'll make up their minds and assign the right meaning and influences to your work and identity. Find the benefits your library brings to people and help them associate those benefits with its name. Tie your brand to what motivates people: feelings first, and then logic.

Another aspect of branding is the use of taglines. Taglines are slogans, phrases, or brief sentences that express the spirit of your organization and are easy to remember. They should be tied to your mission, vision, and values. A tagline should not be changed from year to year, but should support your brand and reputation consistently—no matter how often your campaign themes may change. Sometimes a tagline can be built into your logo. If you have a tagline, use it often. It will remind people of who you are and what you're striving for. Examples of strong taglines are: "Opening Doors Wider," "Here for Good," "We Build Strong Kids, Strong Families, Strong Communities," and "A Mind Is a Terrible Thing to Waste."

## Words to Know

The term *branding* means a collection of functions necessary to make a business or nonprofit successful, requiring ongoing effort to:

- Increase the public's awareness of your organization's name and logo
- Build a strong company "essence" or personality that inspires loyalty and trust in your current customers and provides a level of familiarity and comfort to draw in potential new customers

# Media Relations

One of the most powerful PR tools is *free* media placement. Free publicity on TV, radio, magazines, newspapers, and online is great because people tend to trust and believe articles and stories from the media more than advertisements, so you get better results. Here are some great reasons to send out press/media releases:

- You've just launched a new product or service.
- You just hit a big number (for example, your library's millionth customer served).
- You have a tie-in to a major national story.
- You are opening a new branch.
- You're adding new jobs to the community.
- You just received a major grant, especially if it adds more jobs.
- You've just won an award.
- You've been selected to have your library visited by a leading politician.
- You have more _____ than anyone in town (PhD or MLIS degrees, minority workers, days without accidents, etc.).
- You have something exciting coming up on your calendar.

## OTHER WAYS TO GET FREE MEDIA PLACEMENT

Post content about your library and its services, or articles about issues of interest to all libraries (like advocacy), on multiple websites. Write a regular column in the community paper. Participate in conferences. Contribute to online forums. The goal is to have your name show up repeatedly in search engines. Reporters turn to search engines as their primary source of information when they are looking for experts in any given subject area. If your library's name turns up only once, they have just one chance to see you. But if it comes up repeatedly in their search results, they're likely to think you must be the expert on that topic, so you're the one who will get the phone call. It won't happen overnight, but it can be very valuable once it does happen. Another way to get on the radar of reporters is to sign up at HARO—Help a Reporter Out. Each day you'll receive an e-mail with a list of specific media queries. If you're qualified to respond to a specific query, act fast and watch how fast you become the trusted, go-to authority. Keep it simple. The reporter will contact you for more details.

Libraries and their fund-raising organizations need to be better at marketing. For-profit businesses have big marketing budgets to spend on advertising, and there's no way your library or its fund-raising organization can keep up with their spending. Rather than being focused on big budgets and big plans, however, libraries and their fund-raising organizations need to be focused on *big impacts*. By being creative and keeping the "fun" in fund-raising, you can show people how your library aligns with their values and raise more money to keep your library and your community strong.

# 9

# Fund-Raising for "the Other 95 Percent" of Your Library's Budget

**WHAT IS "THE OTHER 95 PERCENT" OF YOUR LIBRARY'S BUDGET? IF** you're a public library, it's your *public funding.* The public funding provided for a public library will always represent the largest portion of its budget—and rightfully so; yet many library fund-raising groups don't stop to think about the impact they can have on this revenue. It's up to library fund-raising groups to both raise private funds *and* conduct advocacy activities that secure strong public support for the majority of the library's budget. While library fund-raising organizations such as Friends groups can typically raise private money that represents anywhere from 1–10 percent of the library's total budget, in these difficult economic times they can't ignore the other 90–99 percent of the library's budgetary needs.

## What Is Advocacy?

The word *advocacy* is used frequently these days in discussions about the public funding of libraries. Based on the context in which it is used, it can have a number of definitions. There are soft approaches to advocacy that include heightening public awareness of the library and talking with individuals about the importance of library services. However, a more meaningful approach to advocacy for our libraries is to initiate a *formal* process of communicating with elected officials and governing boards about the importance of strong library funding. It also includes making recommendations to elected officials for appropriate levels of public funding support.

In this chapter, therefore, advocacy means the active involvement of citizens serving as lobbyists to communicate to elected officials the need for strong public funding for libraries.

# The Relationship between Advocacy and Fund-Raising

In today's world, adequate funding for many kinds of services is becoming more and more difficult to secure. Budgets are tight, and services get cut as a result. That includes library budgets and library services. By developing meaningful advocacy messages and employing advocacy strategies, you can help others understand the value of your library to the community and motivate them to help ensure that its budget remains strong and healthy. Pairing advocacy with fund-raising is especially effective for any service or institution that is predominantly supported by public funding—like a library.

Here are four reasons why it's important to include advocacy in any discussion about private fund-raising:

1. **To keep the library from being overlooked.** The love that many citizens feel for their library doesn't necessarily equate to strong public funding. Without a voice in support of libraries, elected officials are likely to overlook the need for funding public libraries at a high level. Many libraries are funded from what is called the general fund of a city or county, a fund that also includes services such as police, fire, and public works. In those settings, funding for the library typically can be overlooked as it only represents about 1–3 percent of most cities' or counties' general fund budget. This lack of visibility in the budgeting process is reason enough for citizen advocates to come forward and make a case for the importance of strong public funding of the library.

2. **To ensure that public dollars cover the basics.** Because private donors recognize that the library is a *public* institution, they don't want their private contributions to take the place of government funding. They expect their contributions to provide a margin of excellence and enhanced library services, not make up for lost public dollars. For this reason, the library's fund-raising organization should conduct annual advocacy activities that encourage elected officials to provide *high levels of public support*. In fact, the library's fund-raising organization has an obligation to its private donors to conduct these advocacy activities to ensure that private contributions are being used for *enhancement* of library services. This can be challenging today because many public libraries are experiencing painful budget cuts.

3. **To raise the library's visibility in the community.** An advocacy campaign also brings attention to the library. It creates greater awareness

of the library's services and funding needs. It's a lot like conducting an annual promotional campaign for the library, which always helps in fund-raising efforts.

4. **To leverage politically active people's connections.** Conducting advocacy activities on behalf of the library will have the added benefit of attracting a different type of individual to a library fund-raising team or to a Friends or Foundation board. Politically active people can be a valuable asset for fund-raising. While these individuals may not make large personal gifts, politically active people know and are known by virtually everybody in the community. They can open almost any door in town for your library's fund-raising purposes. In fact, experience has shown that former elected officials, as well as business, civic, and community leaders, make the best spokespeople for the library's needs in an advocacy campaign.

# How to Conduct Advocacy Activities

Learning a few basic guidelines will help you do a better job with advocacy as you weave it into your fund-raising organization's efforts. Here are a few tips:

**The right person should deliver your advocacy message.** One of the most important things to understand about advocacy is that *the person doing the communication is just as critical as the message.* This is similar to fund-raising because the results of fund-raising, as explained in chapter 1, frequently rest upon the relationship between one individual and another. When library directors and library staff approach elected officials about the need for more funding in the library's budget, these individuals are always perceived as self-serving. However, when private individuals, business representatives, and civic leaders bring that same message to the elected officials—with nothing professionally to gain—elected officials view these requests for funding in an entirely different light. These advocates are perceived as interested in the welfare of the community. (Hint: Asking a former elected official to chair your advocacy committee is an excellent idea.)

**Advocacy should be a structured activity.** Advocacy should not be an occasional activity of your library support organization. If you want to be successful at advocacy, create a standing committee (or other formal group) within your library support organization's structure. Just as other fund-raising committees function as year-round committees, so too should the advocacy committee.

**The library director must be directly involved in any advocacy effort.** The involvement of the library director is a critical component in any successful advocacy effort because the last thing that any library needs are citizen advocates who are advocating for funding that is not a priority to the library. The library director should stay in close touch with citizen advocates to educate them about the library's funding needs and to make sure that the message being delivered to the elected officials is one that fully reflects the needs and priorities of the library at this time.

**You'll need a clear, written advocacy platform.** Through a process of several meetings, an advocacy committee—with the library director—should develop a list or "platform" of funding initiatives for which it wishes to advocate. The advocacy platform should also have specific dollar amounts for initiatives being requested because there is nothing harder for an elected official to respond to than an advocacy request which states, "please increase funding for the library." Instead, elected officials will look more favorably upon a request which specifically says, "Please increase the library's materials budget by $25,000 per year because of (1) a 10 percent increase in library utilization, and (2) an increasing variety of formats our community requires today." Draft the advocacy platform into a printed document.

**Personal meetings with elected officials are critical.** After drafting an advocacy platform, the final step of the process is to have advocacy committee members meet personally with each elected official. The meetings are best arranged by a specific official's constituent—someone who lives within the ward or district or county of an individual with whom they are meeting. While the meeting should be set up by a constituent, it is important that one additional member of the advocacy committee be designated to attend each of the meetings so that a continuity of message can be guaranteed. These meetings provide an opportunity for your advocacy committee to speak with the elected official about the importance of the library and its needs *and* to leave behind a copy of the printed advocacy platform. Following visits to elected officials, it is also appropriate for advocates to attend meetings of the budget committee, City Council, or County Commission. This continued visibility in front of the elected officials is critically important for the success of an advocacy effort.

**Advocating for public dollars, like private fund-raising, should be an ongoing activity.** It's extremely important that citizen advocacy efforts are conducted year-round and year after year. An effort launched at the eleventh hour when budget cuts are imminent is almost never successful, nor is a one-year-only process. When elected officials know that the library has an active, *ongoing* advocacy program, and that members of the advocacy committee will be meeting with them every year about the library's needs, your advocacy effort gains real credibility. This approach also raises the consciousness of your elected officials around library needs and funding, keeping it on their "radar screens."

If your library is on a calendar fiscal year, here is a sample schedule:

| Month | Advocacy Activity |
|-------|-------------------|
| *March* | Advocacy committee begins meeting, with goal of developing a clear advocacy platform |
| *June* | Finalize and print advocacy platform |
| *Summer months* | Advocacy committee members hold personal meetings with elected officials and leave behind copies of the advocacy platform |
| *Fall months* | Advocacy committee members attend budget hearings and add public testimony<br>Advocacy committee contacts the media to publicize the advocacy platform |
| *December* | Elected officials adopt a budget after being exposed to nine months of advocacy efforts on behalf of your library |

# The Legality of Lobbying and Advocacy

While effective advocacy is essential to securing public funds, the legality of lobbying and advocacy on the part of nonprofits is often misunderstood by many individuals, including some attorneys. The first thing to understand is that lobbying on the part of a nonprofit 501(c)(3) organization is completely legal.

> **Words to Know**
>
> *Lobbying is one* form of advocacy that involves making formal requests of elected officials for specific policy and funding initiatives.

The IRS has developed guidelines to help nonprofit organizations understand how they may go about lobbying and advocacy legally. In general, the prohibitions against lobbying are quite simple: (1) *Nonprofit organizations are not allowed to endorse a specific candidate for an elected office.* A nonprofit which chooses to do this will definitely be in danger of losing its 501(c)(3) nonprofit status. (2) *Lobbying expenses should not constitute a substantial part of the organization's budget.* The guidelines under these "substantial part" tests are fairly vague, however, and many nonprofits don't feel comfortable with this loose interpretation of lobbying legality. As a result, the expenditure test provided for in Section 501(H) of the IRS rules for charities (see www.irs.gov/charities/article/0,,id=163394,00 .html) allows nonprofit organizations to file an IRS form in which they agree that their annual expenditures for lobbying for the first $500,000 of income will not exceed 20 percent of the total expenditures of the organization. If a nonprofit organization spends more than 20 percent of its income on lobbying in any given year, it does not lose its tax-exempt status. Instead, the organization is taxed for the excess amount of money spent over 20 percent. The taxation rate for this overage in spending is 25 percent.

In addition, lobbying can be classified as either "direct" or "grassroots" lobbying. Direct lobbying is any attempt to influence legislation by communicating with the legislative body. This also includes expenditures for ballot measures. Grassroots lobbying, on the other hand, intends to influence legislation by affecting the opinions of the members of the general public. For example, if a library support organization communicates with its members about legislation of direct interest to the library, this isn't lobbying; but if the communication urges the members to contact their elected officials, then the activity is considered grassroots lobbying.

The total of all direct and grassroots lobbying expenditures should not exceed 20 percent of the total organization's expenditures. In addition, the amount of lobbying expense that can be spent on grassroots lobbying is 25 percent of the total amount allowed for lobbying. Here's an example of an organization's lobbying expenses: If the budget of a library Friends group is $10,000 in any given year, then—using the expenditure test—the organization can spend up to 20 percent of that budget ($2,000) on all of its lobbying activities and 25 percent of the $2,000 ($500) on grassroots lobbying. If the Friends spent $3,000 on lobbying instead of the $2,000 they were entitled to, they would be required to pay a 25 percent tax on the last $1,000 of expenses in excess of the $2,000 allowed, or $250 in taxes.

Although these formulas may sound complicated, the reality is that most non-profit organizations spend a very small percentage of their budgets on lobbying activities because so much of lobbying occurs through volunteer efforts and through electronic communications.

One of the best sources of information about this topic can be found in the archives of the Friends and Foundations of California Libraries. David Guy, an attorney, and former president of the Friends of the Sacramento Public Library and the Sacramento Public Library Foundation, has written an article for the Friends and Foundations of California Libraries that is extremely comprehensive and lays out these guidelines quite well. This article is reproduced in the Fund-Raising Toolkit of this book. See page 187: "Advancing Our Libraries: The Legal Opportunities and Limits for Nonprofit Lobbying."

# Leveraging Private Funds to Secure Public Funds

One of the best cases to be made for lobbying and advocacy by your library's fund-raising organization is the potential to use private support to strengthen the argument for public support. Organizations that don't have their own private resources come to the lobbying table—to elected officials—begging. On the other hand, a fund-raising team, Friends group, or Library Foundation that raises thousands of dollars of private funds for the library comes to the lobbying table from a position of strength. It is viewed in a very different light. Very few elected officials want to turn away private funding which could be made available by the addition of small amounts of public funding. Leveraging can be a powerful tool when raising private money and advocating for strong public funding from elected officials.

When you think about fund-raising for your library, it's easy to limit your thinking to ways you can raise private dollars, but the reality is that you can't ignore the importance of maintaining strong public support at the same time. Effective advocacy raises the visibility of your library in the eyes of elected officials and should complement your private fund-raising efforts. Think of it as a two-pronged approach: public dollars ensure that your library can continue to provide strong, essential services for your community, and private dollars help fund the enhancements that make your library truly special.

**PART TWO**

# Roll Up Your Sleeves—Types of Fund-Raising Activities

# 10

# Creating a Culture of Giving through Annual and Special Appeals

**FUND-RAISING, AS YOU'VE READ IN PREVIOUS CHAPTERS, SHOULD BE A** well-planned, year-round activity—not an occasional hit-or-miss effort. Regular (creative!) fund-raising appeals should be high on your list of priorities of annual tasks for staff and volunteers. The good news is that an appeal that is conducted on a regular basis, such as an *annual appeal,* is one of the easiest ways to incorporate private fund-raising into your library's overall operations. (You may also find that, once an annual appeal has been in place for several years, individuals will begin giving larger amounts as their giving habit solidifies.) *Special appeals,* on the other hand, give your library or its fund-raising organization the opportunity to focus in on specific needs and fill targeted gaps.

The success of *any* appeal—whether annual or special—depends upon your ability to develop a strong case for support and to persuade potential supporters of the worthiness of your library. To start thinking about how you can begin or improve regular fund-raising solicitations, look at the calendar of your library's activities. Are there some that naturally lend themselves to the inclusion of a fund-raising campaign or event? For example:

- Do you send an annual report to your supporters in the spring? While you are telling the world all the great things you did in the previous year, why not ask for a donation?
- Is your summer reading program a huge community draw? Leverage the popularity of that program and tie it to a special fund-raising effort.

- Do you solicit donations in November or December? The end of the year is an obvious time to ask your supporters for a donation because people are used to giving during the month of December. Year-end gifts often tend to be larger because people think about tax deductible donations at that time. Thus, a year-end solicitation has the potential to raise significant revenue for your library.

# Annual Appeals

An annual appeal (or "annual fund") is simply an organized campaign to secure individual donations on an annual basis. Although generally thought of as a year-end appeal, an annual appeal can occur at any time throughout the year. Your library or its fund-raising organization can conduct an effective annual appeal campaign by using direct mail pieces (solicitation letters and brochures), as well as one-on-one "asks" by library volunteers who are willing to make personal solicitations. These materials and personal asks should highlight the good works that your library has accomplished during the year, remind potential donors that a gift to your library or its fund-raising organization is tax deductible, and ask for a generous *unrestricted* donation.

Regardless of when you choose to schedule it, every library should have—at the very least—*one* annual solicitation of individuals asking for unrestricted support of the library and its programs. Focus on the individuals who are ready, willing, and able to make a gift—people who have an interest in what the library is doing—and encourage them to make their gift a large one!

One last important thought: fund-raising is obviously about *gifts*—but what exactly constitutes a "gift"? It's not as easy a question as it may seem. See "What Is a Gift?" (page 191) in the Fund-Raising Toolkit for some thoughts on this topic. In addition, every nonprofit that accepts gifts should have a Gift Acceptance Policy in place. Such a policy will help define what types of gifts will be accepted and how they will be used. A "Sample Gift Acceptance Policy" (page 193) is included in the Fund-Raising Toolkit as well.

> **Words to Know**
>
> An *unrestricted gift* can be used just about anywhere a nonprofit has a need. Because it can be used for general operating expenses, it is always the best kind of gift to receive. A *restricted gift*, on the other hand, must be used according to the terms of the gift. For example, a donor might restrict his or her gift for the purchase of children's books or for funding a specific endowment.

# A Keystone for Your Library's Fund-Raising

A keystone is a wedge-shaped stone that locks together all the other pieces of an arch. (See figure 10.1.) It's a good metaphor for a library or its fund-raising organization's annual appeal because an annual appeal offers:

> **Visibility.** An annual appeal keeps your library "front and center" in people's minds and reminds donors of both your library's critical services and the library staff's good work. In this way, it keeps donors loyal and invested

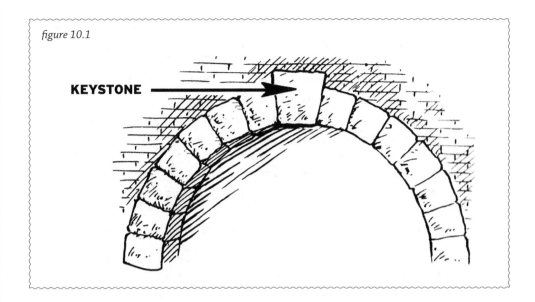

figure 10.1

KEYSTONE

in your library and lays the groundwork for other kinds of fund-raising efforts you might undertake.

**Flexibility.** Because an annual appeal customarily raises *unrestricted* funds, those dollars can be spent wherever they are most needed. An annual appeal, thus, communicates to potential library supporters the importance of giving *unrestricted* dollars.

**Relationship building.** Your annual appeal can become an individual donor's stepping-stone to a higher level of giving, or to other kinds of giving. From regular giving as annual appeal donors, for example, individuals can progress to becoming "major" gift donors (see chapter 13 for more information on major gifts), and finally to "planned gift" donors, leaving gifts to your library in their will or estate plan. See chapter 14 to learn about planned gifts.

# Getting Started

If you've never done any formal fund-raising and currently have no annual or other regular appeal in place, you can begin your first annual appeal campaign with a modest investment of time and effort on the part of a few volunteers and staff.

**Start with a brainstorming session.** Gather together a group of library insiders like key staff, trustees, and volunteers to talk about a fund-raising appeal. Establish a goal and a budget. Ask each individual present to write down the names of five to ten individuals whom they know and to whom they are willing to send a letter, soliciting a contribution. Find out from your governing entity (city/county/township/etc.) whether you are allowed to solicit *all* your library's cardholders. Most libraries differ in their policies regarding patron mailings. If you are allowed access to these names and addresses for solicitation purposes, then use them. Keep in mind, however, that your best donors may not necessarily be library users. Ask everyone who is involved in creating the campaign—*all* your volunteers—to make a personal donation. The size of his or her donation isn't important; but it is much easier to ask for a donation from others when you can say "please join me in making a gift." Ask one volunteer to gather all the names and remove any duplicates. Create a very simple database—perhaps just a basic spreadsheet at this point—with those individuals' names and addresses. Add columns that will indicate whether they respond to your solicitation letter and the amount of their gift.

**Draft a compelling solicitation letter.** It should be no longer than *one page* in length, so be clear and succinct as you develop your case for support. Sing your library's praises, and include highlights of its programming and services. Talk about how the library is used, and by whom. Use bullets to make your points. (They're reader-friendly and require you to boil your statements down into as few words as possible.) Consider quoting a volunteer, or telling a library user's story. Show that your library and its fund-raising organization are good stewards of both public and private dollars. See the tips below for creating an effective solicitation letter, as well as the "Sample Annual Appeal Solicitation Letter" on page 204.

**Create a donation (remittance) card and envelope.** Along with your solicitation letter, you can include a remittance card and a self-addressed return envelope *or* a printed remittance envelope that allows donors to fill out their personal information directly on the envelope's inside flap.

**Use the Web.** Determine how you can use your website, as well as social media, to get your fund-raising appeal's message out there.

**Track all donations.** Create a simple database that records donations of all kinds throughout the year. This database will become the basis of your annual appeal's mailing list. Building your database throughout the year will give you a strong start for your next campaign. Keep it simple. Don't create a database that is difficult for someone else to use. See chapter 7 for information about creating a donor database if you don't already have one.

**Thank your donors immediately.** Timeliness is extremely important. Send a thank-you letter as soon as each gift is received. Set a goal of a forty-eight-hour turnaround time for thanking your annual appeal donors. Whenever possible, make a thank-you phone call too. When donors feel appreciated, they will be motivated to give again. Generally, thank-you calls from volunteers are more effective than those from paid staff. See chapter 7 for advice and tips for thanking your donors in meaningful ways.

**Consider hosting a "thank-you" event for your annual appeal donors.** This can be a low-cost gathering for donors who meet or exceed a specified giving level. See chapter 7 for more information on donor recognition events.

## TIPS FOR EFFECTIVE SOLICITATION LETTERS AND FOLLOW-UP

1. **If you can, hand-address solicitation letters.** It increases the likelihood that the envelope will be opened.

2. **Put a first-class stamp on your solicitation letter.** Anything other than a first-class stamp will get less attention from a potential donor. Bulk mail rates may be cheaper, but remember: you want your mailing piece to make a good impression to increase the likelihood of being opened and read.

3. **Whenever possible, personalize your letters.** Address the donor by name. Never start your letter with "Dear Library Friend." Using the mail merge feature in Microsoft Word is easy. There are also mailing services that can merge data into your letter so that each will be personalized; however, there is a cost to this service.

4. **Add a personal, handwritten note to the letter whenever possible, encouraging giving.** This is best done by someone—a volunteer, not a library staff member—who knows the recipient. A simple note like "Jane, the library would appreciate your support!" (signed by a person Jane knows) will do.

5. **Include a response card and self-addressed return envelope.** No stamp is necessary on the return envelope because most donors are quite happy to pay for the cost of a first-class stamp.

6. **Personalize the return address envelope.** People give to people. If a volunteer has written a personal note of encouragement on the solicitation letter, add that person's name to the return address portion of your mailing envelope.

7. **Don't forget the telephone.** If a volunteer has written a personal note of encouragement on a solicitation letter, ask if he or she will make a follow-up phone call—or even a personal visit. A caller who says, *"I hope you'll take the time to read the library's message and will join me in supporting the library with a personal gift"* can make a real difference in the response rate to your solicitation letter.

## Levels of Personalization

You can personalize a fund-raising solicitation in many ways. The chart below shows a continuum of personalization, ranging from the *least personal* kinds of solicitations to the *most personal* ones.

| | |
|---|---|
| **LEAST PERSONAL** | A word-processed envelope with an indicia or bulk postage stamp, and a letter inside addressed to "Dear Library Friend" |
| | A word-processed envelope with an indicia or bulk postage stamp, and a letter inside addressed to "Dear Jane" |
| | A word-processed envelope with a first-class stamp and a letter addressed to "Dear Jane," *and* signed by someone Jane does not know |
| | A word-processed envelope with a first-class stamp and a letter addressed to "Dear Jane" *and* signed by someone Jane knows |
| | A hand-addressed envelope with a first-class stamp and a letter addressed to "Dear Jane," signed by someone Jane knows, *and* whose name is also written above the return address of the outside envelope |
| | A hand-addressed envelope with a first-class stamp and a letter addressed to "Dear Jane," signed by someone Jane knows, whose name is also written above the return address of the outside envelope *and* a short, handwritten personal note to Jane on the solicitation letter |
| **MOST PERSONAL** | A hand-addressed envelope with a first-class stamp and a letter addressed to "Dear Jane," signed by someone Jane knows, whose name is also written above the return address of the outside envelope, with a short, handwritten personal note to Jane on the solicitation letter *and* a follow-up phone call (or even a visit if you know the individual) |

# Special Appeals

Typically, special appeals raise *restricted* funds that cannot be used for anything other than for a targeted, specified purpose. For example, has your summer reading program budget been eliminated or your collections budget slashed? Do your library users cry out for more computers, but they're not in the budget? It may be time for a special fund-raising appeal to address these specific budget holes.

As state and local governments continue to limit the budgets of libraries, there are more reasons than ever to solicit funds for special needs, but a word of caution is in order. Probably the most important thing to remember about special appeals is that, unlike ongoing appeals, *they should only occur on rare occasions*. Be sure you keep special appeals "special" because it's never a good idea to set the precedent of raising private funds for needs that should be provided by public dollars. Once elected officials determine that public funds can be shifted from your library to other areas of government because the library will raise private dollars to make up the loss, your library will be on a downward budget trajectory. In addition, private donors like to see their money used for *enhancements* of services and materials, not for basic services. It's never a good idea to ask your private donors to provide the funds for salaries or the electric bill!

If you're considering a special appeal, consider timing just as carefully as you would with an annual (or other regularly occurring) appeal campaign. Is there a certain day or month in your community that would be appropriate to ask for special gifts? Your community's Founders Day or its annual Arts Festival, for example, can provide a perfect occasion to spotlight your library and appeal for a special need with which you need help. Does your community have a big homecoming weekend in the fall? That may be a good time to encourage returning family and friends to help renovate a beloved wing of the library.

Special appeals require succinct, effective marketing materials, including letters and brochures, as well as the services of volunteers to personally approach certain individuals you plan to solicit. Use the information above about developing effective annual appeal campaigns to guide you through special appeals. While the message of a special appeal is different from that of an annual or other regularly occurring appeal—because the need is more finely focused—the solicitation process is essentially the same.

For examples of materials created for annual and special appeals, see the Fund-Raising Gallery 10A–10K.

# 11

# Membership Programs

**PERHAPS THE BIGGEST DILEMMA IN THE LIBRARY FUND-RAISING WORLD** is whether or not your Friends group or Foundation should offer memberships. One can easily see the developmental objective for museums, aquariums, and other space to offer paid memberships that allow a member free (or reduced) admission or access to special programs and services, but what are the benefits of "belonging" to a library Friends group or Foundation? And where do simple donations end and memberships begin? This is not an easy question; therefore, if you choose to offer memberships, be prepared to have this conversation often!

*Philanthropy*, as noted in chapter 3, comes from the Greek word *philanthropos*, which means "loving people." We think of philanthropy today as the desire to benefit humanity—to improve the material, social, and spiritual welfare of others—especially through nonprofit giving. Some nonprofits, like museums or zoos, have the ability to give tangible benefits for membership donations. Their members get discounts, free admission, and other perks. These memberships feel more like paying a fee than making a donation, and these kinds of membership donations may not be completely tax deductible when something is given in return.

Other nonprofit organizations (like fund-raising organizations for libraries) must rely on purely philanthropic memberships, because donors cannot expect special privileges from their (free) public library. So what *do* these donors get back? More often than not, philanthropically motivated donors/members receive the assurance that they have done the right thing. Perhaps, too, they "get back" a sense of ownership in an organization—the library—that is truly helping the community. Because they believe that it's their civic duty to support the library, these donors do not expect recognition in return.

# Is a Membership Program Worth Your Effort?

The list of pros and cons in establishing a membership program for a library or its fund-raising organization can be discussed for a long time, especially if you are also conducting an annual fund or other kind of campaign. Why run a membership program when you have nothing really tangible to offer? Read the pros and cons below to help you decide.

## Pros

**Your donors want to be part of something.** Most people like the feeling of belonging to a group, club, or other support organization with which they feel a personal connection–something beyond simply carrying a library card.

**It makes your library friendlier.** Membership brings people a deeper sense of ownership in their library. They will feel better about using the materials and services if they feel they have done their part to support it.

**Membership dues are a great source of unrestricted funds.** Dues contribute more money to support your library's general operating expenses.

**Membership creates a great database of library supporters.** Members provide an excellent pool for future fund-raising efforts and solicitations, as well as for library volunteers.

**The "swag" you distribute is free advertising.** Swag is an inexpensive gift you give members. It is customarily imprinted with your library or its fund-raising organization's name and logo. When your members wear their T-shirts or carry their library book bags, they are walking advertisements for your library or its fund-raising organization. Keep them well informed of your programs and activities so they can also serve as your advocates!

**A Friends or Foundation membership card is concrete.** It says, "I'm affiliated!" Members like to have membership cards as tangible evidence of their association with an organization like your library's Friends group or its Foundation.

**Membership creates a pool of interested volunteers when advocacy needs arise.** When it's time for your library or its fund-raising organization to urge public officials to keep the library's budget strong, your members are your library's army–its hands, feet, and voice.

**Membership numbers impress public officials.** In the public arena, there's strength in numbers. Remember that your members are public officials' constituency and voters in future elections. The higher your membership count, the more influence members will have.

**Members are strong prospects for planned gifts.** Because members can be counted on for regular annual gifts and for repeat gifts, they may be willing to include the library or its fund-raising organization in their estate plans too.

# Cons

**Donors who give large gifts may become confused.** Not all donors to your Friends or Foundation will understand the difference between a donor and a "member," and it can be confusing to donors when you ask them for "membership" dues. They will want to know why they should make an extra payment to be a "member" of an organization they already support.

**Membership may discourage other kinds of giving.** Some feel that membership dues mean smaller donations in other areas of fund-raising.

**Memberships can be confusing when you also have an annual fund.** Members often confuse their membership dues with their annual fund donations. They think their membership dues are their annual donation, or vice versa. This gives rise to a bigger problem if your membership renewals occur in the same month as your annual fund. People may see this as one more fund-raising ploy! (The best practice is to make sure that your membership solicitation and your annual solicitation are spaced six months apart.)

**Membership does not beget "philanthropic" giving.** Most membership organizations receive dues in order for members to have access to certain services and programs. It often costs less to become a member than to pay admission every time one visits. Sometimes membership discourages an interest in giving altruistically in favor of trading dues for access.

**Membership is something extra to keep track of.** Membership requires a system to keep track of your members, and continued updates of the information in that system. This can be a time-consuming process.

**Management of a database—monthly renewals?** Membership renewals are a lot of work. How often will you ask your members to renew? How will you follow up? Getting renewals could take as many as three renewal solicitation letters per member per year. These are (1) an alert that membership is about to expire; (2) an alert that membership has lapsed and is about to expire; and (3) an alert that membership has expired.

**The term "member" seems contradictory to why a library exists.** The library is an egalitarian institution—free and open to all—and the very idea of a "member" seems to contradict this basic belief.

**Memberships do not appeal to Gen X and Gen Y populations.** The general rule, stated above, that people like to belong to something has an exception: the Gen X and Y population does not like to join. Research studies have confirmed that these generations want to know what difference their dollars will make, not what's in it for them.

**The membership mailings may cost more than the membership campaign brings in.** Adding a member to a mailing list can be very expensive. Postage continues to increase, and the cost of printing newsletters and program announcements can also be expensive. Does it make sense to send mailings to someone who is only supporting you with a small annual membership contribution (often $25 or less), but not truly supporting your library in a significant way?

**Your staff will discuss this forever!** The distinction between members and donors will never go away. Your staff will discuss and weigh the details time and time again, and will always reach the same conclusion: *There is no right answer to whether membership is an effective fund-raising program for libraries or their fund-raising organizations.*

# Membership Levels

If you decide that membership is a good idea, you will need to give some thought to membership levels. Most organizations have several levels of membership. Most members start at the most basic level. How do you convince a member to upgrade his or her membership when the benefits are the same? You must approach it from a philanthropic standpoint. What is it that your members want—is it "the desire to benefit humanity," as philanthropy is defined in a previous chapter?

Membership levels should have meaningful names—which is often easier said than done! "Basic" and "Contributor" usually identify lower-level members. "Sponsor," "Patron," and "Benefactor" are terms that sound like someone has given a substantial gift. Many communities will have meaningful words that are unique to them. Names of people or places are often used for membership levels. This matter should be given serious thought, and perhaps some brainstorming sessions. Remember that having ascending membership levels also provides incentives for higher giving. Your "Benefactors" will be seen as an elite group and this may add some subtle peer pressure for some members to give at a higher level.

Always refer to your membership levels when recognizing your donors. Include your membership levels on your website and in your annual report. Think about doing something special for your highest levels. You may want to hold a special lunch or reception. Many organizations recognize the highest levels on a wall of fame in the lobby. Chapter 7 has some good tips for thanking donors in a meaningful way. Most importantly, keep your donor recognition respectful and appropriate. Never include the name of a member or donor who has requested to remain anonymous.

# Selling the Idea of Membership

If you decide that membership is a good idea for your library's fund-raising organization, a well-drafted membership brochure is essential. As discussed above, because membership benefits are questionable, or at least not tangible, it will take some creative writing to make membership sound appealing. The language should be directed at the potential member's philanthropic-driven desire to belong. Articulate how the funds will be used to pursue your mission. Let them know that the simple fact that they are members will help your library. Numbers matter in advocacy. Membership levels should be featured prominently. Make it enticing to be a member at a higher level. Don't forget the swag! Members love their book bags and T-shirts. Perhaps you can convince local bookstores to offer discounts to your members. Other businesses or other organizations with members might also be willing to offer discounts to your members.

The return section of your brochure should request enough membership information needed to form a complete database entry. Remember that this is just the start of your relationship, so make certain you have all of the basic information you need to contact your members by phone, mail, and e-mail. You will be using this information in the future, so make certain it is complete now.

Creating a membership program is a common approach used by Library Friends groups, but it is not always the answer. Weigh the pros and cons of membership and determine whether your library or its fund-raising organization has the time and resources to do it well before embarking on this effort.

For some examples of materials created for membership campaigns, see the Fund-Raising Gallery, 11A–11C.

# 12

# The Gift of Remembrance: Tributes and Memorials

**WHEN SOMEONE DONATES TO YOUR LIBRARY OR ITS FUND-RAISING ORGA-**
nization, they get a great feeling of satisfaction in return. That great feeling goes a
long way toward motivating people to donate to any nonprofit organization. What
can give a donor an *even better* feeling? It's making a donation that honors someone while it supports your library. Tribute (or "honorary") and memorial gifts can
do just that, and they can be a wonderful addition to your library's fund-raising
activities.

Tributes and memorials are like two sides of a coin. *Tributes* honor someone who
is still living—often to mark a special occasion like a birthday, graduation, retirement, and so on. *Memorials* are given to remember someone who is deceased. These
kinds of gifts not only provide great opportunities for giving, they are also very easy
for your library or its fund-raising organization to initiate.

Like any other area of your fund-raising plan, you must let your community know
you accept these types of gifts. Marketing materials, therefore, are very important.
Your first focus should be on developing a brochure (or brochures) explaining the
program:

- When gifts are appropriate
- How to make them
- How the funds will be used
- How the honorees and donors will be recognized

Later on—once your brochures are complete and readily available—you can also
mail solicitation letters that explain this meaningful type of giving.

# Creating a Tributes and Memorials Brochure

When creating a brochure, focus on your message, and keep it simple. Your potential donors love the library and love the person they are honoring. What a perfect fit! Tell your donors how this perfect fit can benefit your library. Tell them how you will use the funds and how you will recognize the honorees and the donors.

Using software your already have, you can create an attractive brochure without the help of a graphic designer. Just follow these simple steps:

**Create a catchy "tagline."** A tagline is simply a slogan, a phrase that will be easy to remember.

**Develop a simple brochure design.** Use letter-size paper for a one-fold or two-fold brochure. Open a simple brochure template in Word. Don't just stick to text. Select digital photos or scan existing ones, and insert those too. Use photos and illustrations that suggest occasions for giving and also give your brochures a little visual punch. If possible, print your brochures in color.

**Include a donation form.** Your brochure should include a simple tear-off or cut-off donation form. It should be quick to fill out and easy to return

---

## Tips for a Great Tribute and/or Memorial Giving Brochure

1. Include a tagline on the front that invites people to read what's inside.

2. Remind the reader that your library is an important community resource.

3. Tell the reader that your library needs support.

4. Explain the opportunity for tribute and memorial gifts, and suggest some occasions when these kinds of gifts would be appropriate.

5. Include a donation form with:
   - Your library's name/address/phone/website
   - Contact info for staff (or your library's fund-raising organization) for tribute and memorial gifts
   - Donor's name and contact information
   - Honoree's name and contact information (if applicable or desired)
   - Space to specify an occasion being honored or remembered
   - Space for payment information
   - A sentence stating that this gift is tax deductible according to IRS guidelines. The following sentence will work: "*(Your library or its fund-raising organization's name)* is a not-for-profit 501(c)(3) organization. Your gift is fully tax deductible as allowable by law."

6. Say thank you on your brochure. You'll send every donor a thank-you letter, but it never hurts to say thank you more than once. Say it prominently in your brochure: "*We appreciate your support!*"

via mail or in person. If you make it possible to download your tributes and memorial gifts brochure from your library's website, be sure you also make it easy for online donors to give.

See the Fund-Raising Gallery that follows the Fund-Raising Toolkit for sample tribute and memorial brochures. Note that the tribute brochure shows younger people and looks more celebratory, while the memorial brochure depicts the warm, loving pictures that speak to the connections between generations. The pictures help convey the message, while the relatively concise text explains each giving program. Too many words will bore a potential donor, so keep it short and clear.

# Using and Recognizing Tribute and Memorial Gifts

How can you best use tribute and memorial gifts? Purchasing books is a very effective use of these kinds of gifts because tribute and memorial donors like the idea that their donations translate directly into books. The very act of remembering and honoring a loved one is often more meaningful and important than the size of the gift itself. The personal touch is essential here, and you can express your appreciation by the methods you choose for recognizing tribute and memorial gifts. Personalized bookplates are a very easy and popular option. The bookplate should indicate who made the donation and who is being honored. Design or purchase bookplates specifically for your tributes and memorials program. Making the bookplates unique to your library will add to the feeling of personalization, something your donor will greatly appreciate.

A word of caution, however. Avoid allowing donors to select *specific books* for their bookplate. This practice will create excessive work for library staff once this program gains popularity. In addition, the library's collection managers know what materials are needed most, and material selection is best left to them.

Don't forget to consider several other basic issues, such as establishing a minimum donation level and determining how the gift will be receipted. Because the donation will be used to purchase a book, for example, there is a cost involved (i.e., the price of the book) that must be covered by the donation. Twenty-five dollars ($25.00) is often required as a minimum gift to receive a personalized bookplate.

A receipt in the form of a thank-you letter should be sent informing your donor that the gift is fully tax deductible. For an added personal touch, enclose a photocopy of the bookplate so the donor can see what the bookplate looks like and will know how the gift has been recognized. Another great idea is to enclose a fresh tribute and memorial brochure with your thank-you letter so donors will have it at hand when they want to make another tribute or memorial gift.

A second letter should be sent to the honoree (or his or her family). The purpose of this letter is to inform the recipient that a gift in an individual's honor or memory was made to the library. Include the donor's name and address (the recipient may wish to send a personal thank-you note to the donor), but do not indicate the dollar amount of the gift. Instead, include a photocopy of the bookplate that bears the name of the honoree.

Give serious consideration to starting a book endowment for tribute and memorial gifts. Rather than money in and money out for the purchase of books, an endowment can be created with very little effort. Money can be collected as it comes in, deposited in the endowment, and once a year, a single distribution can be made for the purchase of books. If you think that starting an endowment for tribute and memorial gifts is a good idea, seek advice from an investment professional. For a basic article from the *Chronicle of Philanthropy*, visit http://philanthropy.com/article/Tips-for-starting-a-charity/63841. Endowments must be established according to specific guidelines and regulations. Do you know a professional who might be willing to help you establish an endowment and determine how it should be managed? Many organizations that are new to endowment investments turn to their community foundations for advice. If you must pay someone, do it. Spending a little money to do it correctly at the outset is extremely important.

> ## Words to Know
>
> An *endowment* is made up of funds permanently invested in a stock and fixed income portfolio which typically appreciate in value. Each year, organizations draw down a percentage of these funds to use as needed or as the endowment directs. Typical drawdown is between 4 and 5 percent of the endowment's market value.

> ## Working with a Community Foundation
>
> If you decide to start an endowment, you must manage the investment of the money, or you will spend it away with your drawdowns. A community foundation is one option for managing your funds. Like any firm, it is likely to charge you fees for this management. However, be aware that, as a rule, you must give community foundations your funds. You can set restrictions on what the funds are to be used for (i.e., for library projects), but those funds are no longer yours—they belong to the community foundation. Consider all your options carefully before you choose how to steward these funds.

There are times when honoring or remembering a person or commemorating an important life event calls for a special kind of gift, and it's important to make your library a receiving point for such gifts. Establishing a simple tribute and memorial giving program makes it easy for a donor to give to your library, honor someone, and feel great about both. You may also find that once a donor has made his or her first tribute or memorial gift, that person will do so again. Make it as easy as possible for donors to give in this way (through a brochure, a phone call, or your library's website), and remember that you can never thank your donors too much.

# 13

# The Big Bang: Major Gifts

**FUND-RAISING, AS STATED IN EARLIER CHAPTERS, IS FIRST AND FORE-**
most about *relationships,* and nowhere is this truer than in the area of major gifts. In the world of professional fund-raising, a great deal of attention is paid to major gifts; in fact, it's possible to write an entire book or develop a fund-raising training program on this topic alone. This chapter will examine the basics of major gift fund-raising—why it's important to your library and how to identify and nurture major gift donors.

## What Is a Major Gift?

Defining a "major gift" isn't as simple as it sounds because the dollar amount required for this designation varies from institution to institution. In large non-profits and universities, a major gift may be as much as $100,000 or more. In some very small organizations or those that have just begun fund-raising, a major gift might be $500, $1,000, or $5,000. For many libraries, a major gift may fall well below the $5,000 range.

The one thing that is a constant, however, is that *major gifts are significantly larger than typical annual gifts to an organization,* perhaps five to ten times the size of an individual's annual gift. For example, if an annual donor to your organization contributes $1,000 each year, a major gift for that individual would be in the neighborhood of $10,000. Note, however, that this formula is simply intended for guidance.

*You* know your donors best, and there may be some for whom a greater or lesser gift is the appropriate amount to ask for.

Don't plan to ask your major gift prospects for significant donations more frequently than every five (or more) years. The donor should understand that the need for which you're requesting a major gift is a special one that cannot be met through annual support alone.

# Using Major Gifts

While annual gifts are typically unrestricted gifts which provide support in whatever area is of greatest need to the organization, major gifts are usually intended for a very specific purpose, one that is critical to the library at that particular time. For instance, a library may wish to create an endowment to purchase books and materials. In this case, it would be appropriate to approach a number of your long-term donors and request a major gift for this endowment fund.

Major gifts may also be used to start a new library program or service, such as specialized workforce resources or outreach services to underserved communities. These kinds of programs and projects are very appropriate for major gift giving, and individuals who have been regular annual donors should be approached for a significant gift.

Major gifts can provide an opportunity for a matching gift challenge. For example, a major donor's large gift can be used to match others' donations, thereby doubling the impact of other donors' gifts. Donors love to know that their gift will have twice the impact, and matching gift challenges are great motivators for giving at all levels.

When identifying individuals who might be willing and able to make a major gift for a special project or new service, it's important to match the donor with the appropriate project or service. A successful entrepreneur, for example, might be very interested in creating a small business center in your library, while a retired librarian might find collection development or technology expansion areas of interest.

# Best Prospects for Major Gifts

Your best prospects for major gifts are people who consider themselves loyal supporters of the library, its mission, and its fund-raising organization. This will include "library insiders" like the board of directors of the fund-raising organization, the Board of Trustees of the library system, and key library staff (including the director). In addition, look for individuals who have been consistent donors year after year. Individuals who have given on an annual basis for five to ten years—even if they are not "library insiders"—make excellent prospects for major gifts to the library. It's good practice to routinely recognize individuals who are regular donors because people who give faithfully to annual appeals tend to be good prospects for both major gifts and planned gifts to the library.

## Words to Know

The *Giving Pyramid* is a model that illustrates how donors are initially attracted by entry-level fund-raising strategies (at the broad base of the pyramid) and cultivated over time, moving up the pyramid to larger gifts. (See figure 13.1.)

In the Giving Pyramid—a tool commonly used in fund-raising—first-time gifts, annual gifts, special gifts, and memberships appear at the bottom half of the pyramid, where the base is wide and the number of individual donors may be large. As you move up the pyramid, the gifts decrease in number but increase in size. At the highest level are planned gifts. Major gifts fall between annual and planned giving in the Giving Pyramid. A solid prospect for major giving will have made an annual gift to your library and/or been a member of your library's fund-raising organization for a number of years.

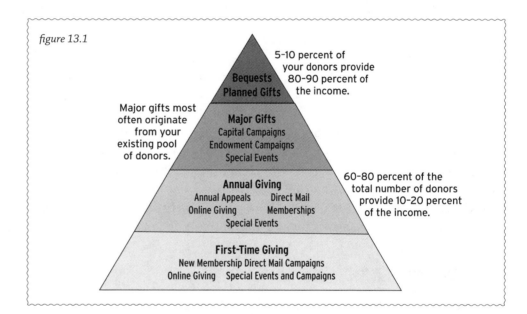

figure 13.1

Bequests
Planned Gifts

5-10 percent of your donors provide 80-90 percent of the income.

Major gifts most often originate from your existing pool of donors.

**Major Gifts**
Capital Campaigns
Endowment Campaigns
Special Events

**Annual Giving**
Annual Appeals    Direct Mail
Online Giving    Memberships
Special Events

60-80 percent of the total number of donors provide 10-20 percent of the income.

**First-Time Giving**
New Membership Direct Mail Campaigns
Online Giving    Special Events and Campaigns

# Soliciting Major Gifts

Fund-raising professionals will tell you that 95 percent of their job involves nurturing donors, and only 5 percent actively asking donors to make a contribution. This is especially true in the area of major gifts.

Even if an individual has contributed to the library or its fund-raising organization for five to ten years in a row, if he or she is suddenly presented with a written or verbal request for a major gift ten times the size of his or her annual gift, the donor isn't likely to be inclined to give. In fact, the donor might be insulted by this kind of request. How do you avoid this mistake? If you want to grow a beautiful garden, you have to first cultivate the soil, enriching it with nutrients. Then you plant; but even then, your work is not finished. Your plants need to be nurtured by water, fertilizer, pest control, trimming, and weed removal. Fund-raising best practices show that individuals who have been regular donors to an organization should be cultivated and nurtured with the same care as this garden before they are ready to be asked for a major gift.

Here is one way to do it. First, identify anywhere from 10 to 50 individuals who might be the most likely prospects for major gifts. These will be individuals who have given the largest annual gifts, as well as those who are closely affiliated with your library or its fund-raising organization (such as board members and key staff). These individuals should be nurtured in ways that *do not involve asking for a contribution,* but rather that build their relationships with the library. For example, you could invite individuals to programs at the library that may be of personal interest. They could get updates on what's happening in the library and what new or special projects are coming up. They could be taken to coffee, breakfast, or lunch as a way to get to know them better. Fund-raisers often refer to this type of activity as "touches," and many people believe that major donors should have at least seven touches for each time that they might be asked for a gift. It's ideal if one person in your organization is designated as the person who will nurture and solicit individuals for major gifts. In very mature fund-raising organizations, this is a full-time position that raises hundreds of thousands of dollars annually in support of the library.

> **Words to Know**
>
> In fund-raising, a *touch* is any personal contact or interaction with a donor that does not include asking for money.

For a library that either has no staff for fund-raising or has just begun fund-raising, a simple approach to major gifts might be to ask the library director, your Friends or Foundation board members, or library trustees to each contact *one* individual who they will agree to nurture with the many touches needed before that individual can be asked for a major gift. Eventually, this activity can be more formalized and staffing can be identified for carrying on this function.

## MAKING THE ASK

Once you have identified a prospective major donor (by matching the donor to the need for which you are asking for support and by having some idea of his or her capability to give):

1. Schedule a one-to-one meeting with this individual.

2. Be able to state your case for support clearly, concisely, and personally:

   - Describe the need
   - Explain how the library's program, service, or project responds to the need
   - Explain why the library is the appropriate service provider
   - Review the costs
   - Explain what success will look like
   - Ask for the individual's support

3. Know ahead of time the dollar amount you are requesting.

4. Ask.

   - Establish rapport and make your case for support
   - Look the individual in the eye when you ask

5. Be prepared for questions and discussion. Have ready answers for objections. It's possible the prospect may suggest giving a different amount, but it's important to go into your personal meeting with a specific dollar figure in mind, as a starting point for discussion.

6. Be gracious whatever the outcome. Even if the prospective donor does not agree to a major gift, he or she has given you the gift of their time, and perhaps you have planted a seed that will sprout later.

---

### Confronting the Three Most Common Fears When Asking for Major Gifts

**Rejection.** Don't take a rejection personally. It is not a reflection of your library's work, the value of your library in the community, or your personal performance. It usually means that the donor has other priorities at this time.

**Embarrassment.** Don't think of yourself coming into the situation from a position of weakness, with your hand out. Remember that the library is a vital part of your community and be proud to ask for support that goes beyond the level generally given. Remember, too, that *people give because they are asked*.

**Failure.** See Rejection! If your ask does not result in a major gift, pick yourself up, continue to cultivate that donor, and plan to ask again. "No" rarely means "never."

---

Major gifts fund-raising (on some scale) should be a part of the long-range fund-raising plan of every library. It is certainly something to which small libraries and those that are just beginning fund-raising can aspire, but not an area of fund-raising that should be part of a small library or Friends group's initial fund-raising plan. Doing it well requires significant time and resources, as well as patience and passion.

# 14

# Leaving a Legacy through Planned Giving

## What Is Planned Giving?

Imagine having faithful donors who continue contributing to your library, your Friends, or your Foundation even after their lives are over. People who love libraries have the opportunity to do just that—to support their library both today *and* tomorrow by making a planned gift, one that provides benefits to the library long after a donor's death. In fact, a planned gift is sometimes called "the ultimate gift" because it can be significant, and it may give in perpetuity. These kinds of gifts are becoming increasingly important to libraries as trillions of dollars transfer from one generation to the next in the first few decades of this century.

If yours is a very small library, or if your library's Friends group or fund-raising organization has little experience in fund-raising, you may feel resistant to venture too far into planned giving. Put your fears aside. The good news is that planned giving can be really *simple*. In fact, it can be as simple as encouraging someone to leave a gift to the library in his or her will. Gifts of life insurance and retirement plans are also very easy—perhaps even easier than wills. Most importantly, regardless of the planned giving methods you choose to promote, *be sure your donors know that you are in the business of accepting planned gifts,* and always remember to recognize your planned givers.

Your library or its fund-raising team should offer your donors the opportunity to include the library in their financial and estate plans. You can do this by providing donors with basic information about making planned gifts to the library (such as writing a newsletter article about planned giving or developing a simple planned giving fact sheet), then encouraging them to seek charitable gift planning advice from professionals who can make certain the planned gift is set up to fulfill their wishes. Someone associated with your library or its Friends or Foundation should be familiar with a variety of planned giving methods.

> ### Words to Know
>
> The terms *planned giving* and *deferred giving* are often used interchangeably. They refer to the process of cultivating, facilitating, and stewarding long-term gifts to charitable organizations such as libraries, their Friends groups, and their Foundations.

When most people think about planned gifts, they imagine a gift that is transferred out of a deceased donor's estate to a charity. The donor is gone and his or her representatives are required to make certain the charitable intent is fulfilled. While that is generally correct, it's not the only means by which planned gifts are completed. Planned gifts may also be made during the donor's lifetime, with the donor retaining use of the assets making up the gift, either before, during, or after the gift is made.

## Why Is Planned Giving Important to Your Library and to Donors?

With planned gifts, donors can help perpetuate the library's mission far into the future. Planned giving allows donors to make much larger gifts to your library than they may be able to give during their lifetime. An effective planned giving program may also have wide-ranging effects that are not immediately apparent, such as strengthening your annual and capital giving programs. Donors who consider entrusting your library or its fund-raising organization with their accumulated assets are usually very willing to support its ongoing operating needs.

### Benefits to the Donor

Make a personally significant gift, perhaps larger than he or she thought possible

Leave a meaningful legacy without giving up assets during his or her lifetime

Save on gift and estate taxes

Pass assets on to family members at reduced tax costs

Reduce (or avoid) capital gains

Possibly receive an income for life

## Developing a Basic Planned Giving Program

Two of the most essential attributes required in developing a planned giving program are *patience and persistence*. Planned giving does not always provide immediate

## Who Is a Likely Candidate for a Planned or Deferred Gift?

An individual who has been a loyal, longtime donor to your library or its fund-raising organization, regardless of the size of his or her gifts

A person who would sincerely like to make a large gift to the library, but cannot afford to do it now

A retired librarian or library employee

Someone whose children are financially successful and not dependent upon their parents' estate for their livelihood

Someone with no spouse, children, or close relatives

Single females over age 65

An individual who wishes to derive income from his or her estate while they are living

An individual whose assets have greatly appreciated and who wants to avoid capital gains

An individual whose assets may bring substantial taxation to heirs

gratification because planned gifts can take a decade or longer to be realized. But planned or deferred gifts can be among the most *cost-effective* gifts that you can raise because they tend to be of significant size and require less total staff time to secure than other types of large donations, such as major gifts.

Planned giving doesn't have to be complicated or intimidating. For small libraries and those with limited or no development staff, there are simple options. If this kind of giving is new to you, start slowly. Begin with the ten steps below:

1. Learn all you can! Attend a basic seminar offered by recognized planned giving professionals. Gather planned giving materials from other non-profit organizations. Talk to people with practical experience in soliciting planned gifts.

2. If necessary, get the backing of your library's governing board and executive staff, and establish a budget for your library's planned giving efforts. Establish a board-level gift planning committee to oversee the activities in this area.

3. If you feel your library has a strong foundation for development activities, take a gradual approach to adding gift planning to your other fund-raising strategies. It makes more sense in the long run to start with the most basic methods of planned giving, then later to venture into more complex methods.

4. Identify some ways that small and large planned gifts could make a positive difference toward supporting your library's mission.

Review the National Committee on Planned Giving's Model Standards of Practice for the Charitable Gift Planner (www.pppnet.org/pdf/modelstandards.pdf) to understand the expectations and context for ethical gift planning activities. Visit the Partnership for Philanthropic Planning's website (www.pppnet.org). This is a nonprofit organization whose mission is to help people and organizations create charitable giving experiences that are the most meaningful in achieving both a charitable mission and the philanthropic, financial, family, and personal goals of the donor.

5. Review your existing fund-raising program and adopt gift planning program policies that compliment it.

6. If possible, seek out a mentor who is experienced in the field and with whom you will feel comfortable being in frequent contact.

7. Obtain legal counsel and form alliances with professional gift and estate planners in your area.

8. Write about planned giving opportunities in your library's newsletter. Create an FAQ sheet about leaving a legacy to your library. Develop planned giving information and marketing materials, such as a simple brochure and response form. See "Creating a Planned Giving Brochure" (page 205).

9. Create a web page on your library's website that explains how planned giving to your library works. Include a PDF of your brochure and a downloadable response form. See the Fund-Raising Gallery 14A for a sample planned giving brochure with a response form included.

10. Use every opportunity you can to spread the word that individuals can support the library they love in a meaningful, effective, and lasting new way. For example, add a message at the bottom of your e-mail signature that will remind people of the importance of planned giving. It can read something like this: *"When you remember (your library or its fund-raising organization's name here) in your will, your commitment to quality library resources extends beyond your lifetime."*

*Note:* These steps will vary depending upon the size, experience, and personnel resources of your library or fund-raising team or organization. If your library is small, some of them may not be necessary. You may never go beyond requesting and receiving simple bequests, and that's just fine.

# The Most Common Planned Giving Methods

A basic understanding of estate administration will help you become familiar with a few ways that your library or its fund-raising organization might receive a planned gift. Following a death, assets may be in the decedent's name alone, jointly held with others, or perhaps held by a separate entity.

## PROBATE ASSETS, NON-PROBATE ASSETS, AND THE TAXABLE ESTATE

The probate estate is made up of assets that were held in the decedent's name and social security number, alone. Through a court administration, and pursuant to a will, some of the assets are transferred to a charity that has been named as a beneficiary, along with distributions to other beneficiaries. The donor may also have non-probate assets consisting of assets held in a trust, jointly held assets (bank accounts and real estate), life insurance, retirement plans, and so on. The distribution of non-probate assets is controlled by a title or contract with an entity holding the asset (for example, accounts payable on death or right of survivor) or by the laws of the state where the decedent resides. These assets are not controlled by the court, and thus, are non-probate. *The **taxable estate** is generally made up of all probate and non-probate assets. Of course, there are exceptions to all of these rules too numerous to include in this general discussion. Seeking the advice of a professional advisor is essential when working with those considering planned giving.*

Here are a few of the most common planned giving methods:

> ## Words to Know
>
> *Probate* is the process by which a judicial authority (a court) establishes the validity of a will. It issues a certificate that states that a will is genuine and confers upon executors the power to administer the estate.

## BEQUESTS

To leave a bequest means to "hand down" or "pass along" something to someone through a will. A bequest is one of the simplest methods of planned giving. A non-profit organization can receive a bequest of cash or property if it is named as a beneficiary in someone's will. A bequest may name a specific item that the beneficiary should receive, a specific dollar amount, a percentage of an entire estate, or some portion of an estate. A bequest may also be for a residual amount that is left after other specific bequests and conditions have been satisfied. Because a bequest is made through a will, beneficiaries do not receive the gift until the donor's death.

## LIFE INSURANCE

A donor may name your library as a beneficiary of a life insurance policy. If the donor wishes to give the entire value of his or her life insurance policy to your library, ownership of the policy may be transferred directly. If the policy has cash value, the transfer of ownership to the charity results in a tax-deductible gift for the donor. If the policy is not paid in full, the donor can be asked to make future donations to your library or fund-raising organization to cover the cost of the policy's premiums. These premiums may also be deductible on the donor's income tax return. Donors who wish to designate your library as a beneficiary of a life insurance policy should talk to their insurance provider.

> **Words to Know**
>
> A *beneficiary* is a person or organization designated to receive funds or other property under the terms of a will, insurance policy, trust, and so on.

## OTHER BENEFICIARY DESIGNATIONS

In addition to donating a life insurance policy, a donor can designate your library to receive all or part of his or her Individual Retirement Account (IRA) or other payable-on-death account by simply completing a beneficiary designation form provided by the individual's plan trustee, custodian, or agent. A beneficiary designation will take precedence over a will or trust. This means that assets distributed by beneficiary designation will never reach the donor's estate unless the estate is specified as the beneficiary. A beneficiary designation from an IRA is often the most tax-efficient way to make a planned gift because it may avoid both income *and* estate taxes.

## TRUSTS

A trust agreement is a legal document—similar to a will—that spells out the rules a donor wants followed for property held in trust for his or her beneficiaries. The main difference between a will and a trust is that most trusts are effective during one's lifetime as well as following death. In addition, trusts do not go through the court system (probate) when a person dies. A decade or two ago there was a big push to place assets in trust because, at that time, the probate process was considered expensive and burdensome. Most state laws have changed, and probate can now be a very informal and a relatively inexpensive process. In some circles, however, trusts remain popular because of their privacy. Because a trust is not a part of the probate process, it never becomes public record.

Specific provisions direct the use of the income generated by the trust, and other provisions control the assets that generate the income. Thus, income and principal are treated and directed separately. Accordingly, in planned giving there are charitable trusts that direct the *income* to be distributed to the charity (charitable lead trusts) and others that direct the *residue or remainder* to the charity (charitable remainder trusts.) The big difference is whether the charity receives the income during the life of the donor, or if it receives what remains following the donor's death.

By creating a *charitable lead trust,* a donor can transfer his or her assets to a trust for a set term of years or the donor's lifetime. Each year, the trust makes payments to the donor's designated charities. It is called a "lead" trust because the charity receives the lead (or first) portion, in the form of income, while non-charitable beneficiaries receive the remaining assets.

A *charitable remainder trust* is created when a donor irrevocably transfers an asset to a trustee who holds and manages the assets for the benefit of the donor and the charity. The donor retains the right to receive the income from the trust. There may be one or more income beneficiaries. Following the required terms or at the donor's death, the trustee will transfer the assets to the charity.

## ANNUITIES

Charitable gift annuities are similar to charitable remainder trusts because the donor receives a specified income for a term of years or his or her lifetime. A contract provides that, following the transfer of assets by the donor to a charity such as your library or its fund-raising organization, the charity is obligated to pay the donor an agreed-upon annual distribution. Annuities differ from trusts by the fact that with annuities, the donor and charity must negotiate and enter into a contractual relationship.

## REAL ESTATE

With this type of planned gift, a donor may donate his or her home, vacation home, parcel of land, farm, and so on to your library, while retaining the right to live in it and use it for the remainder of one or more lifetimes, a fixed term of years, or a combination of the two. Such gifts provide the donor with an immediate federal income tax deduction, even though the charity will not have use of the gift—the "remainder"—for a number of years.

The table on page 108 illustrates the types of gifts that you may encounter if your library begins a serious planned giving program and should help you determine which kinds of gifts are the most beneficial to both the donor and your library.

# Restricted vs. Unrestricted Funds

There are two kinds of gifts that donors can make: restricted and unrestricted. *Restricted* gifts specify a single purpose for which the gift may be used. For example, a donor may specify that his or her planned gift be used only for children's materials, for upkeep of the library's reading garden, or another purpose about which he or she feels a personal passion. *Unrestricted* gifts, on the other hand, allow the library

**SELECTING THE APPROPRIATE CHARITABLE GIFT**

| Donor's Position | Gift Types | Good Assets to Give | Donor Benefits | Charity's Benefits |
|---|---|---|---|---|
| The donor has enough assets now, and wants to see the gift at work. | Outright gift | Cash<br><br>Stock<br><br>Real estate | Income tax deduction<br><br>Estate tax reduction | Charity receives immediate use of funds |
| The donor wants to make a gift but needs all of the assets now. | Charitable bequest<br><br>Life insurance<br><br>"Payable on death" accounts | Cash<br><br>Stock<br><br>Retirement plan assets<br><br>Savings or brokerage account remainders | Estate tax deduction | Charity receives eventual use of funds |
| The donor wants to make a gift and has assets, but needs the income from those assets for now. | Remainder trusts<br><br>Gift annuities<br><br>Pooled income funds<br><br>Your home with a retained use | Cash<br><br>Stock<br><br>Real estate | Partial income tax deduction<br><br>Life income for yourself or heirs | Eventual use of funds |
| The donor wants to make a gift now but wants the donor's beneficiaries to receive something, too. | Lead trust<br><br>Life insurance | Cash<br><br>Business | Income or gift tax deduction<br><br>Reduced taxes on appreciation<br><br>Preservation of assets for children | Immediate use of funds |

to use the gift in any way needed to fulfill its mission. Unrestricted funds allow for a great deal of flexibility and are thus the more desirable of the two kinds of planned gifts you might receive.

# Notification of a Planned Gift

First of all, celebrate! Being notified of a planned gift is a wonderful accomplishment. There is no greater honor than for an individual to entrust his or her support through a legacy gift. The second thing you should do, however, is obtain the donor's intentions in writing. See the "Planned Giving Declaration of Intent Template" (page 206) for an easy form you can adapt for your library or its fund-raising group's use. Remember, however, that notification of a planned gift is a *promise,* and promises can be broken; there is no guarantee the donor will not change his or her mind and direct the gift elsewhere. Donors do this all the time and rarely notify the

charity from which they are withdrawing their promise in favor of another designated recipient.

Your library or its fund-raising organization are now in the business of receiving planned gifts. What next? First of all, get the word out. Publicize the idea that
donors can make planned gifts to support the library. Every mailing to your donors
should include a reference to your planned giving program. Ask your current donors
and members if they have already included your library in their estate plan. You will
be surprised to find out that many have, but have not informed you about it. This
is a very common occurrence. Whenever you have the chance, include your list of
planned givers in your publications. With their permission, feature legacy donors
as a way to encourage others to give. Consider running a series of articles that tell
the stories of a few legacy donors, explaining who they are and why they chose your
library to support now and after their death.

Designate a person on your staff to accept phone calls about planned gifts. Be
sure they have the knowledge and training to answer questions and provide some
guidance. Provide potential planned giving donors with an example of the specific
language that should be included in all wills and trusts.

Create a recognition circle just for your planned givers. Give the circle a meaningful name that describes the group as legacy donors. Design a logo specifically
for the circle. Treat your planned givers above and beyond all others. Have a special
event for them annually that recognizes their support. Special personalized gifts
are always appreciated—certificates, engraved bookends or lapel pins, for example,
or perhaps a framed artist's rendering of your library. Get creative! Make the recognition circle a group that *every* donor strives to be a part of. Remember that legacy
gifts are generally revocable, so continue to make certain your legacy donors know
how much they are appreciated.

Planned giving can add a rich new dimension to your library's private fund-
raising efforts. While it's not the place to *start* raising private dollars (ongoing
appeals, memorial and tribute gifts, and events are more appropriate starting
points), it provides a meaningful way for your most faithful donors to give gifts of
significant size, and gifts that continue in perpetuity. Making a legacy gift is a lot
like planting a tree late in life. You may never enjoy its shade, but you can feel good
knowing that others will.

*Author's Note:* This chapter discusses several legal documents and tools your
library and its fund-raising organization should consider when implementing or
enhancing a planned giving program. The material is intended to provide a very
general overview, *not* to recommend specific planned giving methods.

One of the most important things you can do for a successful planned giving
program is to enlist the services of professionals. A lay person should never undertake to give legal advice or prepare planned giving documents. By all means, have
general discussions with your donors, but direct them to seek professional advice.
If necessary, research resources in your community and put together a list of those
professionals who are willing to talk to your donors. Always remember that the relationship between a donor and his or her professional advisor is theirs alone.

# 15

# Taking the Fear Out of Fund-Raising Events

**THE MENTION OF HOLDING A FUND-RAISING OR SPECIAL EVENT IS ENOUGH** to send some individuals running screaming from the room. It's true, special events can be unpredictably challenging from any number of perspectives—*if* not well planned. Alternatively, they can also be extremely successful vehicles for raising significant unrestricted dollars and getting your library or its fund-raising organization on the radar screen of a much broader audience. Conducting a special event is something you should consider as part of your development plan—think of it as the icing on your fund-raising cake!

## What Can a Special Event Do for Your Library?

There are a number of reasons for conducting a special event, regardless of the amount of money it raises. A special event:

> **Creates a new pool of potential donors into your library.** Once an individual participates in a special event, that individual is much more likely to become a donor, a volunteer, or even a board member. Additional value added by this event attendee is that he or she brings new money, which is traditionally unrestricted. This means that it can be used for programs, services, or even general operating expenses.

**Raises the visibility of your library.** Libraries are known for their programs and services, but holding an event is a great way to invite people who don't use the library into its sphere. Special events are like putting the spotlight on your library and inviting everyone in the community to learn more about all that goes on there.

**Enhances the library's image.** Young adults may view the library as being there for kids and seniors, but a cool and creative event will bring enthusiastic young adults into the library, priming them to become future library supporters. Depending on the target audience, you have an opportunity to send a message through your event that the library is about more than books or other traditional resources.

**Galvanizes and energizes your volunteers and board members.** A fun event can present an opportunity for volunteers to be creative and display their special skills. It also allows volunteers to work across committee lines, allowing them to break out of their organizational "boxes."

**Offers prime opportunities for corporate sponsors.** This is yet another way of bringing new folks into your library's sphere of influence. (There will be more about the great potential between corporate sponsors and special events later in this chapter.)

**Energizes your organization.** As soon as a great event is over, almost everyone wants to start planning the next one.

# Types of Fund-Raising Events

There's no denying it, most library fund-raising events center around books and authors. But, luckily, there are a lot of variations on that theme. Some of the events libraries are hosting include:

- Lunches, cocktail parties, or dinners with author presentations
- Dinners with authors in private homes
- "Mystery dinners" in the library
- Trivia contests in libraries
- Themed events in the library, or elsewhere
- Silent and live auctions (either stand-alone or as part of another event)
- Golf tournaments

Luckily, with a creative planning team, the possibilities for a unique, fun—*profitable!*—event are endless. We've included a listing of great events being held in libraries around the country. See "Cool Special Events to Check Out" on page 207 in the Fund-Raising Toolkit.

The most important consideration is that the event speaks to your community and your potential audience. Who are you trying to attract to your event? Women?

> **TIP:** Nothing increases bidding on auction items like a glass of champagne or good wine!

One library throws a women's-only event on Super Bowl Sunday, featuring chocolate, champagne, chair massages, and a great silent auction.

Another library Friends group's fund-raiser takes place on a riverboat on the Mississippi River. It features a local celebrity posing as Mark Twain, who gives a dramatic presentation (think Hal Holbrook's "Mark Twain Tonight"), and there is great food and wine. It's a wonderful fund-raising event and a fun outing for families and seniors alike. Still another library conducts an event aimed at 20–30-somethings, complete with trivia, a cell phone scavenger hunt, and trendy food trucks. Truly, the possibilities are endless!

# Potential Challenges of Special Events

Before you get too excited, know that there are both pros and cons to conducting a special event that need to be considered before you make the decision to go down this path. You've just read about some of the benefits. Consider some potential pitfalls.

**Special events may not make a lot of money.** This is especially true when you first host an event. It costs money to plan and execute a good event, and there's no guarantee that if you plan it, they will come. Most organizations that decide to include a special event in their fund-raising activities plan for losing money or just breaking even in the first year or two of the event.

**Special events can drain the time and energy of staff and volunteers.** Planning a special event takes a lot of time and energy, often more than you anticipated. Don't even think of conducting a special event if you don't have a dedicated group of volunteers who are capable of planning and executing it. If you can make the investment, it's wise to hire someone whose responsibility will be to coordinate and monitor all the event details to make sure it's a success.

**A special event may draw money away from more lucrative fund-raising efforts.** An individual who pays to come to your event may draw the conclusion that this is his or her only contribution to your library. This *may* happen, but it is unlikely that most individuals who come to your event will see it this way—in fact, a special event is a great way to increase connections and build loyalty with current donors. Remember that one of the main objectives of a special event is to bring new people into the fold of your library's fund-raising activities. A special event will actually increase your potential donor base.

**There can be uncontrollable risks involved in hosting a special event.**
Try as we might, we can't control all of the details surrounding a special event. Bad weather, competing events, tardy special guests or speakers, and other unanticipated glitches happen. Good planning from the very start is critical. Every special event planning committee should ask itself all the "What if . . . ?" questions throughout the planning process and make sure that for every question, there's a Plan B.

# Ten Tips for Conducting a Successful Special Event

1. **Start out with a great concept!** The author luncheon or dinner is tried and true, but it's been done and overdone. That's not to say that it isn't a good vehicle for bringing people together to support your library, especially since it's a natural fit for most library lovers. But spice it up a little! No one wants to spend money to attend an event that's ho-hum, even if it's for a good cause. If you're going to do an author event, make it classy, fun, theme-based, out-of-the box. Host a women's author event with chair massages, makeup "makeovers," and girl-themed silent auction items. Serve cosmopolitans and chocolate. Or turn the tables and host a men's author event. Sell raffle tickets for sporting events or autographed sports paraphernalia. Serve martinis and chicken wings.

2. **Plan, plan, plan . . .** Every aspect of your special event, from creating the concept to celebrating its success, should be included in a detailed, written plan, complete with a timeline and assigned responsibilities.

> **Five Things That Will Kill a Special Event**
>
> There are so many events being held in communities all the time that it's essential that your library event is truly a *special* event. Avoid these common mistakes and you're well on your way.
>
> 1. A ho-hum event with no style, class, or pizzazz
> 2. Insufficient resources (volunteers, staff, budget, and partners)
> 3. No one in charge
> 4. Lack of attention to details
> 5. Failure to have a good time

3. **Check your community calendar for other (competing) events, and avoid religious holidays.** The last thing you want to do is schedule your event for the same day that another local organization is having one. Be sensitive to the fact that your potential guests may choose to take part in religious observances too.

4. **Establish an event budget.** You can't make money on a special event without spending money. Treat your event like any other fund-raising function—determine costs, expenses, and a financial goal for the event.

5. **Create an event committee with clearly defined roles, expectations, and responsibilities.** The committee should be composed mostly of vol-

unteers, but staff should also be on the committee to ensure that there is good communication and collaboration. Recruit a committee chair who is well-connected to the community and who will be a dynamic leader of the group.

6. **Create a committee culture of ownership, creativity, and fun.** This will ensure that your committee members are committed and will do all they can to promote your event, bring their friends and family, and be totally dedicated to making the event a success in every way.

7. **Consider hiring an event coordinator.** This costs money but can be a *priceless* investment as it ensures that someone is in charge at all times and that the burden for managing all the details of the event is not placed solely on staff or even a volunteer chair. Event planners or coordinators are well-trained to know where the pitfalls of an event are and can easily sidestep them to keep your event on track.

8. **Create a "brand" for your event and be consistent in using it.** Give your event a fun, creative name and tagline, design a logo, and use it on all event materials. Make sure that it's interesting and catchy enough so that when someone sees it, they'll want to be part of it. You may want to recruit a marketing professional to your event committee or find a design intern to help with creating your event's brand.

9. **Look for corporate sponsors.** A great way to make a profit is to recruit corporate sponsors who can help defray event costs. This requires planning, as well as establishing a good case for how sponsoring your event will benefit a potential sponsor. You'll read more about corporate sponsors later in the chapter and in chapter 17.

## An Example of a Special Event "Brand"

The Friends of the Saint Paul Public Library hosts "Opus & Olives: Fine Print and Fine Food," a large author gala, every fall. The event logo is an olive with a pen piercing it. This "hip" logo is unique, easily recognizable, and used on everything in print materials, e-mails, and online information about the event. (See figure 15.1.)

figure 15.1

10. **Publicize your event in more ways than one.** In today's communication-crazy world, we get more mail, e-mail, texts, and media messages than we know what to do with. To ensure that your event is well attended, you have to have a marketing plan for the event that includes as many ways as possible to get your event date on people's calendars. This should include direct mail, e-mail blasts, Facebook, Twitter, and local newspapers.

11. **BONUS TIP!** Give your event at least three years to be really successful. It takes time for an event to gather a following and become a "must do" activity. If you have a solid event concept and you give up after the first year, you haven't given it enough time to build a base of support and loyalty. By year three, any really good event should be in the black and on people's calendars as soon as you announce the date. This requires a real commitment on the part of the library or your fund-raising organization to stick it out—even if the early results don't show a significant profit. Remember that the benefits are *more than just dollars* and include potential new donors, corporate relationships, visibility, and other intangibles that are all valuable in the fund-raising world.

# Corporate Sponsorship— The Sweet Spot in a Special Event

One of the best ways to make sure that your special event is profitable is to recruit corporate sponsors. Chapter 17 contains a great deal of helpful information about this, but a few words are in order here. It's very difficult to make much money on a special event without corporate sponsors underwriting most, or all, of the cost of the event. Before you begin to recruit corporate sponsors, you need to take the time to develop the case for why a business should support your event. In other words, you need to spell out what the "win/win" proposition is to be able to persuade a business that they will benefit while supporting your library's event.

Small businesses and large corporations alike want to be part of pivotal community events for a variety of reasons.

- It's good business. Sponsoring special events sends the message that your company or small business is invested in the community.
- It's advertising. Corporate sponsors should be listed on all your event promotions and at the event itself. This gets their name out in front of an audience often, and it's associated with a great cause.
- Corporate sponsorships can come with perks, like free tickets to the event that sponsors can use to invite special clients or customers. Sponsorship provides the opportunity to promote or publicize a business's products or services at the event. It can also be a way to help them directly build their business. For example, if a company offers a service or product as part of

a silent auction, it creates the potential for gaining a new or existing customer for the long term.

- Corporate sponsorship can often be paid from a company's marketing budget, so the cost for "doing good" comes out of a budgeted line item.
- Corporate sponsorship raises a business's profile in the community. It is beneficial to be seen as supporting an organization along with one's competitors. A corporate sponsor may love the library but, in the end, it's always a business decision to sponsor an event.

When soliciting corporate sponsorships, you may want to consider having graduated levels of sponsorship support, whereby a business receives more benefits as the amount of funding or in-kind donation (a gift of goods or services instead of cash) increases. Examples of "Corporate Sponsorship Opportunities and Benefits" are included on page 209 of the Fund-Raising Toolkit.

Having a well-respected lead sponsor for the event validates the importance of the event in many people's minds. This business or corporation has the privilege of having its name at the top of all event promotions. For example, "Guys in the Library is presented by LifeChange Fitness." This privilege also comes with special perks:

- The opportunity to be at your event's podium, leading off the program, or introducing speakers
- Premium seating or extra guest tickets
- Attendance at a "special reception" with featured speakers or authors
- The chance to offer special promotions to your guests

You may also want to consider having a media sponsor for your event, as this connection can be extremely valuable. Newspapers, radio, television, or electronic media can help promote your event through all sorts of venues (print, on-air promotion, social media, etc.). The actual cost for purchasing advertising from a media sponsor (such as your local newspaper) would probably be prohibitive if you have to pay for it, but an in-kind donation of advertising is something that media outlets often give in the course of doing business. The benefit for the media sponsor is visibility as a supporter of one of the community's most valuable assets. If your special event is big enough (in terms of profit), you may want to consider offering to co-host your event with a media sponsor, especially if the sponsor has its own philanthropic program with which you can share a portion of the profits.

Another important corporate sponsor or partner for most library events is a local bookseller. Many library special events center around authors and their books. Working with a local bookseller is a great way to handle the task of ordering and selling books at your event. Often, a bookseller will agree to return a percentage of book sales to your library in exchange for being the exclusive bookseller at your event. These might range anywhere from 10 to 25 percent of gross sales.

Whatever types of corporate sponsors you have recruited, it is important to treat them as partners in your event. Their involvement is important. Once they have committed to a sponsorship, touch base with them before the event to see that their expectations are being addressed (use of corporate logos in advertising or promotion, seating at the event, or any other special—but reasonable!—requests they might have). It's also good partner relations to check in with your corporate sponsors *after* your event to see if everything went smoothly from their perspective and to ask if they have any suggestions for improving the event. At this time, you can also ask if they would consider sponsoring the event the following year.

# Planning Your Event

The best way to ensure that your event will be successful is to pay attention to every detail. Planning for a special event should begin three to twelve months prior to the event, depending on its scope and size. The more parts there are to an event, the more planning is required. For example, if you are planning a simple author luncheon, three to four months is adequate to plan the event. If you're hosting a big gala, with lots of guests, presenters, and sponsors, you need closer to a year to plan it well.

Regardless of the size of your event, you should start by *recruiting a planning committee.* This committee should be able to handle most of the logistics of the event, including recruiting corporate sponsors and encouraging guests to attend the event. Set out the expectations for your committee when you recruit members so you don't end up with an enthusiastic group of volunteers who really only want to decide which author(s) you should invite or what the decorations should look like. Your event committee's chair is a *key* position. Recruit someone who knows lots of people and business owners in your community. It's that individual's job to help set the agenda for your meetings, lead the meetings, keep the event and the committee on track, and help recruit corporate sponsors. Depending on the size of your event, it can be a good idea to have co-chairs.

**Establish a schedule** of all event planning meetings at the first meeting. Determine whether you need to meet weekly, monthly, or more often as you near the event date, and make sure that you include a final meeting *after* the event to debrief—and celebrate! Make sure that all committee members have the meeting calendar. One individual should be responsible for setting meeting agendas and sending them out to all committee members with a reminder of the next meeting. Send these agendas and reminders out a week in advance of each committee meeting.

**Identify all the major tasks** that you will need to accomplish to make your event a smashing success. The list below will give you a good start.

Make sure that someone is assigned the responsibility for oversight for each of these tasks. It is too much to ask that an event chair, or even the committee as a whole, be responsible for all these tasks. Breaking out and sharing responsibilities assures that no one gets burned out by too much work and that there's accountability for each major task.

## Major Tasks Common to Many Special Events

Confirm (in writing) an event date and site.

Invite speakers, performers, or an emcee for the main event.

Identify corporate sponsors you can approach to help underwrite your event. It's important to identify sponsors as early as possible so their brand or logo can appear on event publicity materials.

Print Save-the-Date cards (if applicable), invitations, programs, or other materials that you will use for the event (e.g., a listing of corporate sponsor benefits, a description of the event that you can use to recruit authors or presenters, etc.).

Update your library or its fund-raising organization's website to include information about the event. Make it attention-getting. "COMING SOON!" will catch a browser's eye. Keep the website updated throughout the pre-event period; people who hear about the event will logically go to the website for more details or to reserve a seat.

Mail the event materials listed above.

Publicize the event in as many ways as you can.

Determine event site logistics (rooms, food, beverages, seating, audiovisuals). Imagine your event from start to finish. What should work out smoothly? Where might your challenges be? At one large library fund-raising gala, organizers thought they had every possible detail worked out, until the audio that accompanied the large overhead screens came on and the event's star speakers could hardly be heard.

Determine logistics for a silent or live auction, raffle, or other fund-raising activity associated with the event. In some states, an event raffle is considered gambling, so if you are holding a raffle, check to see whether your state requires any special forms to be filed and approved.

Determine logistics for authors, presenters, or performers (background and biographical information for promotions, travel details, audiovisual needs, handler needs, etc.).

If you plan to sell books at your event, determine how this will be handled.

Track your reservations. Determine ahead of time whether individuals can only reserve by mail or in person, or if they can register online through your website or by using an online payment option such as PayPal or EventBrite.

Staff your event adequately. You might need greeters at the door, assistance with registration, handlers for authors or speakers, photographers, ushers, bartenders, and anyone else who can help ensure that the event goes smoothly.

Plan for efficient handling of guest check-in on the day or evening of your event. Place a check-in table in a prominent location and have pre-printed nametags for easy pickup. Have people on hand who can answer questions and give directions.

**Create a work plan** that is a calendar with deadline dates for all major tasks leading up to the event. This should include dates for:

- All event planning meetings
- Promotion/advertising dates, including copy deadlines
- Printing and mailing (Save-the-Date, invitations)
- Corporate sponsor deadlines
- Author/presenter logistics completed
- Event site meeting with site representatives, caterers, and so on
- Final count for guests/meals to the event site

Make sure that everyone involved in the event knows their assignments. The event planner, staff coordinator, or event committee chair(s) should monitor the work plan and calendar regularly to make sure that no task has been left undone. There are certain elements of the work plan that will emerge or become more complex, depending on the nature of your event. For example, if you are conducting a silent or live auction or a raffle, this will bring details and deadlines of its own; be certain that these are included in your overall work plan. The work plan should also include a countdown plan for the final week before your event since that when all the details come together. Be sure that everyone understands their responsibilities during this critical pre-event time.

**Tracking event sponsors and guests** is an extremely important part of the event. Create a database and include the names of all individuals who were sent an invitation. Note when they made their reservation and how they paid for the reservation (cash, check, credit card). Create a document, spreadsheet, or database that details all of the actions or results for every sponsor and their guests. See page 210 for a "Sample Event Sponsorship Tracking Form."

For example, a corporate sponsor listing might include:

- Names of all potential corporate sponsors and appropriate contacts within their organizations
- Name of event-planning team member who will be contacting and recruiting each sponsor
- Outcome of their solicitation (Yes/No/Next Year . . . )
- Sponsors' guests' names (if appropriate)
- Invoice for sponsorship sent/payment received
- Thank-you letter sent/date

**Hold a post-event debriefing session.** You can't exhale just yet. The final task in conducting a successful event is the wrap-up. When you schedule your event planning meetings, make sure you set aside a date a 7–10 days after the event (when it's still fresh in your minds) to debrief the event and *celebrate!* Make this a festive meeting—everyone's worked hard to present a successful event—pat yourselves on the back. Debriefing is really important because you won't remember important details next year, despite the fact that you may feel sure you'll never forget them. Ask your event planning committee these and other questions:

- How did the event go from a big picture perspective?
- What went really well?
- Were there any glitches?
- What could we have improved?
- Did we hear any complaints from guests or sponsors?
- What would we do differently next year?
- How did we work as a planning team?

Make sure someone notes your responses and put them in the file for planning next year's event. Remember that your library's special event is more than a night out or an enjoyable afternoon with lunch and an author. It's a great opportunity for meeting and cultivating new donors and a valuable component of your fund-raising and development program.

See the Fund-Raising Gallery 15A–15D for examples of special event promotional materials.

# 16

# Donate Now! Getting Started with Online Giving

## Fund-Raising Should Be a Multipronged Effort

Online giving, almost unheard of a decade ago, grows stronger every year. In 2005, half of the giving to Hurricane Katrina relief was done online. Online donors are generally considered to be younger than those used to more traditional methods of charitable giving, which means that online giving is creating the next generation of philanthropists! Blackbaud's *2011 donorCentrics Internet and Multichannel Giving Benchmarking Report* reported that first-time donors often start online and switch in large numbers to direct mail giving in subsequent years. The study found that for large direct marketing organizations, the majority of gifts are still received through direct mail. However, while direct mail is still the dominant channel for new donor acquisitions, it has become increasingly common for new donors to give their first gift online. These younger, online-acquired donors tend to have higher household incomes than mail-acquired donors, and often give much larger gifts than mail-acquired donors. The bad news is that online-acquired donors tend to have slightly lower retention rates than mail-acquired donors. So the Internet is an increasingly important way to acquire donors, but multichannel fund-raising via direct mail, website, telemarketing, and social media is the most cost-effective way to acquire *and retain* new donors.

You may already be using direct mail, but how does your library get started with online fund-raising? It's not enough to just put a "donate now" button on your

Online giving is cost-effective. Compare the cost of raising one dollar:

Direct mail–$1.25

Telemarketing–$.63

Online–can be as little as $.05

SOURCE: The Case Foundation

website and wait for the money to roll in. You must promote your online capacity in your newsletters and put your website address on all of your print materials. Include information about the online giving option in all of your direct mail fund-raising campaigns. Create special promotions for online giving using your e-mail list and your mailing list. Test to see which ones perform best. Use what you learn to continuously improve your messaging and delivery processes.

# Getting Online—DIY or Use a Service?

If you are a registered 501(c)(3) organization, there are easy ways to accept donations online through giving services such as Convio, Just Give, Kintera, or Network for Good. These vendors collect donations and send tax receipts to your donors, then pay you at the end of each month. You are able to download contact information from any donors who have not asked to keep that information private. Each service charges a moderate, one-time fee to cover credit card processing and overhead. While some may charge a monthly fee, their per-transaction fees can be lower, and they usually provide additional services to help you get your message out. It's worth your time to investigate what's available in your area and what services are included for the fees paid.

To take online donations, you need a bank account that accepts online credit card payments, called a merchant account. Some online giving services will allow you to use their account, or you can apply for your own. If you already have a merchant account (for instance, for taking credit card payments over the phone) it's possible that you can use it for online payments as well—but there will still be some verification and paperwork to do.

Why establish your own account? You'll receive the money faster—generally within a few days, rather than in bulk once a month. Also, your organization's name will be shown on the donor's credit card bill, rather than the vendor's name. If you have a high volume of donations, using your own merchant account is usually more economical. In general, it makes sense for organizations that are just getting started with online donations to use a vendor's merchant account, while those who are ready to invest time and money should consider setting up their own account.

Different vendors use different pricing structures. It's important to estimate how many donations you expect to get per month and how large a typical gift will be in order to compare fees across vendors. Some of the fees may include:

> **Setup fees.** A one-time fee, paid before you begin using the tool. What is included varies widely—check to see if it covers everything you will need to have done.

**Annual or monthly maintenance fees.** Consider these "rent" for the system. They usually cover e-mail-marketing services in addition to donation processing.

**Transaction fees.** These fees vary with the number of donations you receive. They are calculated either as a percentage of each donation, a flat fee per donation, or both (i.e., 3% plus $0.40 per donation means that $1.90 would be deducted from a $50 donation).

**Merchant account fees.** If you are using a merchant account of your own, there may be separate fees paid to the company that supplies it to you. These may include monthly fees or "statement fees."

There's a chance that you will pay an additional monthly fee to an Internet gateway provider. Accepting online donations always requires a gateway provider, but their fees are typically included in either the vendor's fees or the merchant account's fees. Ask your vendor to be sure. You may notice that different types of fees are likely to be better for different types of organizations. For instance, if you expect only a few donations, it may be cheaper for you to use a service that charges more per transaction and less per month. If you expect a lot of online donations, the opposite is true—it's worthwhile to pay more in setup and monthly fees if it decreases the transaction fees applied to every donation.

Some vendors' donation forms look nothing like your website, and some may even display the vendor's logos prominently. Others offer forms that are tailored to match your organization's website and navigation—but you typically pay for the privilege. Remember that you will appear more professional and likely raise more money with a donation tool that matches your site's look.

Some tools make data integration much easier than others. (See chapter 7 for information about creating effective donor databases.) Some allow you to create an Excel file that specifically matches your donor database. Others allow you access to your data programmatically so that you can set up an automatic process to synchronize the data. But some might only let you copy and paste text manually, which can be a significant cost when you consider the value of your time.

Decide on which features you want to offer your donors. Is it vital that you are able to accept tribute or memorial gifts? Support employer matching gifts? Do you plan to solicit recurring or sustaining gifts? Define what features you can't live without, and narrow the list to those services that can support these features.

# DIY Online Giving—Take Baby Steps

One popular yet simple way to accept donations online is to place a PayPal donation button on your page. Just sign up for PayPal and get your Donate Now button from them. They do charge a small transaction fee, as well as credit card fees. While donors formerly needed to create a PayPal account to donate, that's no longer true—they can now simply use a credit card, as most donors would typically expect.

With no way to customize the look of the donation form, PayPal's user experience is unmistakably PayPal, however, it's one of the cheapest ways to take donations.

Google allows nonprofits they've approved for a Google Grant (www.google.com/grants) to accept donations through Google Checkout without charging any transaction fees. Free is a hard price to beat, but the interface isn't optimized for donations—it forces the user to create a Google Account, and to associate a credit card with their Google Account before they can actually make a donation. It's a flow that may be off-putting and confusing to less tech-savvy donors—and if people don't donate, it doesn't matter how free it is.

Individuals who are invested in your library can help by setting up a Cause on Facebook. They'll need to have a Facebook account first, and then add Causes to their profile. Other Facebook members will then be able to join the cause and contribute. As a bonus, this builds a community around your library. Facebook charges a per-transaction fee, so check it out when you're ready to get started.

Another company that helps motivated individuals raise funds for the library they support is Firstgiving.com. Anyone can create a free, personalized fund-raising page for nearly any nonprofit. After you create your page you can promote it everywhere you have an online presence (Facebook, Twitter, blogs, etc.) with a widget or a badge. All funds are sent directly to the nonprofit so the person who set up the page doesn't have to worry about where or how the money is being sent.

Depending on the size of your giving community, the preferred access point for online fund-raising could be your library's (or its fund-raising organization's) own website. If you can provide a secure donation page on your site, you'll maintain consistent branding, control the flow of data, and be able to respond directly and immediately to gift donors.

The tables below give you a snapshot of the choices you will have as you consider doing it yourself or hiring a service.

## Words to Know

A *widget* or *badge* is a stand-alone application that can be embedded into third-party sites allowing users to enhance local content with dynamic web applications such as sports scores, weather reports, or devices for accepting payments. An important factor with a widget is that the functionality it provides cannot be modified—it is pre-published by the service provider. The host can either accept that functionality or not use the widget. However, the host does control the placement. Usually created using JavaScript, DHTML or Flash, the code can easily be copied and embedded into a website by someone with authorship access and little or no knowledge of coding.

### USING A SERVICE

Vendor collects donations and sends receipts to donors

Vendor pays you in bulk monthly

You pay one-time fee to cover credit card processing and overhead

You establish a merchant account with your bank to accept online credit card payments, or you may be able to use vendor's account

You can customize your donation form to varying degrees (check with vendor)

You may have to pay setup fees, annual or monthly fees, transaction fees, merchant account fees

**DOING IT YOURSELF**

| PayPal | Google Checkout | Facebook "Cause" | FirstGiving.com |
|---|---|---|---|
| Inexpensive (small transaction fee, credit card fee) | No transaction fees for approved nonprofits | Transaction fee | No fees |
| User does not have to create a special PayPal account to donate | User must create a Google Account and associate a credit card with this account | Users need a Facebook account | User does not have to create a special account to donate |
| No way to customize your donation form to your organization | Donors leave your site to make payment on Google | Builds community around your cause | You can create a free, personalized fund-raising page |
| You receive funds immediately | You receive funds immediately | You receive funds immediately | All funds go directly to the nonprofit |
| You send receipts to donors | You send receipts to donors | You send receipts to donors | You receive funds immediately |

# Landing Pages

A successful landing page has one clear call to action. Everything on the page will focus on getting the visitor to take that one action. Get to know your audience. Find out what motivates them and tap into their passion.

Maintain the same branding on all landing pages. You can have as many landing pages as you have appeals and audiences—each page customized for the segment you're sending there—but be consistent. Your website should have the same logo and colors as your e-mail newsletter or other e-communications, which should use the same logo and colors as your direct mail.

- Include your library's or its fund-raising organization's phone number. Even if they don't use it, knowing they can call a real person helps visitors trust your organization more.
- Focus attention with a brief, compelling headline and a single image of one person. Have them look directly in visitors' eyes. Be sure to use a web-optimized photo to ensure short page-loading times. People will leave the page if it takes more than a couple seconds to load.
- Use big buttons to grab visitors' attention and convert them into donors.
- Keep your story and call to action in the area of the browser that's visible without scrolling down.

Use a second landing page after they complete their donation. Your cause is at the top of your donor's mind right after they give! First thank them, and use that moment to get them to take the next step—share on social media sites, join an e-mail list, or contact their local elected official, and so on.

Measure and act on the data: what works and what doesn't for your website? Use Google Analytics to learn how people are finding you. What pages do they visit? How long do they stay? Where do they exit? Which inner pages direct visitors to the landing page? Take what works and use it to improve website navigation and future appeals. Data means nothing if there's no follow-up. If you don't have the time to analyze your data, see if you have a volunteer who might want to do this, or ask a marketing student if such a project might make a good internship.

# Forms That Follow Function

The donation process begins with a request for donations on your website. This might be a "Donate Now" button or a link with information describing all the good work you do and how you use donors' money. When donors click the button or link, they are taken to a donation form where they can determine how much they would like to give, then enter their billing and credit card information, and provide any other information you request.

The actual look of the form is one of the big differentiating factors between the tools mentioned above. Some tools—such as PayPal and Network for Good's Basic DonateNow—make it obvious to the donor that they have left your site and are now being asked to donate through a different website. Others allow you to tailor the appearance of the donation form to match the colors, fonts, and images to your own website.

Here are six basic rules about online forms to keep in mind when planning fund-raising via your website:

1. **Use a simple donation form.** If you overload the donation form with lots of options, you run the risk of overwhelming your donors. Testing shows that the more complex the form, the higher the abandonment rate. Start with the minimum of required fields and carefully add things. Remove clutter from the rest of the page that may cause distractions.

2. **Use more than one donation form.** Many libraries and their fund-raising organizations have only a single donation form, which is a mistake. Use a combination of a general donation form along with other, campaign-specific forms. In the back-end programming of your website, all the forms route to the same location, but in some cases, such as for memorials and honoraria, you may need to capture additional donor and honoree data. E-mail "blasts" should route donors to a specific form for tracking purposes.

3. **Don't require donors to register.** You should be careful not to force donors to register with your website in order to give. Requiring registration can be a big turn-off to first-time or occasional donors.

4. **Suggest giving amounts.** You can ask for an "Other" amount on the form, but there should always be a clearly displayed minimum gift

amount. Testing has shown that nonprofit donation forms with clear ask amounts perform better than those left blank.

**5. Offer a mobile-friendly donation form.** Check your website stats to find out how many people already visit your site using a mobile device. It is predicted that by 2014 more web browsing will happen on mobile devices than desktop computers. Mobile-friendly forms should be optimized for size and speed. Use less page clutter and eliminate unnecessary extra fields.

**6. Invite comments.** Add a box for the donor's comments or for additional information he or she may want you to know (for example, the name of an individual the donor is honoring with the gift).

# You're Online: Now What?

Once you have your online fund-raising capability in place, make the most of its advantages (cost-effectiveness, timeliness, the ability to find out more about your donors over time) and communicate with your supporters based on what they respond to.

**Build and manage your e-mail list.** Drive traffic to your site, and make sure it's optimized to convert visitors to donors. Send messages to existing supporters, asking them to tell a friend about you and follow you on social networks like Facebook and Twitter. If you don't have e-mail addresses for all your current donors and members, consider purchasing a service that finds e-mail addresses to match the postal addresses in your existing database.

**Develop relationships with your supporters.** Over time, you can survey your members to find out more about them and their interests (useful for list segmentation), and create special messages and landing pages based on what they tell you.

**Create compelling campaigns.** Clearly communicate your goals, share your progress, and thank people for contributing. Ask them to share their involvement across their social networks. Communicating at every step can improve response rates significantly and keep your supporters returning.

**Engage your supporters as volunteer fund-raisers.** Many organizations have been successful with peer-to-peer campaigns such as walk/run/ride events, but consider virtual events too, since traditional events like races can be expensive to organize. Plan a one-day online giving event. Provide incentives for supporters who raise the most money, or the largest number of gifts. You can strengthen your relationships with supporters by engaging them in this way, and expand your organization's visibility in their networks.

**Measure your success at every step.** How many visitors to your site are signing up and/or donating? How many people are opening your e-mails? Who's clicking through and taking action? How many of your supporters stick with you over time? Online methods allow you to more easily test different messaging strategies with different groups of supporters, so hone your efforts.

**Finally, you're heard it before, but it bears repeating: *tell a great story.*** Without smart, creative, clear and compelling content you'll never be able to attract, retain, or convert your donors online or offline.

## REFERENCES

Case, Scott, and Katya Andresen. *Online Giving: Donors Are Younger, More Generous, and in a Hurry to Help.* The Case Foundation, n.d. www.casefoundation.org/spotlight/holiday/online_giving.

Flannery, Helen, and Robb Harris. 2011 *donorCentrics Internet and Multichannel Giving Benchmarking Report.* Target Analytics, Blackbaud. www.blackbaud.com/files/resources/downloads/WhitePaper_MultiChannelGivingAnalysis.pdf.

# 17

# Building Relationships with Businesses for Library Fund-Raising

**FUND-RAISING IS ALL ABOUT RELATIONSHIPS; AND BUSINESS SPONSOR-**ships or underwriting constitute another kind of relationship—one between your library and a for-profit (business) organization. Because libraries and their services are highly valued by our society in specific as well as intangible ways, sponsorships and underwriting of library or Friends/Foundation activities are appealing because they allow a business to connect itself to people's positive feelings about the library. It's important to remember, however, that while the business may have affection for the library, philanthropy is *not* a driving reason for this mutual exchange. Sponsorship and underwriting are business-to-business relationships—partnerships that ideally produce valuable benefits for *both* organizations.

## Sponsorships, Underwriting, and Libraries (No Reason to Cringe)

Library, Friends, and Foundation sponsorships and underwriting are increasing as primary marketing tools for businesses. The reason for this can be summed up in three words: cause-related marketing.

**Note:** *For this chapter, "sponsorship" refers to opportunities that are finite, such as events or series of events that may occur annually, but are not continuous. "Underwriting" refers to opportunities that are ongoing—specific services, such as the bookmobile. This chapter will focus primarily on sponsorship because, in the library world, sponsorship occurs much more frequently than underwriting.*

Cause-related marketing is a relatively new phenomenon, first conceived in the early 1980s. Today it seems ubiquitous. Look around at local and national special events, sporting activities, and public spaces, and you will see the brands and imprints of businesses that are (at best) tangentially associated with providing those experiences. (The corporate culture of "pink" created by Susan G. Komen for the Cure—in this case of breast cancer—is an example of cause-related marketing on a grand scale. Coca Cola's redesign of its iconic red can in support of the World Wildlife Fund in 2011 is another.) The nature of this potential win-win relationship is that you give the sponsor or underwriter the right to be associated with your library or its fund-raising organization and its work in exchange for something your library, Friends, or Foundation needs—such as cash, goods, or services. In other words, you leverage your library's reputation and community reach in order to gain critical resources.

> **Words to Know**
>
> *Cause-related marketing* is a partnership between a for-profit business and a nonprofit for mutual benefit. In the case of libraries or their fund-raising organizations, business sponsorships allow access to resources the library or its fund-raising organization would not have otherwise. In return, the business expects to profit by selling more products and gaining favorable publicity because of the "halo effect" of being associated with a respected community organization such as the library.

A very important point to remember is that neither sponsorship nor underwriting requires giving away the right to control any content, nor bowing to outside influence upon the activities your library conducts. This is understood in the business industry, but not always by librarians or the public; hence, it can become a unique obstacle to finding sponsors and underwriters for library (or Friends/Foundation) needs. Businesses really do recognize the great brand value of the library, and they want their sponsorship to respect and reflect that value. However, some library staff or library users may fear that a business's logo or imprint on a library program or item sends the message that the business, not the library, is in charge. Nothing is further from the truth.

Here is an actual example of this kind of misunderstanding: One Midwest library made an agreement with an Internet provider to create mouse pads to be placed at each public access computer. The mouse pads were branded with the logo of the library, the library's Friends group, and the business sponsor (a generous Friends supporter), who paid for them. When library staff became upset that this arrangement was agreed upon, it was found that all kinds of branded mouse pads were already at the computers! These previously accepted mouse pads had been provided free of charge, although none carried any library or Friends identification (and no fee had been paid). Interestingly, neither library staff nor users objected to the mouse pads they had become accustomed to seeing.

One lesson here is that most libraries do not have policies about accepting in-kind gifts, such as the mouse pads in the above example. Therefore, if your library or fund-raising organization is considering seeking corporate sponsorships (including in-kind gifts) for library programs or products, creating a sponsorship policy may be the first thing you need to think about. See page 211 for a "Sample Sponsorship Policy."

# Why Do Businesses Choose Library Sponsorships?

In many businesses, it is the individuals in the marketing or community relations department who are charged with creating and reinforcing their company's brand and key messages. They emphasize positive brand aspects (such as trustworthy, reliable, fast, or cutting edge) and often highlight a specific product or service. Their messages build brand loyalty, which is as important as brand recognition. In cases where your library's patrons are also the potential customers of a business, you have a tailor-made sponsorship opportunity. Marketing or community relations departments will pay for library sponsorships because they seek brand loyalty through their association with your library. Consumers today increasingly demand that businesses show community responsibility, and sponsorship of a nonprofit is a very effective way to achieve this. It can be seen as a form of advertising that is altruistic and more subtle than typical methods.

In some instances, there are specific benefits a business may be looking for that your library can easily provide. If you hold excellent events and have a standout facility, these attributes present opportunities for business leaders to entertain clients. (This is why major sports venues have suites or boxes.) In certain instances, your library can also provide names of potential customers for a sponsoring business. Typically, libraries are hyper-concerned about privacy, but if your library holds a drawing, raffle, or door prize, it is perfectly acceptable to share the names of contest entrants with the sponsoring business as long as you offer a disclaimer to entrants that explains how entry forms will be used.

## Potential Opportunities for Sponsorship

- Programs
    - Author readings
    - Programming at a single library location, or a program series or theme
- Series of workshops
    - Computer training for seniors
    - Technology training for teens
    - Home or car maintenance/repair
    - Personal financial management
- Any "special" services
    - Bilingual programming
    - Films
- Events
    - Donor recognition
    - Volunteer recognition
    - Special fund-raising events
- Print materials
    - Newsletters
    - Calendars
    - Brochures/reprints
    - Reading lists
    - Maps
- Book bags
- Special library cards

## Finding a Sponsor

There are two steps to finding a sponsor. First, decide what you are willing to have branded by the sponsor, then determine which business is likely to desire association with that activity, service, or item (such as mouse pads, book bags, pens, etc.). If you are just beginning to consider sponsorship, it may be helpful to focus on one kind of activity first that allows you some flexibility with the sponsor—an event, perhaps, or print materials that are costly to provide. When exploring sponsorship, it can be advantageous to look for a sponsor for something for which you already have a well-defined audience, such as an evening meet-the-author series. Another strategy is to first ask potential sponsors about the kind of programs and activities *they* are interested in, then identify or develop library or Friends/Foundation programs or activities that meet their interests. The list that follows illustrates the kinds of library or Friends/Foundation activities which typically attract business sponsorships.

Once you have decided what you want to have sponsored, look around at which organizations in your community might want to reach the same audience that a library activity or service reaches. For instance, if you decide to seek a business sponsor for your summer reading program, start by making a list of businesses that primarily serve families. Are any of these businesses already sponsoring activities and programs in your community? If your first sponsored activity is with an organization that already has experience in nonprofit sponsorships, you will quickly learn some of the routine practices in your community.

It's important to know who to ask. The *best* way to get to the right person in the business is to use a relationship you have. Ask people who know your library's, Friends,' or Foundation's good work (a member of your Friends group or library fund-raising committee, one of your board members, volunteers, or frequent users) whether they have personal connections with decision makers inside the targeted company. As in other types of fund-raising, the person making the request is an important consideration when asking for a business sponsorship, and a champion on the inside is always extremely valuable. Your first contact with the potential sponsor might sound like this. "I'd like to bring a sponsorship proposal to you, but I want to be sure it fits your priorities. Could we talk about your needs?"

> ## What Would You Do If You Had the Money to Do It?
> ### A Real-Life Example
>
> A public library had a relationship with a local food co-op and approached co-op managers about creating a new program series in partnership with the library. The co-op agreed to pay a sponsorship fee in order to be part of a high-quality library program series with a food theme. Both parties decided that the series would be exclusively sponsored by the co-op and cross-promoted by both organizations through all available media. Library staff suggested a sustainability theme (which the co-op liked) and selected all of the books, speakers, films, and associated program content. Most programs in the series took place at the library, with one at the co-op.
>
> The partnership was a great success for both parties and is now in its third year of focusing on farming, nutrition, and healthy cooking practices. The fee the sponsor (the co-op) paid the library was enough to cover staff time, speaker fees, and promotional expenses, and (happily!) the library made a modest profit for its effort as well.

# Securing a Sponsor

Your job is to make it easy for the business to see how your opportunity will help them meet their marketing goals—and easy for them to say yes. You should be thinking win-win and long term. Be prepared to negotiate. You will want to present the potential sponsor with a written document that specifies what the library (or its Friends/Foundation) will provide to the sponsor, as well as what cash, products, or services the library or its fund-raising organization will receive in turn. As you negotiate, you can add or remove provisions from both sides of the equation until you have an agreement—or agree that you don't have the right match.

## What's in It for Your library?

In-kind items of value a library or its fund-raising organization might accept in addition to (or in lieu of) cash:

**Printing.** Many large businesses have in-house printing capabilities and can produce brochures, bookmarks, promotional materials, and so on for the library, Friends, or Foundation.

**Advertising.** Media partners can be newspapers, radio, TV, and websites. Be sure you have the opportunity to leverage media exposure with other sponsors by offering to list them in a newspaper ad, for example, or mention them in a public service announcement.

**Design.** Media partners and others may have design professionals who can help you make your library's (or its fund-raising organization's) publications more attractive and more likely to be read.

**Marketing and Publicity.** If your sponsor sends monthly bills or newsletters, would they promote your event or program through an insert with the bill? If your sponsor has many locations, would they put information about you there as a regular part of their business?

**Product donations.** If your sponsor is a retailer, are any of their products ones that your library, Friends, or Foundation would otherwise have to purchase?

**Giveaways.** If your library will distribute them, will your sponsor produce co-branded items that can be given away for free?

Your proposal should clearly state the sponsorship fee the library, Friends, or Foundation expects. Base this sponsorship fee on value and the cost of similar marketing exposure, not on your library's budget or need. This is an important distinction. In the case of underwriting an ongoing library service, like the bookmobile, you can't base the sponsorship fee on what it costs to run the bookmobile. However, you *can* base it on comparable advertising expenses. For example, if your sponsor wants to underwrite your bookmobile by putting the business's logo on it, price out what it costs to wrap a bus or delivery truck in your area. Use that cost to determine a fee for making your bookmobile a moving advertisement for the underwriter. For help with the kinds of points you should discuss and the language to use, see 213, "Sample Business Sponsorship Agreements."

# Sponsorship Agreements

When your library or its fund-raising organization and a business partner hit upon that win-win situation, it's time to write a letter of agreement. This letter allows you to state in writing exactly what each party is willing to do, and what each expects in return. This document ensures that, as you move forward, there are no surprises or misunderstandings. Be as specific as possible in your letter of agreement. Include dates, deadlines, how often promotion will take place, and so on. This is a business arrangement, so include invoicing and payment information too. It's usually a good idea to include an "escape clause" that will allow either party to break the agreement in the event of an unforeseen change or event. (For example, if your Friends' business partner was found to be engaging in an illicit activity, or if a high-profile individual from that business made a political statement that reflected poorly on your library, these might be grounds to use your escape clause.) See page 213 for "Sample Business Sponsorship Agreements."

Once the agreement is signed by both parties, that's when the real work begins and when your library or its fund-raising organization begins fulfillment.

You should already have an idea of how many times your library, Friends, or Foundation intends to carry out certain activities, and the key to successful fulfillment is sitting down with the people who will actually do them, and making concrete plans. Depending on the activity or item to be sponsored, fulfillment may occur before, during, or after the fact. For example, you will make sure the sponsor's logo is included on the invitation *before* an event; you'll provide a script or talking points for use *during* an event; and you'll send out thank-you correspondence *after* an event. It's important to communicate regularly with your business sponsor to ensure that they know what your library or its fund-raising organization is doing. Quantify your efforts whenever possible and report these results to your sponsor. Include copies of press coverage. Remember that the businessperson you are working with has a supervisor, and part of your job is to help that person shine. For help with all the steps of doing business sponsorships well, see the checklist in the sidebar below:

> ### Words to Know
>
> *Fulfillment* describes the actions your library, Friends group, or Foundation takes to make the sponsorship a success.

Communicate internally and with close stakeholders why you are pursuing sponsorships. (Assure everyone that you are not "selling out" the library's brand.)

Determine what your library or its fund-raising organization has to offer and what benefit(s) you need in order to offer it.

Thoroughly research prospects who will value what you have to offer.

Determine who the right contacts are—at your library, within its fund-raising organization, and at the business from which you are seeking sponsorship.

Develop a proposal that shows your library's strengths. Include your best materials and most impressive information targeted to their market. Showcase your pride, and use third-party info if possible, such as national return on investment (ROI) studies on the value of libraries.

Be clear that you are *not* asking for a contribution, you are establishing a business relationship.

Be prepared to follow up with a "sales" call—ready to discuss the proposal in more detail. Be flexible, but be clear about your boundaries.

- If you are really nervous, identify a business that you *do not* plan to solicit for sponsorship, and ask someone there to serve as a reviewer to read your materials and review your solicitation process, then make suggestions.

- If you hear "no thank you," don't assume it's over forever! Ask for help—"What would get you fired up about a sponsorship opportunity?"

Meet with key people, and seal the deal!

Send letter of agreement and be sure to say thank you.

Start working on fulfillment.

Communicate with your sponsor. Do they have what they need from you?

Create a portfolio of outputs and results.

Communicate with your sponsor. Find out what is working and what is not.

Write the story and provide photos for your sponsor to use in internal and external communications. Make it easy for the sponsor to promote this great partnership!

Remember that this is a business transaction, and the way to collect your library's fee is to send the sponsoring business an invoice.

Get to know your sponsors. They are fun people! This might just be the start of a beautiful relationship.

If your sponsorship is event-related, be sure to follow up the next day.

Send the full portfolio of outputs and results, report anecdotal responses, and say thank you one more time.

Does this seem like a lot of work? Remember that this is a two-way association, and be sure to ask for enough to make it a win-win. This means that your library or its fund-raising organization gets what it needs as well. Sometimes you may choose not to renew the partnership if you decide it is not worth your staff time; however, it's more likely that you'll find yourself able to offer new activities or raise additional funds from people who attend sponsored events.

# 18

# Securing a Grant (It's Not Just about Writing)

A *GRANT* IS A SUM OF MONEY GIVEN BY AN ORGANIZATION (USUALLY A government, corporation, or foundation) to a recipient (typically a nonprofit organization, educational institution, or an individual) for a particular purpose. Grants are awarded because a funder wants to create change or sustain something valuable. In many cases, when a foundation is created, the funder defines areas of interest—such as youth, education, environment, or health. Sometimes funders are even more specific with their interests, for instance: supporting mentoring, middle school science curriculum, habitat protection, or heart disease prevention. The foundation may also define the types of grants it will award (see sidebar on next page). Some foundations give multiple types of grants to address a variety of interests, but almost never to a single organization at the same time.

The way to get a grant is to apply for it by writing a *grant proposal*. This is a formal application for funding that is often lengthy, requiring budgets and supporting documentation. Many people consider grant writing to be an impersonal form of fund-raising because funders' rules are clear, and their priorities and guidelines are carefully spelled out. There is even a sense of anonymity in submitting a proposal that parallels the absolute egalitarianism of library service. While this is true, *successful* grant writing shares important traits with other fund-raising strategies. It's about relationships too, about creating win-win situations. As a grant writer, you must align yourself with what funders are interested in and leverage the relationships of your current supporters. An unknown organization's request is rarely funded.

# Before You Start Writing

Because your time and resources are limited, you must have a way to prioritize the grant opportunities you will pursue. There are three principal components to consider *before* applying for grant funds:

1. Identifying a need and developing a plan to address it

2. Finding appropriate potential funders

3. Communicating effectively with the funders

Please note that finding funders *does not* come first! It is ineffective to begin researching the hundreds of thousands of grant makers in existence without first having some idea of what you will try to accomplish with their funding.

# Identifying a Need ... or Why Should You Receive Grant Funds?

## Types of Grant Funding

**General operating support.** A grant given to an organization to use as it determines within the scope of its mission. A general operating (or "gen op") grant is like an unrestricted gift from a donor, but it's also the hardest kind of funding to get. This type of grant usually must be reapplied for annually. Example: a grant that can be used to add to the collection, support Sunday hours, purchase new public access computers, or for any other high-priority need that cannot be funded by other means.

**Program support.** A grant given to continue or expand a specific set of activities done by the organization. Demonstrated effectiveness is key to a successful request. Example: a grant for the summer reading program, which for years has been helping children retain the reading skills they developed during the school year.

**Project support.** A grant given to initiate a new activity or achieve a specific, time-limited goal. Although normally given annually, a grant may occasionally be extended if you need additional time to achieve your goal. Example: a grant to develop a curriculum for digital literacy, with staff training to ensure effective teaching, and a new laptop, digital projector, and screen.

**Capital support.** A grant given to build a new facility or enrich an existing facility via redesign, furnishings, or structural or technology upgrades. These grants can be given to the project as a whole, or to an identifiable area. Example: a grant for the refurbishing of a specific branch or to create an area specifically for computer use.

In a general operating request, you will describe many of the services your library provides, with data to support how and by whom those services are used. Thinking about the spectrum of services you provide should also help identify the greatest needs or goals of your community that you have a role in addressing. These are likely the areas in which you will want to submit a program or project request. If you are cutting hours or staff, the greatest need may be to minimize the effect on the community through staff training or automation technology. If your schools have many children entering kindergarten unprepared to learn, the greatest need may be for early literacy activities and education. Almost every library serves job seekers, and the community may need services specifically in English language learning, technology training for adults, or twenty-first-century skills for teens.

Brainstorming with your library's leadership team may produce a list of twenty or more activities you currently do or want to try. However, you will quickly want

> **TIP:** If there are a wide variety of marketing opportunities attached to one of your needs—for instance, you want to produce printed materials that could include the funder's logo—you may want to consider underwriting or sponsorship instead of foundation funding. See chapter 17 for more on corporate underwriting and sponsorships.

to prioritize the two or three greatest needs and set aside activities that don't fall under those priorities. When you have this list compiled, consider which items fit with *grant funding,* as opposed to other fund-raising activities.

With project or program proposals, once you have some ideas about what you want to accomplish, it helps to do a bit of preliminary planning to ascertain what is needed to successfully start the project. This includes thinking about

- Project leadership
- Staff time
- Production expenses
- Marketing the project to the intended audience
- Evaluation

Whether you have a dedicated grant writer or a clerk in the youth services area who wants to write a proposal, there are a number of items to be considered in order to be prepared to carry out your project successfully if you are funded. See the "Grant Project Concept Worksheet" (page 216) for a tool that can guide your thinking. This project concept form can also help when an opportunity arises for which you have not planned, but want to pursue. For instance, grant opportunities from the American Library Association may excite someone on your staff, and thinking through implementation realities will quickly bring focus to a discussion.

# Finding Appropriate Funders . . . or Who Will Support Your Work?

Once you have determined the role your library plays in meeting the community's greatest needs, it's time to begin thinking about who might provide the funds to help you strengthen or expand your efforts.

Research is essential to finding the right prospective funders, and also to avoid wasting both your time and the funder's time if your goals do not overlap. There are many databases you can use, including the Foundation Directory Online (http://fconline.foundationcenter.org), compiled by the national Foundation Center. Look to see if your state has a database of its own. Often these are subscription-based services, but your state library office or even your public library may have a subscription. A few examples of state databases are the Minnesota Council on Foundations' Guide to Grantmakers (www.mcf.org), the Iowa Foundation DataBook (www.foundationdatabook.com/Pages/ia/ia1.html), and the New Mexico Grantmakers' Directory (http://nmgrantmakers.org). Such databases will typically provide you with contact information, areas of interest, giving history, and trustees. However, the data is often at least six months old; so, if a website is listed, visit it and study it carefully. The information on the funding organizations' own websites will be the most accurate and up-to-date. Be mindful that most foundations receive far more requests for funding than they can fulfill. If their areas of interest do not fit with your goals, don't bother to apply. It indicates to them that you did not do your research and gives them a negative first impression.

There are six major types of organizations that provide funds through grants.

> Many foundations will grant funds only to 501(c)(3) nonprofit organizations (such as your library's Foundation or Friends group); however, some will give directly to the library for a project. Some foundations will give a grant to the nonprofit with the understanding that the funds will be passed through to the library, restricting those funds for a very specific use. Although general operating support is unlikely to be available for a government-supported library, your nonprofit fund-raising organization can apply for these unrestricted funds for activities conducted in support of the library (fund-raising, programming, advocacy). These grants are usually awarded because the funder believes your organization is valuable in meeting community needs. They believe this because you can provide convincing information to that effect.

1. **Community foundations.** A community foundation may hold many different funds from individual donors, which together are overseen by foundation staff and can be used to support different needs within the defined community or region. Sometimes the donor indicates issues of interest, and the foundation serves as a conduit to the community. In some cases, the donor retains the right to direct where the funds will be spent. Because libraries are critical to community vitality, community foundations are likely to partner with you on initiatives that will build your capacity or that dovetail with the work of other successful organizations in the community. There are often other assets held by a community foundation which the staff have jurisdiction to allocate, with approval from a board of directors.

2. **Cause-focused organizations.** This kind of organization exists to advance a certain cause in one or many communities. These organizations typically have professional staff who are experts in the areas of interest they fund. Foundations that focus on education, youth development, literacy, arts, humanities, civics, or employment may be good prospects for libraries. American Library Association grants are "cause-focused."

3. **Government.** Your local government unit and each of the progressively larger units around you (including your state and the federal government) may have funds for which you can apply. Specifically for libraries, there are national grants available from the Institute of Museum and Library Services (IMLS), as well as funds that IMLS distributes through state library offices. In addition, some cities and states have funds dedicated to arts opportunities. Your library almost certainly provides access to the arts through your collection, and possibly your programs, so these opportunities are worth looking into.

4. **Family foundations.** These are formed when one or more persons in a family form a legal entity to which they give their money, but typically retain some rights concerning what it can support. Depending on the

amount of money involved, this family foundation may be created as a fund within a community foundation, at a financial institution, or as an independent foundation. Often these foundations are overseen by family members, while some have professional staff. Traditionally, the family of the original donor is involved in decision making.

5. **Corporate foundations.** These are foundations that receive funds from a corporation and then distribute them to support causes they feel directly or indirectly affect their business. Frequently they receive an amount every year from the business, based on annual profits. They are typically staffed by a person who does other community relations work for the company.

6. **Corporate giving.** Some corporations do not have an actual foundation, but do still make charitable gifts. With larger businesses, this is often through matching the gifts that their employees give, and sometimes matching employees' volunteer time with funds. Independently owned businesses may make donations at the sole discretion of the owner, or in consultation with a sales team.

There are pros and cons to each of these types of funders. The table below will give you a snapshot of what those might be.

| Type of Funding Source | Pros | Cons |
| --- | --- | --- |
| Community Foundation | Typically staff see and understand the library as a critical connector in the community.  Donor-advised funds of your supporters are a good opportunity to open the door. | May have their own agendas, and can be risk-adverse. May choose to fund organizations they have funded in the past. |
| Cause-Focused Organization | If you are part of the solution to the problem they are focused on, you are likely to at least have a good conversation with them. | High expectations regarding reporting of outcomes. |
| Government | Largest amount of funds available. | Largest amount of requirements, paperwork, and reporting. |
| Family Foundation | If you have a connection, you are very likely to get the direction you need for a successful application. | If you don't have a connection, it is almost impossible to get funded. |
| Corporate Foundation | Guidelines typically are written very clearly. It is usually easy to discern if you are likely to be funded. | These budgets have been shrinking. Corporations have a very strong need to see outcomes. |
| Corporate Giving | If you have a champion on a corporation's staff, they can have tremendous influence. | Typically not driven by philanthropy, but by marketing. |

A word about in-kind giving. A common charitable practice in business is to provide in-kind gifts of products or services in lieu of cash. This can be very beneficial, *if you need the in-kind gift or service*. For instance, it may be very valuable to you to have a local media company produce a training video you can put on your website, or for a printing company to produce posters for a book sale. However, if the item or service is something you would never consider paying for, think through the costs and benefits to in-kind support before you accept it. (Be aware that accepting "giveaways" might dilute your own brand and value. For example, if you accept promotional bookmarks from a business, the library patrons who use those bookmarks are being marketed to by that business via your library.) See chapter 17 for more information about in-kind donations and promotional giveaways.

Finding the right funder for your goals depends on two complementary components: research and relationships. Although combing databases for potential funders can be exciting, it is essential to your success to think about (1) who knows you *and* this funder, and (2) who knows you at this funder. This is where research comes into the picture, and who could be more skilled at this task than a librarian?

Ideally, your research will help you determine how much time will go into the application, and what the odds are of being funded. If you have identified a potential funder, there is still one last question you must ask yourself. Will you write the proposal in-house, or hire a grant writer? If you have no grant-writing experience, a professional grant writer can serve as a mentor or provide you with basic materials you can reuse as needed. Grant writers sometimes call this a "mother proposal" because all or part of it can be cut and pasted into other proposals. A professional can also help you with complex applications such as government proposals that often require information to be submitted in very specific formats. If you decide you want to hire help, understand that you will probably still need to do some writing yourself, and you will certainly have to spend time working with the grant writer and reviewing the proposal. When negotiating fees for grant writing, be aware that professional fund-raisers are ethically prohibited from accepting work on a commission basis. You will pay an hourly rate for their work whether you are approved for the grant or not.

## Communicating Effectively . . . or How Do You Build Relationships with Your Funders?

Fund-raising is about relationships, and relationships are often as important to securing grant funding as they are to securing gifts from individual donors. There aren't many foundations that will respond favorably to your request without knowing you or believing that you can deliver what you promise. Effective communication builds the relationship and allows you to demonstrate your credibility, either directly or indirectly (through association with leaders in your community).

Use a two-pronged approach to determine how to best communicate with a potential funder. First, start with your fund-raising board or committee. Ask these individuals whether they also serve on foundation boards in the community, now or in the recent past. They may be able to introduce you to the right people at the foundations with which they have a connection. For a second approach, identify a prospective foundation based on alignment of priorities, then send the list of that foundation's leadership to your fund-raising board or committee. Find out who among your fund-raising team may have friends or colleagues on the list, then ask that fund-raising team or board member to champion your cause. (This can be as simple as putting the names of the funders' leadership group in an e-mail to your fund-raising team and asking if any have a connection that is strong enough for them to contact a person on your behalf.) These two approaches may seem similar, but they are actually based on different methodologies. In the first case, you are using the volunteers and board members you already have and following those leads. In the second, you are researching prospects based on your goals, locating potential opportunities, then using your volunteers' and board members' connections to strengthen your grant request.

The contact can occur in a variety of ways. Your fund-raising team member's willingness to pursue it will depend on his or her belief in your organization and the depth of their relationship with the individual he or she is asked to contact. Talk to your fund-raising team member about your proposal, and send him or her a copy. Ask if they will arrange a meeting to introduce you to their contact at the foundation, so the three of you can discuss an application. If not, see if they will call their contact at the foundation and talk to him or her about your organization and the application you wish to submit. If your fund-raising team member is too busy or does not have success reaching the foundation contact, ask if he or she will write a letter of support that you can submit with your application. You may have to draft this letter, or at the very least suggest a few key points the letter should make. See the "Template for a Letter of Support" on page 218.

Whether there are contacts within your fund-raising team or not, you, your grant writer, or your project manager should talk personally to a staff member at the potential funding organization early in the process. If you cannot get an introduction from one of your volunteers, call a foundation staff member, such as a program officer, and share what you are thinking. He or she will provide valuable feedback about whether you have a likelihood of being funded, what parts of your plans fit best with the funder's goals and priorities, and whether there are any deadlines you need to be aware of that are not part of their published material. It is the job of the foundation's staff to distribute its money to the best organizations. It helps them to associate a person with the written information they receive, and some foundations even require that you call and talk to staff before you can send anything in writing.

# Writing a Great Grant Proposal

Most foundations will have guidelines and specific questions they want you to answer. Some will request a letter of inquiry (LOI), a two-page summary of your project that includes the amount of support you are seeking. These are used to weed out weak proposals and are thus submitted well before a full proposal. Refer to your "Grant Project Concept Worksheet" (page 216) for basic information to include in your LOI. If the funder likes your idea, they will invite you to submit a full proposal.

Other funders invite full proposals with no letter of inquiry needed. The components below are common to most proposals, although they may be identified in different ways. It is crucial that you answer all the questions a funder asks, as leaving something blank can hinder your chances of getting a grant. Be sure to read through all the requirements before you get started, and follow all of the instructions to the letter.

---

### What Is a Common Grant Application?

Grant makers in a number of states have instituted a "common" application form that they will all accept. This has benefits for both those applying and those reading the applications because it streamlines the application and grant review processes. Check to see if funders in your state accept a common application form.

---

## Six Basic Components of a Grant Proposal

There is a "Sample Grant Proposal" in the Fund-Raising Toolkit of this book (page 219). It is an actual proposal for one public library's summer reading program. Use it to get an idea of the kind of information that funders find useful when determining the importance of the program or service for which you are seeking support.

Most grant proposals can be broken down into the following sections:

1. **Organization information.** This can be up to one page in which you brag about your organization. Everyone has an idea of what a library is and does, but you cannot assume people know what happens in a library *today*. It is insufficient to say you have x locations open y hours per week. Use this section to talk about things you do that will not come up later in the proposal. What happens because you exist? How many students are able to complete their homework because you have an after-school help program? How many questions and requests for help do you answer? What kinds of awards have you received? You should also highlight your key program partners. In a general operating request, you may want to list the organizations you work with to provide services both in and outside library facilities.

2. **Need or situation.** Here you should state the need you want to address, and present statistics or anecdotes that demonstrate the need. There is some sort of data out there to support everything you do. Use the Web to locate the most recent studies on the need or effectiveness of the kind of program for which you are seeking support. If possible, use information relevant to your service area. Using demographic information, school testing results, or scholarly studies validates the need. If you cannot find an impartial source, look for information that may have come from a community focus group, or other libraries' best practices.

If you are seeking general operating or program support for something you already do, at the minimum you should reference current usage statistics. Also, use any feedback you have collected regarding the programs you already conduct, especially as they relate to results or impact. For instance, you might include a quote such as, "My second grade son reads more during the summer because we are at the library for the summer reading program."

3. **Solution or activities.** This is often the largest part of the proposal, where you describe what specific activities you plan to accomplish and how those activities will lead to change. If you have a history of offering the activity, highlight your previous successes and relate what you have learned through your prior efforts. Also be sure to include

   • Goals and objectives

   In many proposals you will include your goals and objectives as part of the activities section, but as they are a critical point for funders, they can also be presented separately. You should state one to three overarching goals that relate to your library's community. An example of a *goal* statement is, "to increase the recreational reading of at-risk teenagers during the summer months." Each goal can have one or many *objectives,* which outline the methods used to achieve the goal. For instance, an objective related to the example goal is to "partner with community agencies that serve at-risk teenagers." *Activities* are the specific actions that you will do to make each objective occur, for example, "Create and implement a plan to deliver materials to public summer school locations."

   • Timeline

   A timeline is a compelling tool that shows the potential funder you have thought through how and when the activities will be accomplished. It can be as simple as a spreadsheet with one axis representing a month and the other axis representing a key goal.

   • Personnel

   In applications where the funder does not ask for personnel information separately, be sure to highlight the skills and experience of the key project person or persons, as they relate to their role in this proposal. In particular, if a person has engaged in similar activities, these should be emphasized.

---

**TIP:** A great way to quickly develop grant-writing skills is to volunteer to serve as a reviewer for a funding organization. You will not only read other proposals, but also have the opportunity to sit in on a grant review session that can give you insight into what a funder considers important and fundable. For example, most states have review panels for LSTA (Library Services and Technology Act) grants funded by IMLS. These are useful grant panels on which to serve and could directly lead to your own successful LSTA application.

**4. Measurement and evaluation.** There are entire books available on program evaluation, and they all support the same point: if you receive grant money, you must report to your funder what difference the money made. If you have a program or initiative already in existence, start doing some measurement of its impact! Attendance figures are not enough in the information age—you must have some evidence that indicates attending had a positive effect. (The good news is that many funders are willing to pay for you to hire an outside expert to help with this.) The challenge is that your proposal will need to provide at least an outline of how you plan to measure your success.

Common evaluation tools used by libraries are surveys, focus groups, and interviews. Surveys of participants can be as straightforward as asking "Was it helpful?" and "How do you know it was helpful?" You can conduct these without worrying about breaching any confidentiality standards, stating in your proposal that you will only provide cumulative data and any individual responses will be collected anonymously. The purpose of the evaluation section of a proposal is to prove to the potential funder that

- You have thought about how you will measure impact
- You will report back to the funder
- If you are successful, other organizations can replicate what you have done

**5. Budget and budget narrative.** The purpose of the budget is to demonstrate to the potential funder that you know what financial resources will be needed for success and that you have a plan for securing them. No funder wants to give money, and then have the grantee come back saying, "We couldn't get the project done because we didn't realize we would need $x$." Most funders also have clear rules about what they will not support—for example, the salary of a person who already works full-time. The expense budget allows them to look closely at what you see as the components critical to success. The income budget allows them to see what portion they are being asked to fund, what you will provide, and whether other funders will be sharing their risk. For general operating proposals, you can simply include your organization's annual budget. For project or program grants, you must also provide a project or program budget that includes the items you've included in your "Grant Project Concept Worksheet," but in significantly more detail.

**6. Attachments.** Finally, there are a number of additional pieces of information a funder may request. Most will not accept media of any kind (such as a DVD that highlights your library or explains a program), but it is common to be asked to provide a website address. The following are attachments you may see requested:

- Cover letter—this is a one- to three-paragraph summary of your proposal that includes the dollar amount you are requesting, the reason you feel you are a good fit with the funder, a snapshot of the proposal, and your contact information. Compose your cover letter with care. It is often a funder's first introduction to you. See page 224, "Sample Grant Proposal Cover Letter."
- Cover sheet—a specific form the funder has developed that you must complete. A funder may have a specific form for you to complete. The cover sheet should be located between the cover letter and the actual proposal.
- Financial statements, preferably audited, or IRS Form 990
- List of additional funders, including those from the previous year, or funders that have already committed to the current project request
- List of your board members and their affiliations
- IRS determination letter (proof of nonprofit status)
- If a fiscal agent is being used, confirmation letter of fiscal agent, if required
- Other information as requested

The grant application process may seem like a lot of work—and it is. That is why it is essential to leverage all your relationships to help your proposal receive serious consideration. Use the information you find through research to choose the circumstances under which it is most worth your time to apply. However, remember that once you have written a proposal from scratch, you can often copy a great deal of the information into additional requests to other funding organizations.

With all of your submissions, but especially if you are reusing information from a previous proposal, you must double- and triple-check the requirements. Be sure you are also clear about who should receive the application, and when. What is the maximum number of pages per section or for the entire proposal? Does the funder request certain font and margin sizes in the document you submit? Page numbers? Does the funder want multiple copies of the proposal narrative and budget, but only one copy of the list of additional funders? If the funder does not accept a common grant application form, have you provided all of the information asked for? Make it easy for your reviewer to find the information. Use headers that correspond to each item requested.

## Words to Know

A *fiscal agent*, also called a *fiscal sponsor*, is a third-party organization that serves as your "bank" and "accountant." This step is only necessary if you do not have 501(c)(3) nonprofit status, but the funder will only give to a 501(c)(3). Fiscal agents are generally considered by funders to reduce accountability. If you choose to pursue this path, be sure to research the terms of contracts and legality that will assure the funder that strict oversight is present at multiple points.

# Drumroll, Please!
# Grant Proposal Follow-up

"Congratulations . . . You have been awarded a grant!" This is wonderful news and well worth celebrating, but don't forget to

**Call and say "thank you."** This should be done by your fund-raising volunteer who assisted with the process, or by you or your organization chair or president—preferably on the same day you receive notification.

**Write a thank-you letter.** If you have received the funds, the letter should also include language about tax deductibility.

**Call the project manager** and arrange a time to sit down and discuss the actual implementation. Ask that person to decide who else should attend this meeting.

**Mark your calendar** with the dates when interim and/or final reports are due.

**Share** the fact that you have received this grant—and why—with your volunteers, staff, and the community.

**Communicate.** Depending on the scope of the project, check back with the project manager monthly to ensure that things are moving ahead as planned. If you start to recognize problems or doubt the project will happen within the proposed timeline, communicate with your funder by the halfway point. Don't wait too long to alert your funder to a serious challenge.

**Remember to stay in touch with your funder** as time goes by. That staff member(s) will likely appreciate an e-mail with an anecdote about the project.

What happens if you've gone to all this trouble, and you *don't* get the grant?

**Don't take it personally.** Funders commonly receive applications requesting far more than they have to distribute. Rejection of your proposal doesn't mean it isn't worthwhile or well-written. It just means that decision makers' priorities caused others' needs to be considered more urgent than yours.

**Find out why your proposal was rejected.** Call the same foundation staff member you spoke with earlier and ask him or her to help you understand why your proposal was not accepted, and what you could have done to make it stronger. (There might not be anything you could have done differently.) Some funders will let you read the proposals that *were* approved for funding, so you can always ask to see those too.

**Say thank you.** A gracious and sincere letter of thanks is always in order. Take the time to write the foundation (address it to someone in particular, perhaps the program officer) and express your appreciation for the opportunity to have your request considered. Thank them for the time spent on it and say that you are looking forward to applying again in the future. This final piece of communication is another way to build a positive relationship.

## Six Common Reasons Why Grant Proposals Do Not Get Funded

1.  **Your request did not match the funder's priorities.** Avoid this by doing your research first. If you're still in doubt, consider phoning a program officer or other staff member at the funding organization and ask him or her if your library's program or service fits within their guidelines.

2.  **Your proposal did not follow the funder's required format.** This can give a funder the idea that you are careless. Do not let this happen.

3.  **Your proposal was poorly written and hard to understand.** Avoid this by asking an outside reader to review your proposal and find any parts that do not flow well or are otherwise unclear.

4.  **Your proposal did not convince the funder that it serves an urgent need.** Make sure you write with passion and persuasion.

5.  **Your proposal requested more money than the funder normally gives.** Do your research and ask for an appropriate amount.

6.  **The funder has allocated all funds for this grant cycle.** Look up the funder's next deadline and try again.

After reading this chapter, you may realize that securing a grant is not as easy as you once thought. But grants can be a vital part of library fund-raising, and they are worth going after. The more you try, the better you'll get at it! There are resources at your own library on grant writing, and there are experienced grant writers in your community who can guide you as you learn. Don't be afraid to ask questions, and don't get discouraged by rejections. Persistence *will* pay off, and you will gain visibility in the community and learn valuable fund-raising skills by knocking on as many foundation doors as you can.

# 19

# Capital Campaigns Are Not Just for Dreamers

**CAPITAL CAMPAIGNS ARE A LITTLE LIKE SWAN DIVING OFF THE HIGH** board: terrifying, exhilarating, and oh, so beautiful when executed well. In this age of shrinking library budgets, you might think that this kind of fund-raising is only for dreamers, but the truth is that libraries still need physical upgrades and healthy endowments if they're going to respond to the changing needs of their communities. (Believe it or not, capital campaigns can have another value. Libraries and other nonprofits often report that their *annual giving increases* during a capital campaign period. That is why it is important to continue with regular fund-raising activities while a capital campaign is underway.)

Although we usually associate capital campaigns with building renovations and expansions, they can also help build or acquire new buildings, fund endowments, or even cover extraordinary expenditures such as user accessibility or the purchase of specialized equipment or technology.

The capital campaign is unique among fund-raising activities because its goal is usually a *big* one, measured in six or seven figures. It's also different from the other fund-raising your library undertakes because it generally has specified beginning and end points and is usually a multi-year effort. It requires both an early "quiet phase," when you will solicit large lead gifts, and a later "public phase," when you will engage in all kinds of solicitations to foundations, corporations, and individuals in your community. Because of the size of donations that are solicited, a capital campaign allows—and even *encourages*—donors

> ### Words to Know
>
> In fund-raising, the term *capital* can refer to any tangible physical need, from bricks and mortar to equipment, technology, or furnishings.

153

to make multiyear pledges as a way of encouraging extraordinary generosity. The capital campaign is also a process that must be executed in carefully planned steps. This chapter will walk you through those:

1. Pre-Campaign—Getting Ready for a Capital Campaign

2. Pre-Campaign—Conducting a Feasibility Study

3. Pre-Campaign—Refining Your Campaign and Recruiting Leadership

4. Your Quiet Phase: Securing Large Lead Gifts

5. Launching the Public Phase

6. Wrapping Up

## A Word about Endowment Campaigns

Endowment campaigns are first cousins to capital campaigns. They are launched to establish new endowments or to raise additional funds for existing endowments. An endowment, defined in chapter 12, is made up of funds permanently invested in a stock and fixed-income portfolio that typically appreciate in value. Each year, organizations withdraw a percentage of these funds to use as needed or as the endowment directs. This action is called a "drawdown." Typical drawdown is between 4 and 5 percent of the endowment's market value. Endowment drawdowns can be used to add materials to a library's collection, fund technology purchases, support programming, or for another well-defined purpose.

Endowment funds are probably the *most difficult* funds to raise, particularly in today's economy. The reason is that donors are far less inclined to give to soft initiatives such as endowments. They prefer to see their funds support something tangible, such as capital projects. One way around this problem is to include an endowment campaign within a capital campaign. For example, if your library is trying to raise $3 million for building improvements, increase your campaign goal to $3.5 million and include a $500,000 endowment for the special purpose you feel has the highest priority. Another effective way to raise endowment funds is through special gifts, such as memorials, tributes, and planned gifts.

If your library wants to launch a special campaign just for endowment, follow the steps for capital campaigns since the process for both kinds of campaigns is nearly identical.

# Pre-Campaign—Getting Ready for a Capital Campaign

Start the planning process one to two years prior to the anticipated date your campaign will start. Why so long? Sound strategic planning must drive any capital campaign, so it's critical to first identify your most pressing needs and priorities, as well as your goals. It takes time to plan and develop a realistic budget and timetable, as well as to articulate your library's case for support. Expenses you will incur include a consultant for a feasibility study, conceptual architectural drawings, design and printing costs, and meeting costs. In fact, a rule of thumb is to budget 5–7 percent of your campaign goal for campaign and fund-raising costs, depending on the sizes of both your campaign goal and your community.

Spend time researching and analyzing your library's supporters, both current and prospective. You will need a clear idea of how likely your current supporters are to stretch their giving. Identify how and where you can begin cultivating new supporters. Plan on recruiting plenty of volunteers to provide leadership, to help get your message out, and to generate interest and enthusiasm. Build in sufficient time to recruit and engage them.

Don't rush this process! Remember that careful planning and analysis up front can save you from fund-raising disasters down the road. If you wish to get an idea of how close you might be to embarking on a capital campaign plan, see page 225, the "'Are We Ready?' Test."

| Why capital campaigns FAIL | Why capital campaigns SUCCEED |
|---|---|
| Wishful thinking | Clear vision |
| Unrealistic expectations | Careful analysis of likelihood of success |
| Inadequate preparation | Clear case for support, plan, timetable |
| No history of annual fund-raising | Successful annual fund-raising for several years |
| No feasibility study | Feasibility study |
| No large gift prospects | Adequate large gift prospects |
| Inadequate funds to conduct a campaign | Adequate budget for campaign activities |
| Lack of leadership | Passionate, influential campaign leadership |
| Lack of board buy-in | Committed, enthusiastic board |
| Lack of volunteers | Adequate committed volunteers |

# Pre-Campaign—Conducting a Feasibility Study

A feasibility study is essential for any library that is considering a capital campaign. It validates both the credibility of the library and its fund-raising organization and the confidence in its leadership. The feasibility study can also (a) determine whether a capital campaign has a chance of success, (b) identify individuals who could be asked to provide campaign leadership, (c) assess the importance of your library's project in relation to other privately funded projects underway in your community, and (d) determine whether the campaign goal you have identified (dollar amount) is achievable. It also plants a seed in the minds of individuals of affluence and influence, a seed that might one day germinate into a generous contribution to your capital campaign.

The information you include in your feasibility study should be carefully discussed, fleshed out, and articulated in a written document that states your library's case for support. This document is called a *case presentation,* and it should be clear, concise, and persuasive. The best person to write a case presentation is a library, Foundation, or Friends staff member. The case presentation should be brief, bulleted for easy scanning, and it should cover these basic points:

- Your library's history, mission, and its role in the community
- The community need(s) that your plans address

- Your library's goals and objectives
- Your library's accomplishments and successes
- Your library's current programs and services
- Your library's requirements (physical or other) in order to meet needs and respond to opportunities
- Your campaign (dollar) goal
- The reasons why anyone would want to support your library's campaign

A feasibility study should be conducted by *an outside consultant*, not someone from within your library or its fund-raising organization. One reason is because confidentiality is essential. An interviewee is more likely to answer questions frankly and honestly if he or she is conversing with a neutral party and feels comfortable that individual comments will not be reported to people who might feel sensitive about them. To find a feasibility study consultant in your area, ask around. Do you know of other libraries (or other nonprofits) that have conducted capital campaigns? Find out who helped them determine the feasibility of their campaign. Search "library capital campaign feasibility studies" on the Internet and look for leads there.

Your consultant should plan to personally interview 20–30 individuals whom you select. (This number will be determined by the size of your campaign goal and the size of your community.) These will largely be people who already have a relationship with your library or its fund-raising organization, either as extraordinary personal donors or as representatives of organizations that have made (or can make) large gifts. However, not all interviewees must have a preexisting relationship with your library. A feasibility study is an excellent opportunity for your consultant to meet with influential people who are not yet connected with your library, but with whom you would like to develop a connection. Two things interviewees will have in common are *personal influence* and *access to substantial funding*. Your fund-raising committee, library director, library trustees, and your Foundation or Friends board should all be asked to identify individuals who should be interviewed as part of your feasibility study.

For the personal interviews, your consultant will use the brief case presentation you have prepared to explain the library's needs, opportunities, and plans. If you have conceptual drawings by architects, these should be included as well. The consultant will ask interviewees how such a project fits into their funding priorities and, if possible, find out the financial level at which they might be able to support your capital campaign. This interview is *not* a solicitation for a campaign pledge, but rather a general conversation that is intended to gauge each interviewee's level of interest and capacity to give. The goal of this interview process is to answer the following questions:

- How are the library and its leadership perceived?
- Can we raise the funds required to achieve our library's goals?
- How much can we raise?
- Who has the capacity to make large lead gifts?
- Who can provide campaign leadership?
- Is now a good time for a capital campaign?

- How does our campaign compare with other projects against which we might be competing for major gifts?

Your feasibility study consultant will also develop a gift table. This is a valuable tool that will tell you how many contributions you will need at various giving levels to achieve your dollar fund-raising goal. See page 226, "Sample Gift Table," in the Fund-Raising Toolkit. Your consultant's final deliverable should be a feasibility study report that will tell you

- The level of confidence interviewees have in your library and/or its fund-raising organization
- The level of interest in the rationale and plans expressed in your case presentation
- The likelihood of an adequate constituency of contributors who can support your fund-raising goal
- The potential availability of capable, enthusiastic campaign leadership

What if your feasibility study report indicates that you will not be successful? Consider this money well spent to avoid an embarrassing failure! If success is not likely, reevaluate your campaign parameters. Reduce your campaign goal. Ask yourself if you need to step back and increase public relations and advocacy efforts, or whether you should initiate an annual giving campaign first, and delay a capital campaign until your library or its fund-raising organization is in a stronger position.

# Pre-Campaign— Refining Your Campaign and Recruiting Leadership

This step and those following assume that your feasibility study's results were favorable and that library or fund-raising leaders have made the decision to move forward. In this phase (which may be 12–18 months before you announce your campaign to the general public), your library or its fund-raising organization should undertake actions in response to what you've learned from your feasibility study report. Use that report to determine strategies for your capital campaign, and, if necessary, do some course correction from your original plan. Here are some additional activities that should take place in this pre-campaign phase:

1. **Obtain the approval of your board to launch a capital campaign.** Your board is your strongest partner. Educate members about the need for a campaign (and the costs), and keep them updated throughout the months that follow.

2. **Budget for a campaign.** Budget for meeting costs, architectural costs, printed materials, and extra staff time if necessary.

3. **Create a "case statement."** Expand the brief case presentation you developed for your feasibility study to an 8–10 page document. Elaborate upon each of the points you made in the case presentation and add other important details, such as:

- Architectural renderings
- An analysis of your library's service area and the major factors impacting it
- A summary of your library's demographic and socioeconomic data
- A snapshot of your library's current financial picture
- A history of your library's public and private support
- An idea of anticipated long-range needs
- Information about naming opportunities

4. **Increase your library's visibility in the community through positive public relations.**

5. **Redo your gift table if necessary.** If your feasibility study report told you that there is capacity for raising more (or less) than the original figure you tested, develop a new gift table that reflects a realistic campaign goal.

6. **Add staff if needed.** One person (your "capital campaign coordinator") must be able to set aside 10–20 hours per week for capital campaign activities. If you have a staff member who can do this, you are fortunate. If you do not, hire someone with special skills such as project management, writing, and organization. This individual can identify prospective donors, write grants, develop compelling campaign materials, and keep up with deadlines and details.

7. **Recruit a campaign chair (or co-chairs).** Your chair should be a person who is known in your community, perceived as a leader, well-regarded, and comfortable speaking about your campaign. This person should have a passion for the campaign and a capacity to make a significant personal gift. See 229, "Checklist for a Great Capital Campaign Chair," in the Fund-Raising Toolkit.

8. **Recruit a Capital Campaign Steering Committee of about 8-12 people.** These individuals should be well-respected community members who believe in the library's mission, possess influence and/or affluence, and whose personal involvement with your campaign will inspire the confidence of others and open doors to potential funders. It should include, but not be limited to, members of your board and your fund-raising com-

> **Words to Know**
>
> *Naming opportunities* are instances whereby a library's special or unique feature(s) can bear the names of the campaign's most generous donors. Examples include naming a wing, a room, or a garden area after someone, or installing public art as a recognition tool. If you wish to offer donors the opportunity for a special area or feature to bear personal names, it is important to have a "naming opportunity policy" in place and to remember that these almost always require the approval of your library's trustees or other governing body . See page 227, "Sample Naming Opportunity Policy," in the Fund-Raising Toolkit.

mittee. Ideally, your feasibility study will yield fresh people who will have found the idea of a library capital campaign exciting enough to want to play a leadership role. Look, too, to local businesses for potential Steering Committee members. One of the jobs of a dynamic campaign chair and a Steering Committee is to provide an inroad for lead gifts (more on this in the next step). Ask them to use their personal networks to develop suggestions of individuals who may be willing and able to make large gifts early in the campaign. Do the same with your board.

9. **Develop a campaign plan and theme.** Your theme should be short and catchy, using words that are rich with meaning, for example, "Renewing the Library," or "A New Age of Service."

10. **Recruit volunteers at all levels,** from positions of visible leadership to those who can help with community involvement and the miscellaneous tasks necessary for the campaign's success (such as helping with mailings, delivering campaign materials to library branches, etc.).

11. **Develop a campaign logo and print letterhead.** Include the names of your Steering Committee and chair or co-chairs on your letterhead.

12. **Secure final plans and drawings from the architects.**

13. **Begin promoting your capital campaign in-house:** to your staff, board, and volunteers. Be sure staff and board meeting agendas include a campaign update. Develop a short campaign fact sheet for volunteers and be sure to talk about the campaign at volunteer recognition events.

14. **Drill into your donor database and the greater community** as deeply as you can for potential large donors. You will have identified many of these for your feasibility study interviews, but are there still more who can be pursued for gifts?

# Your Quiet Phase: Securing Large Lead Gifts

The lead gift phase is a critical one, and it should take place during the year (or more) before you announce your campaign to the general public. It is sometimes called "the quiet phase" and is the period when half to three-quarters of your campaign goal will be realized. The first gifts given or promised are called "lead gifts" because they are committed early in the campaign and thus lead the way for other gifts that follow. Lead gifts are also *major gifts;* that is, they are gifts of extraordinary generosity. (Read more about major gifts in chapter 13.)

**Why do people give large gifts to a capital campaign?** The biggest motivator for a campaign donor is a belief that your library's plan and vision matches his or her own vision for how community needs and opportunities should be met. Other motivating factors include

- Confidence in the leadership of your library and its fund-raising organization
- Confidence in your fiscal responsibility and integrity
- A positive personal experience with your library or its fund-raising organization
- A feeling of wanting to make a big impact—and a big difference
- The inspiration of other donors' generosity
- A desire for the good feeling derived from a generous gift
- A desire for public recognition as a donor

Less compelling reasons are the desire for a tax deduction, or a feeling of guilt if one does not participate.

It is important to identify potential lead donors early in the campaign. Continually mine your donor database for potential lead gift donors. People who already have a relationship with your library and have a track record of generous gift giving are always good prospects. Research your giving records and create a list of your strongest possibilities.

Approach individuals, foundations, and corporations for lead gifts. This may involve grant writing, so be sure you have someone on hand with grant writing skills. (See chapter 18 on grant writing if you need help with that activity.) Seek challenging and matching gifts. These are great motivators to individuals considering whether to support your campaign. Who doesn't like the idea of giving a gift that goes farther than the actual dollar amount?

Remembering that fund-raising is all about relationships; the best way to get a "yes" is to have the right person ask the question. Look at your list of potential lead gift donors and determine which individual(s) should actually "make the ask." It may be a member of your Steering Committee, someone from your library or fund-raising organization's board, or an individual who has a relationship with either of these groups and who also knows the potential donor well. You don't have a second chance to do this right, so plan your strategy carefully, and once the ask has been made, remember that it can take time for the request for a gift to mature into an actual gift. During this time, it's important to keep the potential donor informed about the campaign and about the positive things that are happening in your library.

## Words to Know

In a *challenge grant*, a funder issues a challenge. That challenge states, "I/we will donate a specified amount of money to you if you can raise the same amount (or a specified amount) by a specified date." For example, if the Friends of the Library can raise $5,000 before the end of the year, the XYZ Foundation will donate another $5,000. This is sometimes called a *matching grant*. Not all matches are dollar-for-dollar as in the example above, however. A funder may say, "If you can raise $2,000, we will give you $1,000 more." This is a 2:1 match (i.e., for every $2 you raise, the funder gives you $1 more). If the funder says, "If you can raise $2,000, we will give you $500 more," this is a 4:1 match. A funder may also say, "If you can raise 80 percent of your goal, we will give you the remaining 20 percent." Regardless of the funder's specifications, the point is the same—that with challenge or matching grants, every dollar raised is leveraged to bring in more dollars.

While you are working on lead gifts, it is important to continue with your regular fund-raising, advocacy, marketing, and public relations. Don't let your capital campaign distract you from those vitally important activities!

# Launching the Public Phase

After a successful "quiet" phase, you will be eager to move forward and announce your capital campaign to the public. This is your opportunity to invite general contributions from everyone who values the library. When should you do this? Experts say that you should not make your campaign public until you have anywhere from 50–75 percent of your goal reached through lead gifts, and your board members have all made pledges.

One of the main reasons for waiting so long to announce your campaign is that most donors don't want to help you reach the halfway point—they want to take you over the top! In addition, knowing that you have been so successful thus far will motivate undecided individuals to contribute something to the library's effort.

You will want to create engaging printed information (brochures and collateral materials such as pledge cards and envelopes) and have them ready to disseminate, and you will want lots of colorful information—and quick, easy opportunities to give—on your library and its fund-raising organization's websites. Do an exceptionally good job with all your graphic and website materials because well-designed, professional-looking collateral materials will enhance the credibility of your library and your campaign.

Many libraries like to hold a "launch" event to generate excitement and media interest. You can too! Invite the public to a party on the library's lawn or a nearby park; host open houses; let people view your plan and architectural renderings; get kids and teens involved; invite your local business owners to the festivities . . . come up with great ideas that will work for *your* library and *your* community. Use your volunteers to keep the campaign visible and energized. Have them ask neighbors, businesses, and anyone they know who wants to see your library be the best it can be. Start a telephone campaign. Expect the public phase to take as long as a year, and continue with all your regular communication and fund-raising activities during this time.

Once you're in the public phase, people will be curious about how well the campaign is progressing and how close you are to reaching your goal. Don't miss any opportunities to report on the campaign, particularly as you close in on your goal. Use all of your library's regular communication tools (website, newsletter, press releases, etc.) to keep people informed. The old-fashioned "thermometer" that shows the goal on top and allows you to color the thermometer as you inch higher and higher toward that goal is still a popular way of telling people at a glance how well you're doing.

# Wrapping Up

"Are we there yet?" Well, not quite. Your capital campaign is reaching the end, but you still have several months of work to do.

**Ask.** Continue asking for donations and pledges until you reach your goal.

**Thank.** Remember to say thank you promptly.

**Update.** Take special care with your database of donors and pledges, making sure to keep it accurate and up-to-date.

**Evaluate.** Look carefully at your results. Did you meet your campaign goal? What did you learn? What were your greatest achievements and challenges?

**Recognize.** Honor all those who have helped make your capital campaign a reality—your donors, staff, board members, volunteers, and anyone else who helped along the way. Certain donors will deserve special recognition. How will you recognize these individuals? Give serious thought to recognizing people in a meaningful way. Many capital campaigns include a donor recognition wall, which could be an area that features a large plaque, where names of campaign leaders and major donors are listed. Brick pavers have also been used for decades for this purpose.

**Celebrate!** Make it fun. Throw a party in your new or newly renovated library space. Invite a local author or celebrity for a ribbon cutting or other special event. Grab a grill and host a cookout on the library's front lawn. Be creative! You have made your library and your community a better place. You have potentially touched the life of everyone in your library's community, whether or not they ever walk through your door. *Most of all, you have made a difference.*

## REFERENCES

*Designing a Successful Capital Campaign.* 2001. Chicago: Institute for Charitable Giving.

Dove, Kenneth. *Conducting a Successful Capital Campaign.* Jossey-Bass, 2000.

# afterword

## What Does It All Mean?

**F YOU ARE READING THIS PAGE, YOU HAVE LIKELY** waded through a great deal of information and advice. The authors hope you have found the scope of *Beyond Book Sales: The Complete Guide to Raising Real Money for Your Library* to be broad enough to meet your fund-raising needs and helpful in its approach to raising private dollars for your library. And we desire something more—that the ideas and techniques in this book inspire you to step beyond your current fund-raising practices and try new ones. Every topic covered between these pages can be done on a small or grand scale, and you are the best judge of where your library fits on that continuum.

If you finish this book with just one thought, it should be that successful fund-raising stems from healthy, mutually valued relationships. Whether you are seeking members for your Friends group or Foundation, asking for planned gifts, or soliciting a business for event sponsorship, the process is the same: build the relationship first, and the money will follow.

Perhaps the second thought should be: Don't go it alone! Fund-raising doesn't have to be complicated or intimidating. Enlist the assistance and enthusiasm of everyone who values the library—your staff, board, fund-raising committee, Friends and Foundation, volunteers, and library lovers of all stripes. This is the only way you'll make the connections you need to achieve your fund-raising goals and make your library the best it can be. We live in times of challenge that show no signs of abating, so today is the day to start ensuring your library's future through private fund-raising.

APPENDIX A

# Fund-Raising Toolkit

# Toolkit Contents

The chapter listings below refer to the book chapter in which the items are referenced.

# How to Start a Nonprofit 501(c)(3) Library Foundation

1. Go to your secretary of state's website and familiarize yourself with the regulations for starting a nonprofit organization in your state.

2. Decide on your Library Foundation's purpose and mission.

   Develop a mission statement. It should be brief, descriptive of what your Library Foundation wishes to accomplish, and not limited to a specific time period.

3. Recruit board members.

   See if your state requires a minimum number of board members in order to begin this process. The initial board of directors will assume much of the responsibility for starting your foundation. They will determine the direction and goals of the foundation, as well as criteria for recruiting additional board members. They will also write the foundation's articles of incorporation, approve initial bylaws, begin fund-raising, and hire staff as the organization develops.

4. Choose a name and check for availability of that name.

   Your Library Foundation will need a name that is not being used by any other organization. The most logical name is to take the name of your library, and add the word "Foundation" after it. (For example, the Seaside Public Library's nonprofit foundation will be the Seaside Public Library Foundation.) Check name availability through your secretary of state's office. Chances are, you will do this by completing a form, and there may be a nominal filing fee for this service. Once you have reserved your Library Foundation's name, no other organization will be allowed to use it.

5. Write your Library Foundation's articles of incorporation.

   Your initial board members will write this document, which is the legal record of how the foundation is to be managed. The articles of incorporation formally names the entity and states its location and purpose. The articles may also include corporate limitations, corporate existence, the name and address of the incorporator, a list of the initial board of directors, specification about membership, liability of officers and directors, dissolution, and written action. You may find it helpful to enlist professional legal assistance if this is the first time your board members have written articles of incorporation.

   (These articles must be filed prior to applying for tax-exempt status, and the IRS requires specific language in articles of incorporation. Check with your secretary of state's office for guidance or with an attorney when drafting your articles of incorporation.)

6. Incorporate as a nonprofit institution.

   The purpose of incorporation is risk management. Filing articles of incorporation with your secretary of state's office provides limited liability for the Library Foundation's governing body. It also provides stability during personnel changes, eases further relationships with funders/contractors/employees, and provides the means by which the Library Foundation will receive a certificate of incorporation from your secretary of state's office. This certificate will contain a charter number that is unique to your Library Foundation. Check with your secretary of state's office to see where to send your articles of incorporation. There will probably be a filing fee for these.

7. Create a business plan and a budget.

   A thoughtful business plan will help determine your foundation's direction. It should include your goals, what programs will operate, how and where the foundation will get funding, staffing, volunteers, and more.

   The business plan should specify income sources (memberships, fund-raising events, grants, individual donations, etc.) and expenses.

8. Draft your foundation's bylaws.

   Think of these as your rule book. Your bylaws should be more detailed than your articles of incorporation. They should be written flexibly to allow for easy amending as the foundation grows and develops. They should address the following organizational issues:

   **Membership.** Will you have members? Who will they be? How and when will they meet? What notice is required for meetings? How will members vote? What constitutes a quorum?

   **Board of directors.** Number of directors,* election process, meetings, length of term, number of terms allowed, vacancies, removals, quorum, officers, standing committees. (*Don't artificially limit the number of directors at this stage because the larger your board, the greater the range of expertise and contacts you can access. In addition, if you limit your board size now, then wish to increase it later, you will have to amend your bylaws to do so.)

   **Fiscal management.** Fiscal year, committee/officer responsibilities, reporting requirements.

   **Amendments.** How will amendments be made and approved?

   After your bylaws are complete, they must be approved by your Library Foundation's initial board of directors.

9. Apply for a federal Employer Identification Number (EIN)

   Nonprofits need an Employer Identification Number even if they have no employees. It's an ID number that functions like a social security number for individuals. It may be requested when opening a bank account or in other fiscal matters. Your Library Foundation must be incorporated before it can apply for its EIN, and it must receive its EIN before it can go on to the next step of filing Federal Form 1023.

To apply for an EIN, use IRS Form SS-4—Application for Employer Identification Number (EIN). That form can be found at this location: www.irs.gov/pub/irs-pdf/fss4.pdf. Instructions are readily available on the IRS website. There are no filing fees for this form.

The SS-4 can be handled by mail, fax, or toll-free by phone. Mail can take up to five weeks for processing. Go to this IRS website for information on applying for an EIN: www.irs.gov/businesses/small/article/0,,id=97860,00.html. If you wish to obtain an EIN number immediately, call the Business & Specialty Tax Line at (800) 829–4933. The hours of operation are 7:00 a.m.—10:00 p.m. local time, Monday through Friday. An assistor takes the information, assigns the EIN, and provides the number to an authorized individual over the telephone.

10. Obtain income tax-exempt status from the IRS.

Once the articles of incorporation have been filed, the bylaws have been approved by the initial directors, and you have an EIN number, it's time to apply for federal tax-exempt status. First, obtain IRS Publication 557—Tax-Exempt Status for Your Organization. This 55-page document spells out the federal laws governing 501(c)(3) tax-except nonprofit organizations. It is free on the IRS website (www.irs.gov/publications/p557/index.html).

Next, locate IRS Form 1023—Application for Recognition of Exemption under 501(c)(3) of the Internal Revenue Code (www.irs.gov/pub/irs-pdf/f1023.pdf) and Form 8718, User Fee for Exempt Organizations Determination Letter Request (www.irs.gov/pub/irs-pdf/f8718.pdf). Form 1023 applies for a ruling or determination letter, and Form 8718 is used to process the fee for applying for tax-exempt status. *These two forms must be submitted together.* Instructions for both of these forms can be found on the IRS website.

The cost of filing these forms is $750 for organizations anticipating gross receipts averaging more than $10,000 during their first four years and $300 for organizations anticipating gross receipts averaging less than $10,000 during this time period. The forms are filed by mail (check the IRS website for the mailing address for your state). Processing time varies, but it can take up to six months.

11. Apply for sales tax exemption from your state.

This exemption allows you to purchase office supplies, furniture, computer equipment, and other taxed items without paying your state sales tax. To apply for sales tax exemption, check your state's Department of Revenue website to see how to apply for a Certificate of Exempt Status. There will be a form for this purpose.

12. Receive a state tax identification number, if needed.

If your Library Foundation will sell products (such as T-shirts or books) that would normally be subject to your state's sales tax, you will want a tax ID number. You will also need this if you withhold state income taxes from employees, or are a vendor of goods or services to a state government agency. Tax ID numbers come from your State Department of Revenue. Go to that website and search for appropriate forms. There are usually no filing fees for this service.

13. Register as a charity.

Your state's attorney general's office may require that you register your Library Foundation as a charity. State rules vary, and not all nonprofits are required to register, so check with your state attorney general's website to see what the regulations are requiring registration.

*Congratulations!* You have now completed the steps required to establish a 501(c)(3) nonprofit Library Foundation. However, there are still annual reporting and filing requirements of which you must be aware. Keep your financial records in detail and up-to-date. Don't wait until you're asked for financial information because it can be very difficult to go back and find required documentation.

- If your Library Foundation has received monetary grants, certain funders may require post-grant reports.
- Your state may or may not require an independent audit. Research the nonprofit income level at which your state requires such an audit.

    **IRS Form 990.** An organization's 990 is the most complete documentation of its financial history and is often used to hold organizations responsible for past actions and future decisions. Even though your Library Foundation may be tax-exempt, it must still file an annual tax return with the IRS. Usually, charities with more than $100,000 in gross revenues and more than $250,000 in total assets must file Form 990. Smaller charities may file the EZ Form.

    See a sample Form 990 at this web address: www.irs.gov/pub/irs-pdf/f990.pdf. You will want professional financial assistance when filing your Form 990.

- Your state will probably have additional annual filing requirements. It is very important to keep abreast of these requirements and file your reports and registrations in a timely fashion.

Here is a snapshot of the entire process:

| Form | Fee | Submit to | Description |
| --- | --- | --- | --- |
| Publication 557 | None | -NA- | IRS publication that details the rules and procedures for seeking exemption from federal income taxes |
| Request to reserve a name | Check with your secretary of state | Your state's secretary of state | Reserves a unique name for your library foundation |
| Articles of incorporation | Check with your secretary of state | Your state's secretary of state | Legally incorporates your foundation as a nonprofit |
| Form SS-4 | None | IRS | Applies for Employer Identification Number (EIN) |
| Form 1023 and Form 8718 | $750 or $300 | IRS | Applies for federal tax exemptions under Section 501(c)(3) of the IRS tax code. Forms must be filed together. |
| Your state's tax-exemption form | Probably none | Your state's Department of Revenue | Applies for state sales tax exemption |
| Get a state tax ID number | Probably none | Your state's Department of Revenue | Registers a tax ID number for selling products, withholding taxes from employees, and so on |
| Register as a charity | Check with your state attorney general's office | Your state's attorney general | Registers your foundation for charitable solicitation |
| Form 990 | None | IRS | File annually, serves as a tax return for tax-exempt organizations |
| Other state filings as required | Check with your state's secretary of state and attorney general's offices | Your state's secretary of state and/or attorney general's office | These may vary from state to state, so check with your state |

# Fund-Raising Board or Committee Recruitment Worksheet

| FIRST NAME | LAST NAME | Connections to philanthropic organizations | Fund-raising experience | Marketing/PR or media experience or connections | Legal experience | Financial experience | Connections to businesses or foundations | Connections to people of means | Current library donor or likely donor? | Other |
|---|---|---|---|---|---|---|---|---|---|---|
| | | | | | | | | | | |
| | | | | | | | | | | |
| | | | | | | | | | | |
| | | | | | | | | | | |
| | | | | | | | | | | |
| | | | | | | | | | | |
| | | | | | | | | | | |
| | | | | | | | | | | |
| | | | | | | | | | | |

# Board Member Job Description Template

The board of directors of *(your Library Foundation's name)* is a volunteer unpaid group of individuals who assume fiscal oversight and policy direction for the organization. In general, the responsibilities of board members include:

1. Hiring and evaluating the performance of the (title of the Foundation head) of the Foundation;

2. Setting policies for the operation of the organization (not day-to-day management of the business);

3. Approving the organization's operating budget and overseeing its implementation;

4. Assisting the organization with its fund-raising responsibilities through personal contributions at a level consistent with ability and through providing fund-raising contacts to outside funding sources;

5. Serving as an advocate and spokesperson for *(your Library Foundation's name)* and the library.

## Criteria for Selection of Board Members

1. Individuals who are interested and enthusiastic about libraries.

2. Individuals who are knowledgeable about *(your library's name)*.

3. Individuals who are able to participate in meetings of the board and its committees.

4. Individuals who possess skills in the areas of programming, fund-raising, public relations, and advocacy.

5. Individuals who represent racial, ethnic, geographic, and age diversity in *(name of your city/county/township/village)*.

6. Individuals who are invested in and connected to *(name of your city/county/township/village)* through employment or residence.

## Expectations of Board Members

1. Attend (frequency, i.e., quarterly) board meetings (total hours per year).

2. Serve on at least one standing committee of the board (total hours per year).

3. Develop policy recommendations for the organization.

4. Provide fund-raising advice and contacts to the extent possible.

5. Make a personal financial contribution to the organization annually.

6. Consider making a planned gift to the organization.

7. Serve as a spokesperson for *(your Library Foundation's name)* and the library.

8. Attend at least two Foundation-funded (or coordinated) cultural programs annually.

# Sample Consultant Memorandum of Agreement

To:     Consultant
From:   Your Library or its Fund-Raising Organization
Re:     Consulting Services (Describe)
Date:

This Memorandum constitutes an Agreement between *(the name of your library, Friends group, or Foundation)* and *(your consultant/consultant group name)*.

## SCOPE OF THE CONTRACT

The Consultant agrees to provide consulting services to assist the Library (or Library Friends or Foundation) with (general description of services to be contracted for).

## TERMS OF THE AGREEMENT

This Agreement will begin xx/xx/xxxx *(date)* and end no later than xx/xx/xxxx *(date)*.

## SERVICES TO BE PERFORMED

(LIST SPECIFIC SERVICES/TASKS IN THE SCOPE OF THE CONTRACT)

Consultant will . . . . . . . . . . . . .

Consultant will . . . . . . . . . . . .

Consultant will . . . . . . . . . . . .

## RESPONSIBILITIES AND DELIVERABLES

The Library (or Library Friends or Foundation) is responsible for . . . (providing information, scheduling meetings, etc.).
The Consultant is responsible for . . . (general services and deliverables).

## FEES AND EXPENSES

Consulting fees will not exceed $xxxx (project cost may also include hourly rate). Expenses (over and above consulting fees) will include:

- transportation (airfare, car rental or ground transportation, personal transportation billed at the current IRS mileage rate);
- hotel and meals (or per diem stipend);
- miscellaneous expenses (parking, gratuities, printing, phone charges, etc.)

Fees and expenses will be invoiced by the Consultant *(monthly, at the end of the project, after established benchmarks)*. Invoices will be submitted to. . . . . *(where?)* and will be paid within 30 days of receipt of invoice.

## TERMINATION AND NOTICE

Either party may terminate this Agreement within 30 days' written notice.

Please sign in the space provided to verify your acceptance of this Agreement and provide us with your Taxpayer Identification Number or Social Security Number to meet IRS requirements.

A copy will be provided for your records.

_____     _____

For the Library (or Library Friends/Foundation) Consultant

Date: xx/xx/xxxx

Taxpayer Identification

Number: _____

Social Security Number: _____

# Assessing Your Library Worksheet

| 1<br>Constituency Group | 2<br>Their Needs | 3<br>Current Library Services Addressing Those Needs | 4<br>Unmet Needs | 5<br>Priority | 6<br>Estimated Cost | 7<br>Public or Private Funds? |
|---|---|---|---|---|---|---|
| | | | | | | |
| | | | | | | |
| | | | | | | |
| | | | | | | |
| | | | | | | |
| | | | | | | |
| | | | | | | |
| | | | | | | |
| | | | | | | |
| | | | | | | |
| | | | | | | |
| | | | | | | |
| | | | | | | |

# Current Library Fund-Raising Activities Worksheet

| Fund-Raising Activity or Solicitation | When Do You Do It? | Dollars Raised Last Year | Worth Continuing? (yes/no/maybe, and why) |
|---|---|---|---|
| | | | |
| | | | |
| | | | |
| | | | |
| | | | |
| | | | |
| | | | |
| | | | |
| | | | |
| | | | |
| | | | |
| | | | |
| | | | |
| | | | |
| | | | |
| | | | |
| | | | |
| | | | |
| | | | |
| | | | |
| | | | |

# Your Library's Fund-Raising Plan

| Fund-Raising Activity | When? | Strategies to Expand | Goal Year 1 | Goal Year 2 | Goal Year 3 |
|---|---|---|---|---|---|
| | | | | | |
| | | | | | |
| | | | | | |
| | | | | | |
| | | | | | |
| | | | | | |
| | | | | | |
| | | | | | |
| | | | | | |
| | | | | | |
| | | | | | |
| | | | | | |
| | | | | | |
| | | | | | |
| | | | | | |
| | | | | | |
| | | | | | |
| | | | | | |
| | | | | | |

# Checklist of Sources of Private Support

List your library's unique sources under each category:

- ☐ *Members of your volunteer library fund-raising committee or board* need to be the first donors to any fund-raising effort. The dollar amount of their donation matters far less than the fact that they are donors. It is extremely difficult to ask others to support a cause unless you support it yourself. List them here.

- ☐ *Your library's governing board.* While they are not a fund-raising board, they can still be donors.

- ☐ *Other "insiders," such as key library staff and Friends' members* (if your library has a Friends group). If you have a Friends group, those members should be asked to make annual contributions over and above their Friends membership dues, which should be paid at a separate time of the year.

- ☐ *Frequent/regular library users.* (Note: Local policies sometimes dictate whether or not library cardholder addresses can be used to solicit donations for your library, so be sure to check your library's ability to solicit active cardholders.)

- ☐ *The broader contacts of your library board, Friends, staff, and volunteers.*

- ☐ *Local businesses.*

- ☐ *Small family foundations,* typically found in bank trust departments.

- ☐ *Corporate foundations,* which are typically found in larger towns and cities.

- ☐ *Community foundations.* Communities of almost every size have a community foundation, which is a grant-making institution that uses pooled donations for its grant awards.

- ☐ *Large foundations* (that are not linked to a corporation) for which philanthropy is their business.

- ☐ *Government grants* (city/county/state/federal). Who will write your grant applications?

- ☐ *Corporate sponsorships* that involve receiving money, usually from a corporation's marketing dollars, in exchange for recognition within the library for a particular program, service, or collection.

- ☐ *Library vendors.*

- ☐ *Can you think of others?*

# Evaluating Your Fund-Raising Activities

Date _____

Fund-raising activity (book sale, author event, mailing, etc.)

_____

1. Was this a friend-raising or a fund-raising activity?

2. What was your goal for this activity?

3. Did you achieve this goal? Circle **Y** or **N**

4. If yes, what worked especially well?

5. If no, what factors worked against you?

6. Did this activity strengthen individual and/or community relationships? Explain.

7. Did it require excessive staff hours or volunteer help? Explain.

8. Was it labor-intensive for the return it yielded? Circle **Y** or **N**

9. If yes, what were the problem areas?

10. Is this activity worth continuing? Circle **Y** or **N**

11. Was it successful enough to warrant hiring help next time? Circle **Y** or **N**

12. If yes, who could you hire and how much could you spend?

13. Other thoughts:

# (Standard) Thank-You Letter Template

Your library, Friends group, or Foundation's letterhead

Date:

Donor's name:

Donor's address:

Donor's city/state/zip:

Dear _____

On behalf of *(the name of your library, Friends group, or Foundation)*, thank you so much for your contribution of ($ amount). Your support will help build and sustain the success the Library has enjoyed for many years.

   *(Add a paragraph here about how private donations are helping support library programs, resources, and services, or share some news about your library.)*

   As always, we encourage your comments and suggestions about how *(the name of your library, Friends group, or Foundation)* can best meet your needs. A great way to keep in touch is through our website at (your library's, Friends group's, or Foundation's website).

   Please know that we truly appreciate your generosity, and we hope you will continue to help keep our Library strong in the years to come.

Best regards,



P. S. For your tax records, your contribution of $_____ was dated _____ and was processed on _____. You did not receive any goods or services for this gift and it is tax deductible to the full extent of the law.

Below you'll find a comprehensive checklist of suggested fields of information *you might find helpful as you build your donor database:*

Primary Donor (in a multi-person household):

> Title
>
> First name
>
> Middle name or initial
>
> Last name
>
> Gender
>
> Date of death (if applicable)

Partner:

> Title
>
> First name
>
> Middle name or initial
>
> Last name
>
> Gender
>
> Date of death (if applicable)

Address:

> Primary Donor and Partner's home address
>
> Secondary/vacation home address

Contact Information:

> E-mail
>
> Home phone
>
> Cell phone
>
> Work phone
>
> Vacation phone

Name/address of employer for Primary Donor and Partner

Primary addressee information and salutation—used for merging letters, labels, envelopes, lists, etc. (for example, Mr. and Mrs. John Doe *or* John and Jane Doe).

Miscellaneous information:

Marital status

Birthday(s) (if known)

Special requests (such as no solicitation mailings or no phone calls)

Constituent type:

Individual

Organization/Company

Volunteer

Media

Other (you determine)

Gift Information:

Date of gift

Date processed

Amount

Purpose of the gift

Type of receipt/thank-you letter

Does Donor's employer offer a matching gift?

Solicitations (list mailings and other solicitations Donor has received, with dates)

Relationships (is Donor related to another Donor, or a business or other organization you would like to note?)

Notes (add miscellaneous Donor attributes here, such as his/her interests, dietary preferences, hobbies, activities, committees, and so on. You can customize your notes to meet your library's fund-raising team's needs).

# Advancing Our Libraries: The Legal Opportunities and Limits for Nonprofit Lobbying

### By David J. Guy, Attorney at Law

As "Friends of the Library" and similar organizations formed around a passion for libraries and Friends organizations continue to seek the most effective ways to support, promote, and advance libraries, the prospect of influencing governmental entities to support libraries with more robust funding inevitably arises. Questions naturally follow about the extent to which a Friends organization can advocate for libraries without jeopardizing its tax-exempt status. To be sure, Friends organizations have always been tremendous advocates for libraries and they can become even more aggressive advocates for libraries, but, to do so, will require additional analysis, planning, and accounting to retain their tax-exempt status.

This article will serve as a general guide for Friends to begin thinking about options and the various considerations involved in becoming more aggressive in advocating for libraries. Most Friends organizations are set up as tax-exempt public charities under Internal Revenue Code 501(c)(3). This provision provides the greatest flexibility to Friends organizations as they are exempt from most taxes and members' contributions are tax deductible. In exchange for these tax benefits, 501(c)(3) organizations basically agree to be subject to stringent prohibitions on political activity. This means Friends organizations that engage in lobbying or participate in a campaign must do so knowing the boundaries of their allowable actions, and the potential consequences of such actions.

## Candidate Endorsements

Friends organized as a 501(c)(3) may *not* participate, or contribute, or intervene (including the publishing or distribution of statements) in support or opposition of candidates for public office without jeopardizing its tax-exempt status. Although this clearly prohibits Friends from endorsing or otherwise supporting a candidate for office, it does not seem to preclude Friends from preparing a published report card in its newsletter rating elected officials on their votes regarding library matters. Friends can also host forums where the candidates are invited to present their perspectives on libraries and other issues.

## Legislative Advocacy

Friends can influence political activity at the local, state, and even the federal level, although there are limits on the extent to which Friends can lobby. To determine the limits, Friends must first elect whether to proceed under either (1) the "substantial part" test or (2) the expenditure test.

1. Substantial Part Test

   The "substantial part" test applies to all organizations that do not file the proper Internal Revenue Service (IRS) forms necessary to elect the expenditure test discussed below. Section 501(c)(3) states that a charitable organization is exempt from taxation as long as "no *substantial part* of [its] activities . . . is carrying on propaganda, or otherwise attempting, to influence legislation" (emphasis added). Lobbying, which is defined here as attempting to influence legislation, includes contacting, or urging the public to contact, members of a legislative body for the purpose of proposing, supporting, or opposing legislation. Legislation generally includes federal, state, and local government actions, including funding for libraries. Public action involving an initiative, constitutional amendment, city charter amendment, or similar proceeding also qualifies as legislation. Clearly this applies to the state legislature, a county (a board of supervisors or commissioners), and a city council. More specifically, it also appears to apply to actions by a library district or a joint power authority governing libraries. Without a specific legal opinion to the contrary, it is probably best to assume that any action by a Friends organization to influence official government bodies, both directly and indirectly, are subject to the "substantial part" limitation.

Importantly, under the substantial part test, there is no bright line formula to determine what constitutes either "influencing legislation" or a "substantial part" of the activities. Instead, a balancing of all of the facts and circumstances, including the percentage of the total budget spent on lobbying, the amount of volunteerism dedicated to lobbying, and the overall objectives of the organization and the expenditures are to be considered. When filing its IRS Form 990-EZ (or other 990 Form), a Friends organization must state whether it has "engaged in any lobbying activities" and, if so, complete Schedule C, Part II-B (2010 990-EZ, Part VI).

2. Expenditure Test

The ambiguity of the "substantial part" test led Congress to provide a way in which 501(c)(3) organizations desiring to engage in certain lobbying activities could be assured that they would not lose their tax-exempt status. The result was the expenditure test, provided for in §501(h). To make this election a Friends organization simply needs to file IRS Form 5768. By electing to proceed under this test, Friends will have specified limits on contributions made to lobbying. In other words, the "substantial part" standard is essentially quantified by using expenditures as the measure of the activity. For example, Friends organizations that have annual expenditures under $500,000 can spend up to 20 percent of their exempt purpose expenditures on lobbying. There is a sliding scale for organizations with larger expenditures. Importantly, if the Friends spend more than the 20 percent limit on lobbying, then the organization will not lose its tax-exempt status, but will instead be taxed for that excess amount at the rate of 25 percent. Section 501(h) definitions may also exclude certain activities that might be treated as lobbying under the "substantial part" test.

Going a step further, lobbying is classified as either direct or grass roots. Direct lobbying is any attempt to influence legislation by communicating with the legislative body. This also includes expenditures for ballot measures. Grassroots lobbying intends to influence legislation by affecting the opinions of members or the general public. If a Friends organization communicates with its members on legislation of direct interest to the organization, this is not lobbying, but if the communication urges the members to contact a legislative body, the activity is considered grass-roots lobbying. As previously mentioned, the total of all direct and grass-roots expenditures that are not subject to tax must not exceed 20 percent of the expenditures, but additionally, the allowable levels of grassroots lobbying without paying taxes is 25 percent of the amount allowed for total lobbying. As an example, if a Friends organization spends $10,000 in a given year for books and other library programs, then under the expenditure test, this organization can spend $2,000 (20%) total on all lobbying, and $500 (25% of $2,000) on grassroots lobbying, without paying taxes. If the Friends then spent $3,000 on total lobbying, they would be required to pay $250 (25% of $1,000) in excise taxes. Note that volunteer efforts are not accounted for in this process.

With respect to the election procedure, Friends will file IRS Form 5768, a one-page check-the-box form that can be filed online. The form can be filed at any time before the end of the tax year for which it will be effective, which means that Friends can wait to see how much it lobbies during the first tax year. Once filed, the form remains in place unless revoked. It is important to keep a copy of the filed form as the IRS does not acknowledge its receipt. The form and all other IRS documents referenced here are available on the IRS website under the forms section. When filing its IRS Form 990-EZ (or other 990 Form), a Friends organization that has elected to proceed under §501(h) (filed the Form 5768) must state whether it has "engaged in any lobbying activities" during that tax year and, if so, account for its lobbying activities in Schedule C, Part II-A.

## Conclusion

The future of libraries will depend upon the success of Friends organizations and their ability to influence library funding, through both public and private sources. This article describes the importance of Friends organizations making decisions on how to influence public funding within the legal structure surrounding nonprofit organizations. Although the process may seem complicated at first sight, a concerted effort to comply with these provisions can help Friends serve its ultimate purpose—the support and advancement of libraries in the most effective manner possible. Although both options are described here, most Friends organizations that seriously intend to influence public funding for libraries will likely consider electing to proceed under §501(h) because of the vagueness and uncertainties in the "substantial part" test and the certain advantages contained in the §501(h) process.

The legal requirements governing nonprofit lobbying are very detailed and Friends organizations should therefore consult a tax counselor prior to making any major decisions that could jeopardize the tax-exempt status of their organization. In most communities, small nonprofit organizations can actively seek pro bono assistance from attorneys and accountants in helping Friends organizations work through this process.

David Guy is an attorney at law and he is currently the president of the Northern California Water Association in Sacramento, California. For the past several decades he has worked in various capacities to advance economic interests that promote the conservation of California's special places and their precious water and land resources.

With respect to libraries, he served in the 1990s as the president of the Friends of the Sacramento Public Libraries, the secretary of the Board of Directors of the Sacramento Public Library Foundation, a trustee for the Friends of California Libraries, the chairman of the Library Advocacy Committee and the Sacramento Law Library Advisory Committee. He has vivid memories from an early age of helping his parents carry and sort books for the annual Friends' book sale at the Casper, Wyoming, Carnegie library.

We all know that when you write a check to your favorite charity for your annual donation, it is a *gift* to that charity. You intend to give it without the expectation of receiving anything. (This is assuming you are not receiving membership benefits, which is another conversation altogether!) The definition of a gift is: *the transfer of something without the expectation of receiving something in return.* In other words, a gift should have no strings attached.

We generally think of gifts to nonprofits as gifts of money. What if you have a donor who arrives at your library with a Rembrandt? What about a prize sheep? Are those donations? You bet! And you'd better be prepared to accept them—*within reason*—and offer a receipt. Keep in mind, however, that there may be gifts you do not want to accept because managing or selling them (necessitating expertise and resources) may be too problematic. Think carefully before accepting some kinds of gifts. You may be taking on more trouble than the gift is worth . . . literally and figuratively!

This is where a well-drafted "gift acceptance policy" becomes essential. A non-profit's gift acceptance policy must address issues related to the types of property that will be accepted. The review function is best performed by a committee. See "Sample Gift Acceptance Policy" in the Fund-Raising Toolkit for help and guidelines.

So, back to the question: *what is a gift?* Gifts can take several different forms. The most common are:

**Liquid Assets.** These may be in the form of cash, check, money order, or securities.

**In-kind Donations.** These are material goods that help the organization fulfill its mission.

**Tangible Personal Property.** This category includes (but is not limited to) art, furniture, coin and stamp collections, livestock, jewelry, equipment, cars, boats, clothes, and any other personal property item owned by a donor. The sky is the limit—or perhaps the limits of your gift acceptance policy!

**Real Estate.** This may seem like an incredible opportunity, but real estate gifts may be some of the most dangerous gifts for charity. It is a likely gift because real estate is one of the most commonly owned assets; but there may be serious liability issues associated with acceptance. Environmental liability and practical issues related to owning and disposing of real estate are two very big and very real problems related to real estate ownership.

**Appraisals.** Responsibility for appraisals usually lies with the donor, both to obtain an appraisal, as well as to pay for it. There are specific tax laws governing when an appraisal is necessary and who may prepare one. Professional advice is a must. Your gift acceptance policy should clearly define how appraisals will be handled, acknowledging the gift, but not listing a value on the receipt. The reason for this is that it is up to *the donor* to value the gift.

**Legal Fees and Professional Fees.** Legal fees for completion of the gift are the responsibility of the donor. This responsibility should also be incorporated in the gift acceptance policy, as well as any exceptions. When in doubt, discuss this with a professional because a conflict of interest may become a real problem.

The Friends of the Saint Paul Public Library
Gift Acceptance Policy

## Overview

The Friends strongly encourages the solicitation and acceptance of gifts which enable the fulfillment of its mission to support the library financially and present free cultural programming to the general public. We acknowledge that gifts are essential to the overall success of The Friends.

This policy is designed to provide guidance to The Friends and the general public to facilitate the gift-giving process. Gifts may be solicited and accepted from individuals; corporations; foundations; organizations; federated workplace campaigns; and federal, state, and local governments. Gifts may be obtained, however, only for programs consistent with the mission of The Friends of the Saint Paul Public Library.

The Friends is unable to accept gifts which are overly restrictive in purpose. The most desirable gifts are those with the least restrictions, as unrestricted funds allow The Friends to address its most pressing needs. It is also important that gifts accepted by The Friends do not inhibit the solicitation of gifts from other donors.

Various methods of gift giving can provide flexibility, security, and tax advantages to donors. Development staff from The Friends are available to provide assistance to donors seeking to understand and choose from the wide range of gift-giving vehicles. The development staff can also inform donors about the specific protocols involved in Friends approval and acceptance of various gift vehicles.

While The Friends' development staff strives to maintain a high level of familiarity with current giving vehicles, they are not able to give legal advice to donors. The information that those officers provide, and the information provided in this policy, is presented for discussion purposes only and should not be considered or used as legal advice. Donors and prospective donors should always confer with their own legal counsel or tax advisor for opinions about the tax or other legal consequences of specific giving scenarios.

## Development Planning Committee

The Development Planning Committee is currently divided into three strands: current giving, planned/deferred giving, and corporate partnership. The current giving strand will work with gifts that are made immediately or pledged over a discreet period of time. The planned/deferred giving strand will work to secure gifts that will be realized at some undetermined point in the future. The corporate partnership strand will work to secure financial agreements from the business/labor community and other entities in exchange for marketing or publicity opportunities associated with The Friends or the Saint Paul Public Library.

Routine gifts are accepted and administered through The Friends' office with The Friends' President having final authority to accept routine gifts. Proposed gifts that may expose The Friends to adverse publicity, require undue expenditures, or involve The Friends in unexpected responsibilities because of their source, conditions, or purposes will be reviewed by the Development Planning Committee. The final decision-making authority on gifts brought to the Development Planning Committee rests with the Development Planning Committee Chair who will make recommendations to the full Board for approval.

The Friends' Board of Trustees, upon recommendations made by the Development Planning Committee, governs the acceptance of unusual gifts made to The Friends of Saint Paul Public Library. Development staff will meet with the committee to develop recommendations for Board approval.

The committee will review the acceptance of gifts that have unusual restrictions or requests placed upon them, for example, gifts that are made in order to have a room or a service permanently named in honor of the donor. The Development Planning Committee will also review the acceptance of planned gifts that are more complex than simple bequests or that place unusual restrictions on the gift.

## I. Methods of Giving

### A. CURRENT GIFTS

Outright gifts are those placed at the immediate disposal of The Friends and in which the donor retains no interest. Gifts which are donated to The Friends without any expressed limitations placed upon them will be credited to the appropriate accounts. Because of the numerous and evolving needs of The Friends and the library, unrestricted gifts which permit the exercise of discretion in the use of the funds are strongly encouraged.

#### 1. Cash Gifts/Checks

The most frequent method used to make a gift to The Friends is a personal check, made payable to The Friends of the Saint Paul Public Library. The day the gift is received by The Friends will be the gift date for the contribution, with the exception of year-end gifts, when the check date is used to determine receipt. In no instance will a gift date be earlier than the check date.

#### 2. Credit Card Gifts

The Friends will accept gifts charged on MasterCard, American Express, or Visa. Such gifts are considered a cash donation. The date of gift for federal income tax purposes is the date the donor authorizes the charge (card number, expiration date) if by phone, the date of the call, if by mail, the date listed on the check, and if submitted online, the date the electronic transaction is received.

#### 3. Matching Gifts

Employers may match an employee's gift to The Friends. The ratio of the match and the designation of the matching gift are entirely at the discretion of the employer.

## 4. Gifts of Securities

Securities are the most common form of non-cash gifts. When a donor contributes appreciated stock held long term, the donor avoids paying the capital gains tax which would have been incurred if the stocks or bonds had been sold. For securities held short term, the donor should consult his/her tax advisor to determine the value of the deduction.

Most donors contribute securities which are traded regularly on national or local stock exchanges. The value of a gift of securities is the average of the high and the low on the date of gift.

When a gift of securities is made, The Friends always sells the securities immediately. Additionally, any interest or dividends earned subsequent to the gift date is considered income to The Friends, not a gift.

## 5. Gift Date/Valuation of Securities Gifts

a. If securities are hand-delivered to The Friends, the gift date is the day the securities are delivered, and the value of the gift will be the average of its fair market value on that date. Donors should endorse security certificates only upon delivery to The Friends.

b. If the securities are mailed to The Friends, the value of the gift will be its fair market value on the date that the donor signs the certificate over to The Friends. Signature(s) must be guaranteed by the donor's broker.

c. Most of the time, the transfer of securities will occur through the donor's broker. The donor contacts his/her broker asking that a specific number of shares be transferred to The Friends as a gift. The broker contacts The Friends for transfer instructions. The gift date is the day the donor's stock is transferred to The Friends account, and the gift value will be based on the average fair market value on that date.

## 6. Tangible Personal Property

Gifts of tangible personal property, including, but not limited to, works of art, manuscripts, literary works, boats, horses, motor vehicles, and computer hardware, can be accepted by The Friends after a thorough review indicates that the property is readily marketable or needed by The Friends for use in a manner which is related to its mission. Once tangible personal property is accepted and given to The Friends, The Friends reserves the right to sell the property and treat the proceeds as an unrestricted gift.

## 7. Real Property

The Friends will consider gifts of real property, both improved and unimproved (e.g., detached single-family residences, time shares, condominiums, apartment buildings, rental property, commercial property, farms, acreage, etc.), only after a thorough review of the criteria for acceptance outlined below.

a. Acceptance Criteria for Real Property

Market Value and Marketability. The Development Planning Committee must receive a current appraisal of the fair market value of the property. Development staff must communicate to donors that The Friends reserves the right to dispose of all gifts of real estate as quickly as possible. Thus, regardless of the value placed on the property or asset by the donor's appraisal, The Friends will attempt to sell at a reasonable price given market conditions.

b. Approval/Acceptance Process

(1) Development staff will prepare a written summary of the gift proposal and submit it to the Development Planning Committee. At a minimum, the summary will include:

(a) a description of the property;

(b) the purpose of the gift (to fund an endowment, a deferred gift, an unrestricted gift);

(c) an appraisal of the property, including its fair market value and marketability;

(d) any potential income or expenses incurred prior to selling the property;

(e) any potential Friends use;

(f) any special arrangements requested by the donor concerning selling the property (price considerations, time duration prior to the sale, potential buyers, realtors, or brokers with whom the donor would like The Friends to list the property, etc.);

(g) a plan for funding any additional expenses incurred by the acceptance of the gift; and,

(h) all gifts of real estate are contingent upon completion of the attached environmental inspection checklist and verification that no further investigation is required concerning environmental issues.

(2) The Development Planning Committee will review the material presented and decide to accept or reject the proposed gift or to postpone a decision pending the receipt of additional information. The final determination will be communicated to the development staff, who will communicate The Friends' decision to the donor in writing, including any conditions imposed prior to acceptance.

(3) If a proposed gift of real property is approved, The Friends will acknowledge receipt of the gift upon notice that the property has been legally transferred to The Friends. The Friends will not appraise or assign a value for the gift property. It is the donor's responsibility to obtain and assign a value for the gift and to provide, at the donor's expense, the qualified appraisal required by the IRS in the case of assets valued in excess of $5,000.

(4) The gift will be completed with the transfer of a deed or other appropriate conveyance, and the delivery of the property, if applicable.

## 8. Honor and Memorial Gifts

The Friends promotes an honor and memorial giving program for donors to remember and honor loved ones. Gifts collected through this program are added to the book endowment fund and each year the drawdown from this fund is used to purchase new materials for the library. For each gift of $25.00, a bookplate will be placed in a newly purchased book to recognize the donor and the purpose of the gift. For gifts of $500.00 or more, a bookplate will be placed in a newly purchased book once a year in perpetuity. The Friends will accept honor and memorial gifts of any size. However, if a donor wishes to make a memorial gift of $25,000 or more, staff will advise the donor of the possibility of having a named endowment fund created to remember the donor's loved one.

## 9. Restricted Donor-Directed Fund

The Friends will establish a restricted endowment fund with a gift of $100,000 or more. The fund will be invested like any other Friends endowment. The donor can direct the general purpose of the fund, but it must be approved by The Friends Board. Friends staff will make recommendations each year to the donor that highlights the current needs of the library or The Friends. Once the gift is made, the assets become the property of The Friends, though the donor continues to direct the use of the drawdown. At the donor's death, the fund either becomes unrestricted or is designated to a particular use before the donor's passing.

## B. PLANNED/DEFERRED GIFTS

Planned gifts generally are not given from a donor's current earnings, but rather involve the transfer of substantial assets from the donor's estate typically at his/her death. Because income from planned gifts usually represents the wishes of a lifetime supporter of The Friends or the Saint Paul Public Library, the gifts are generally placed in an endowment fund. The acceptable methods of creating deferred gifts to The Friends are described below.

## 1. Will/Bequest

A bequest is a gift of any amount or form made to The Friends in a donor's will. Bequests may provide for a specific dollar amount in cash, specific securities, specific articles of tangible personal property, or a specific percentage of the donor's estate to be given to The Friends. A gift in any amount may be accepted as a contribution to an existing endowment fund so long as the terms and conditions of that fund permit additional gifts. When money is left as an unrestricted bequest, it is deposited into an unrestricted endowment account to be used at the discretion of The Friends.

The Friends always attempts to abide by the wishes of a donor. Should a donor request that his/her bequest be spent immediately instead of placed into an endowment fund, The Friends will treat the gift as an unrestricted contribution to the general operating fund. If the donor instructs the gift to be spent immediately and restricted to a specific purpose, the gift would be directed as instructed.

Donors may also establish, by will, an annuity trust or unitrust. The bequest can be arranged so as to provide a life income for a designated beneficiary or beneficiaries by directing that the bequest be used to establish a charitable remainder annuity trust or charitable remainder unitrust. If such a gift is made by will, the principal will pass to The Friends only after the death of the life income beneficiary.

Donors are encouraged to recognize that over the many years following the establishment of an endowment fund, the needs, policies, and circumstances of The Friends can change in unforeseen ways. The Friends must have the flexibility to make use of funds in the best interest of the organization and in accord with donor interests and specifications. Thus, donors are advised to describe the specific purposes of their gifts as broadly as possible and to avoid detailed limitations and restrictions. Donors considering bequests for a specific purpose are encouraged to consult with development staff.

## 2. Remainder Interest—Personal Residence
With review and approval by the Development Planning Committee, a donor can give a remainder interest in a personal residence to The Friends. The donor or other occupants may continue to occupy the residence without disruption for the duration of the donor's life. Thereafter, the residence will either be sold or used by The Friends for purposes specified by the donor, if any. The procedures for evaluating proposed gifts of real property, as outlined above, also apply to gifts of a remainder interest in property.

## 3. Charitable Gift Annuity
The charitable gift annuity is a lifetime contract between the donor and The Friends. The donor makes a gift to The Friends and receives a fixed amount of income for the remainder of his/her life, and if desired, for another beneficiary's lifetime. Upon the death of the last beneficiary, The Friends receives the remainder. A minimum gift of $250,000 is required to establish a charitable gift annuity. The donor may not make additional contributions to a charitable gift annuity; however, the donor may enter into additional annuities. A donor may also establish a Charitable Deferred Gift Annuity, in which case a gift is made currently, and the donor (or other beneficiary) receives an income stream beginning at a point in the future.

## 4. Charitable Remainder Unitrust
The primary feature of a charitable remainder unitrust is that it provides for periodic payment of income to the donor or a person specified by the donor, for life or a specified term of years, after which the trust assets pass to The Friends.

During the lifetime of the donor, s/he creates a formal trust agreement under which assets such as cash and/or appreciated securities are irrevocably transferred to a trustee, typically a bank or an individual, who then pays the donor or person specified by the donor a regular payment based on a percentage of the value of the assets. Donors may make subsequent additions to the unitrust during their lifetime or by bequest upon their death.

A charitable remainder unitrust may be established with a gift of $250,000 or more.

### 5. *Charitable Remainder Annuity Trust*

The annuity trust shares many common features with the unitrust, the principal difference being the manner used to calculate the payment to the income beneficiary. Whereas the unitrust provides for a payout that varies with each annual valuation, the annuity trust provides for fixed payments based upon the fair market value on the date the trust is initially funded. Additional contributions cannot be made to an annuity trust.

The donor during his or her lifetime irrevocably transfers assets to a trustee, who pays the donor or a person specified by the donor a fixed dollar amount annually for life. The trust can also provide income for the donor's survivors for life; however, the trust assets become the sole property of The Friends.

A charitable remainder annuity trust for The Friends may be established with a gift of $250,000 or more.

### 6. *Charitable Lead Trust*

The primary feature of a charitable lead trust is that it provides for the immediate support of The Friends through income generated by the assets in trust for a set period of time, after which the assets pass to a noncharitable beneficiary, such as the donor, the donor's children, or other persons the donor specifies. A charitable lead trust is conceptually the opposite of a charitable remainder trust. In a lead trust, the donor gives The Friends the current economic benefit of the transferred assets and retains the right to reacquire possession and control of the assets at a future date.

The donor during his or her lifetime creates an irrevocable trust agreement. The agreement may take effect during the donor's lifetime or be part of the donor's will. Assets are transferred to a trustee, with the stipulation that the income from the assets be paid to The Friends for the life of the trust, after which the principal or corpus of the trust reverts back to the donor or others of his or her choosing. A lead trust may be advantageous for donors who have a larger income than they currently need and who desire to transfer assets to heirs.

A charitable lead trust for The Friends may be established with a gift of $250,000 or more.

### 7. *Life insurance*

The Friends will accept gifts of life insurance policies which designate The Friends as the sole or partial beneficiary of the policy. The Friends will also accept transfers of ownership of existing life insurance policies. However, if premiums remain to be paid, the donor must agree in writing to give sufficient funds annually on a timely basis to the Friends in order for it to pay the premiums, or the donor must agree to pay the premiums directly. The Friends reserves the right to cash in a policy or take other actions available to the owner of a policy at any time.

## C. CORPORATE PARTNERSHIP

The Friends recognizes that corporate partnership could prove to be a valuable revenue-generating tool, and acknowledges the difference between corporate charitable giving and corporate partnership. The Friends welcomes and encourages the business/labor community and other entities to establish partnerships that will provide The Friends with the resources, including revenue and/or in-kind contributions, to enhance events, programs, and activities and services to the community.

1. Agreements will only be made when the primary product or service of the entity is not in contradiction to the mission of the Library or The Friends, or the particular activity.

2. The partnering entity may not be involved in activities which purposefully oppose the mission of either the Library or The Friends.

3. The final determination upon entering an agreement will be made by the Library Director (when appropriate) and The Friends President, based on the recommendation of the Corporate Partnership Committee.

## II. Gift Designation/Restriction

### A. CURRENT OPERATING FUNDS

Current operating gifts are those given to The Friends for use during the current fiscal year. These gifts are especially valuable to The Friends because they allow the organization to relieve the general operating budget.

### 1. Unrestricted Funds

Unrestricted gifts are those placed at the immediate disposal of The Friends and in which the donor retains no interest. Gifts which are donated to The Friends without any express limitations placed upon them by the donor will be credited to the unrestricted fund accounts and applied to The Friends' most immediate needs.

### 2. Restricted Funds

Gifts to restricted funds support current operating purposes of The Friends or the library but are restricted by donors as to the specific purpose for which the funds may be expended, i.e., designated for a specific program, the collection, outreach, or other purpose.

### B. ENDOWMENT FUNDS

Endowment funds provide support to The Friends or the Library in perpetuity. These funds provide ongoing yearly support for The Friends by providing a percentage of the value of the fund for use each fiscal year. In ideal market conditions the percent drawn from the funds is less than the amount of growth experienced by the fund, meaning that the principal or corpus of the gift continues to grow annually and thus provides greater support each year.

### 1. Unrestricted Funds

Unrestricted endowments create funds without any express limitations placed upon them by the donor and are applied to The Friends' most immediate needs.

### 2. Restricted Funds

Restricted endowment funds are spent in compliance with specific restrictions placed on the funds by the donor at the creation of the fund. Restricted endowment funds might be designated for a specific program, the collection, outreach, or other purpose.

### 3. Required Minimum Gift

Donors establishing endowment funds of $100,000 or more may specify the name of the fund (e.g., to honor their relationship with The Friends or to memorialize a loved one) and may also specify reasonable restrictions as to the use of the money generated by the endowment. Gifts of $25,000 up to $100,000 will be added to an endowment fund, and the donor's name will remained attached to the portion of the endowment that his/her gift represents; the donor will receive ongoing recognition on a yearly basis in The Friends' annual report. Gifts of less than $25,000 will be placed in an unrestricted endowment set up to receive similar gifts, and the donor will receive recognition for this gift the year that it is made.

### 4. Required Information

New endowment accounts can be created with the following information:

1. Pledge/gift document signed by the donor.

2. Signed endowment fund language describing purpose of the endowment and appropriate fund management information including:

   endowment fund name (formal name approved by donor);

   description of fund, including preferences or restrictions (tight restrictions or unrealistic requirements may make endowments difficult to administer); and,

   additional information as appropriate:

   minimum funding level required prior to activation;

   build-up period;

   instructions re: allocation of fund income during fund build-up period (if any);

   disposition of funds in the event the endowment is never fully funded;

   reporting requirements to the donor concerning fund; and,

   future obligations for fund-raising.

*5. Budget Support from Endowments*

Income will be drawn from endowments each year. The Friends' Board of Trustees has currently set the draw rate on all endowment funds at no more than 6 percent of the fair market value of the endowment as valued over the last twelve quarters.

## III. Stewardship and Acknowledgments

### A. ACKNOWLEDGMENT OF GIFTS

The Friends must provide prompt written gift acknowledgments for individual gifts of $250 or more in any calendar year as required by the 1993 Tax Act. However, The Friends chooses to thank and acknowledge all the gifts they receive. Friends staff strive to acknowledge and thank all donors within two days of receiving a gift.

### B. DONOR RECOGNITION

*1. Recognition of Gifts*

Individuals making gifts for any purpose are entitled to become members of The Friends for a period of one year from the date of the gift. The total amount given by an individual in the course of one fiscal year will determine the individual's membership level.

*2. Credit for Matching Gift Money*

Matching gifts from an individual donor's employer will count towards gift level membership. A donor could give $500 and have it matched by his/her employer to become a member in the $1,000 gift level membership. The rationale behind this policy is that without the donor's $500 gift, the $500 from his/her employer would not have been given to The Friends, therefore, we give credit to the donor for the funds leveraged by their gift.

*3. The Friends' Donor Society / Recognition Circles*

The Donor Society recognizes individuals who have chosen to make a substantial commitment to The Friends through a planned gift or major annual gift and includes two recognition circles. Donors giving at least $500 annually will be included as members in the Perrie Jones Circle. Donors who have made a planned giving provision to The Friends will be included as members of the John and Myrtle Briggs Circle. Donor Society members will be invited to an annual recognition luncheon. In addition to the Donor Society recognition circles, The Friends Loyalty Circle is created to recognize those individuals who have made a donation to The Friends of any amount annually, over a period of ten or more years.

*4. Anonymous Gifts*

The Friends respects the wishes of any donor who would like to remain anonymous.

*5. Planned Gifts*

Actualized planned gifts of $100,000 or more will be recognized on the donor wall at the Central Library.

## C. NAMING OF LIBRARY BUILDINGS AND INTERIOR SPACES

The naming of buildings and spaces is one of the ways in which The Friends can acknowledge the generosity of donors or honor those who have provided extensive service to The Friends and/or the library.

Any proposal for the naming of a library building or space must be submitted to the Library Director and the Friends' President. The proposal must include a description of the building or space to be named, its current use and a description of the name proposed, as well as information about gifts and/or donors who are being recognized. Approval by both the City and the Library Director is required for any naming opportunities.

## D. DATA PRIVACY

The Friends respects its donors' rights to privacy, and encourages donors to request to remain anonymous if they do not want their gift to be acknowledged in any public way. Each year The Friends will publish an annual report that lists donors by their giving levels. Donors who request to remain anonymous will not be included in this report.

The Friends reserves the right to trade names and addresses of its donors with other local nonprofit organizations in an effort to identify additional Friends' supporters. The donor's giving history is always confidential and will never be shared with other organizations. Donors are regularly offered the opportunity to request that their name and address not be traded to other organizations. The Friends respects this request and promptly notes that the name and address cannot be traded.

# Sample Annual Appeal Solicitation Letter

November 2010

Dear Mr. and Mrs. XXXXX,

The Friends of the Saint Paul Public Library is fortunate to have supporters like you. Because I know you value the Library and the services it provides to our community, please consider a year-end gift to The Friends. It is all about continuing, and even increasing, your support for the Library, an essential institution in the city of Saint Paul, and a personally important place for many who live here.

Your generous past gifts have enabled The Friends to

- provide the Library with funds needed for after-school programs and homework assistance for thousands of children and teens;
- continue strong annual support of the Summer Reading Program, children's events, adult cultural programs, and the purchase of thousands of books; and
- assist the Library in offering computers and the Internet to patrons who would not otherwise have access.

We have made certain that the Saint Paul Public Library is there for everyone to use and enjoy. If we want the library to continue to be there, now is the time to make a gift. In 2009, your year-end gift was $____.__. This year, I hope you will consider a gift of $____.__. If you can give more, I would be very grateful.

A donation form and return envelope are enclosed for your convenience. The Friends' goal is to raise $180,000 during our year-end campaign, which will provide much-needed annual support for Friends' and Library Programs.

Thank you for your continued generosity and support. Your gift ensures that the Library will be there for you now and for generations to come.

Best Regards,

Peter D. Pearson
President
Encl.

You can create a simple brochure that your library and its fund-raising organization can use to explain how planned giving works and to solicit planned gifts. It can be a simple two-or-three-fold flyer on 8½" × 11" paper. Follow the following steps and see the sample planned giving brochure included in the Fund-Raising Gallery (14A).

1. Develop a title or tagline for the cover of your brochure.

2. Define "planned giving."

3. Tell readers why planned giving is for *everyone*, not just the wealthy.

4. Tell readers why planned gifts are important to the library.

5. List some of the ways a donor can make a planned gift.

6. Provide a response form that potential planned givers can complete and return to your library or its fund-raising organization.

7. Instruct readers to contact their estate planners when considering a planned gift to your library.

8. Add photos or other illustrations to your brochure to make it attractive and eye-catching so that it invites people to pick it up and read it.

# Planned Giving Declaration of Intent Template

As an expression of my commitment to the mission of

*Your library or fund-raising organization's name here*

I am pleased to declare my intention to help provide for future needs with a gift through:

> Bequest through my Will
>
> Life Insurance Policy
>
> Individual Retirement Account (IRA)
>
> Trust
>
> Real Estate
>
> Other: _____
>
> As of this date, the approximate value of this gift is $_____
> (Indication of amount is optional and will be used for long-term planning)

Though this declaration of intent is an expression of my current plans, I understand that I may modify or revoke it and that it is not a legal obligation binding on me or my estate.

Signature: _____ Date: _____

Name(s):_____

Address:_____

City: _____ State: _____ Zip: _____

Phone: _____

There are fun, profitable special events being hosted by libraries and library organizations across the country. Here is a sampling of cool events to check out.

### AViD (Authors Visiting in Des Moines)—Des Moines, Iowa

AViD is a series of author visits spread over the summer. The event is a discussion of each author's latest work with local public figures serving as moderators and facilitators.

www.pldminfo.org/events_news/AViD/2011

### BOOKMARKS ( BookArt of Johnson County)— Iowa City Public Library, Iowa

Local artists create book statues, with financial support from sponsors, based on a novel. The statues are intended to illustrate the plot and theme, or simply replicate the book. Statues are placed around the city periodically between June and October and are auctioned off in November.

http://bookmarksiowa.org

### Dewey After Hours & the Book Lovers Ball— Denver Public Library, Colorado

These events work in concert with each other. At Dewey After Hours, guests spend an evening at the top of the Art Museum Residences in downtown Denver while sampling new, exotic cocktails. The cocktails are voted on and the winner becomes the signature drink of that year's Book Lovers Ball, which is a themed event in the central library with dinner and dancing among the shelves.

http://denverlibrary.org/content/dewey-after-hours

www.dplfriends.org/events/ball.html

### Dine Out for a Cause—Del Ray Public Library, Florida

Dine Out is a program held once a month during the summer. It features several local restaurants as well as a local author serving as a "Celebrity Chef" for the evening.

### Laugh—Del Ray Public Library, Florida

Laugh is an annual fund-raising event featuring different well-known comedians billed as "a casual, fun-filled night of comedy, cocktails and supper by the bite."

www.delraylibrary.org/dineout

www.delraylibrary.org/laugh with librarychapter6

## Literary Sojourn—Bud Werner Memorial Library (Steamboat Springs, Colorado)

Literary Sojourn is an all-day author and reader festival that draws authors and guests from across the country for readings, book sales and signings, a buffet, wine, and more.

www.literarysojourn.org

## Opus & Olives (Fine Print & Fine Food)—Saint Paul, Minnesota

Opus & Olives is an author gala featuring four best-selling authors and an author emcee. The event includes a cocktail reception, book sales and signing, a four-course dinner, and an author program.

# Corporate Sponsorship Opportunities and Benefits

Corporate sponsorship opportunities and benefits differ greatly depending on the size and cost of the event, but there should be an incentive for any business to sponsor your event at some level.

If you are fortunate enough to have a corporate sponsor who is willing to underwrite the entire cost of the event, you can ask that sponsor if they would allow other sponsors to support the event at lower levels. This would increase your profit; however, businesses may wish to be exclusive in their sponsorship.

You can denote sponsorship levels in your promotional materials by giving names or titles to your levels, rather than specifying the financial level of sponsorship.

Here is an example of sponsorship opportunities and benefits for an author program that will cost $5,000, with a goal of making a $10,000 profit. Make sure that your corporate sponsor benefits are tangible—but also in line with your event budget.

## Presenting Sponsor—$5,000

(Sponsorship at this level should cover at least 50 percent of the cost of your event.)

### BENEFITS

- Naming rights ("Your event is presented by . . . XYZ Corporation")
- X tables/tickets for the event/preferred seating
- Copies of author's book for sponsor's guests
- Logo and corporate name recognition in all event advertising and publications
- Private reception with the author prior/after the event

## First Edition Sponsors—$2,500

### BENEFITS

- 1 table/x tickets for the event
- X copies of the author's book (same number as tickets given the sponsor)
- Logo and corporate name recognition in all event advertising and publications

## Best-seller Sponsors—$1,000

- X tickets for the event
- Corporate name recognition in all event advertising and publications

## Bookstore Sponsor—25% of Book Sales

- 2–3 tickets for the event
- Logo, corporate name recognition in all event advertising and publications, and acknowledgment that a percentage of all book sales from the event are donated to the library.

# Sample Event Sponsorship Tracking Form

Insert these fields (and any other you would find useful) into a spreadsheet, table, or database to track your event sponsors and their guests, as well as payment and acknowledgment information.

| Name/address and contact information of potential business sponsor | Contact at sponsor | Contact on event-planning team | Outcome of solicitation | Guest names | Amount due | Invoice (date) | Payment received (date) | Confirmation letter (date) | Post-event thank-you letter (date) |
|---|---|---|---|---|---|---|---|---|---|
| Fast-trak Printing 200 Main Street City/State/Zip Phone/e-mail | George Nelson | Amy Anderson | Will donate program printing | | NA | | | 1/6/12 | |
| XYZ Bank 450 Main Street City/State/Zip Phone/e-mail | Susan Cooper | Patrick Hall | Will purchase (1) $300 table for 6 | | $300 | 1/15/12 | 2/20/12 | 2/21/12 | |
| | | | | Wendy Grant | NA | | | | |
| | | | | Peter Cole | NA | | | | |
| | | | | Sue Rich | NA | | | | |
| | | | | Liz Harris | NA | | | | |
| | | | | Ann Smith | NA | | | | |
| | | | | Sharon Wilson | NA | | | | |
| XYZ Newspaper 690 Main Street City/State/Zip Phone/e-mail | Alayne Johnson | Lynn Mitchell | Will sponsor at $100 level | | $100 | 1/25/12 | | | |
| Wallace and Green Attorneys at Law 525 Main Street City/State/Zip Phone/e-mail | Jim Wallace | Matt Fredericks | Unable to help, ask next yr. | | NA | | | | |

(Your library, Friends' group, or Foundation's letterhead)

*(The name of your library, Friends group, and/or Foundation)* welcomes and encourages the business community, and other external organizations, to support its work through the establishment of partnerships that will provide resources, including revenue and/or in-kind contributions, to enhance events, programs, activities, and services to the community.

This policy is established with the following in mind:

1. The mission of the Library is to . . .

2. *(Your Friends group and/or Foundation's)* mission is to . . .

3. Any partner, while engaging contractually with *(your Friends group and/or Foundation)* will also be associated with the Library.

4. The reputation and public perception of the Library and *(your Friends group and/or Foundation)* are valuable, though intangible, resources.

*(Your Friends group and/or Foundation)* and the Library are committed to partnering with appropriate sponsors for programs, events, services, and activities. Before signing an agreement letter with any for the purpose of sponsorship, the following criteria will be considered. Each situation will be reviewed on an individual basis.

1. The primary product or service of the entity may not be in contradiction to the mission of the Library or *(your Friends group and/or Foundation)*, or the particular activity to be sponsored.

2. The entity may not be involved in activities which purposefully oppose the mission of either the Library or *(your Friends group and/or Foundation)*.

3. Neither *(your Friends group and/or Foundation)* nor the Library endorse any products or services. The decision to associate with a product, service, or program is not deemed an endorsement.

All letters of agreement will include language that reserves the right of the Library, *(Friends group and/or Foundation)* or the partner entity to withdraw from the agreement in any instance in which the behavior of the organization or its officers will negatively affect the other partner by association. The final determination in all instances will be made by the Library Director and *(leader of your Friends group and/or Foundation)*, as outlined in the procedures below.

## Procedures

1. A representative of *(your Friends group and/or Foundation)* will research and pursue potential partners.

2. If a potential partner indicates an interest in proceeding, the representative of *(your Friends group and/or Foundation)* will submit the name of the organization to a designated Library staff person.

3. The designated Library staff person will research the potential partner's public reputation and will return a summary to the representative of *(your Friends group and/or Foundation)*.

4. If there are no clear barriers to proceeding with a partnership, the representative of *(your Friends group and/or Foundation)* will forward the summary and a recommendation to *(the leader of your Friends group and/or Foundation)* and the Library Director.

5. *(The leader of your Friends group and/or Foundation)* and the Library Director will make the final decision, and respond with recommended actions.

6. In instances where a partnership is agreed upon, the Letter of Agreement shall serve as the binding document of the partnership, and it shall be reviewed and signed by *(the leader of your Friends group and/or Foundation)* and/or the Library Director.

*Note:* Additional language to be considered might include . . .

The Library's and *(your Friends group and/or Foundation's)*, decision-making processes are independent and free of all bias from any sponsor. The Library and *(your Friends group and/or Foundation)* maintain their independence on issues affecting the delivery of Library services to the residents of *(your town)*.

# Sample Business Sponsorship Agreements

## 1. Sample Agreement for Lead Sponsorship of an Event

(Your library, Friends' group or Foundation's letterhead)

This letter will confirm the terms and conditions on which *(name of sponsor)* ("sponsor" or "you") has agreed to sponsor *(event name)* organized by *(the name of your library, Friends group, and/or Foundation)* ("The Friends" or "we").

*(Event name)* attendance in *(year)* is anticipated to reach *(#)*. It will be held on *(date)* at *(location)*. In consideration for the sponsorship fee of *(agreed-upon fee amount)*, the following benefits will be provided to sponsor by The Friends:

- Opportunity for a private reception with author(s) for up to *(#)* guests of sponsor prior to the event.
- Opportunity for sponsor to host an additional event at which the authors will be present.
- Opportunity for sponsor organization representative to open or close the event program.
- *(#)* tables for ten in first two rows, and *(#)* additional tables with preferred seating. Authors to be seated at *(#)* tables.
- Logo and name recognition on all print and electronic materials, including:

  Save the date postcard (quantity mailed)

  Invitation (quantity mailed)

  Preview advertising in (name of confirmed media) (list number and size)

  Half-page thank you in (name of confirmed media)

  Printed program at the event (quantity produced)

  Thank-you correspondence (quantity mailed)

  *(The name of your library, Friends group, and/or Foundation)* newsletter (# of issues, distributed throughout library system + quantity mailed)

  *(The name of your library, Friends group and/or Foundation)* website (# of pages, how long)

  *(The name of your library, Friends group, and/or Foundation)* social media (# of mentions, venues)

- Article highlighting the partnership in *(the name of your library, Friends group, and/or Foundation)* newsletter and on website
- Opportunity to give away sponsor-branded products or samples at the event
- *(The name of your library, Friends group, and/or Foundation)* assistance in promoting sponsorship (copy for sponsor newsletter, photos, etc.)

Upon receipt of this agreement with your signature, we grant you the right to be the lead sponsor of *(event name)*. This sponsorship fee associated with this agreement shall be payable to The Friends under the following terms, for which you shall receive invoices at least 30 days in advance:

| | | |
|---|---|---|
| 1st Payment: | On or before (date) | $ |
| 2nd Payment: | On or before (date) | $ |
| Total Fee: | | $ |

If this accurately sets forth our Agreement, please sign below and return a copy to me. I will return a fully executed copy to you upon receipt.

**REPRESENTING (SPONSOR ORGANIZATION):**

Print Name, Title:

Signature, Date:

**REPRESENTING (LIBRARY OR FRIENDS GROUP):**

Print Name, Title:

Signature, Date:

## 2. Sample Agreement When a Sponsor Pays for Items that the Library Will Offer or Distribute

(Your library, Friends' group, or Foundation's letterhead)

This letter will confirm the terms and conditions on which *(name of sponsor)* ("sponsor" or "you") has agreed to sponsor production of *(newsletters, reading lists, Bookmobile schedule)* (the "Items") for the Library, organized by *(the name of your library, Friends group, and/or Foundation)* ("The Friends" or "we").

The Items will be produced under subcontract by *(the name of your library, Friends group, and/or Foundation)*, for use throughout the *(#)* facilities and bookmobile of the Library system. The quantity of the Items ordered will be *(#)*, with *(a % overage run of up to )*. The Items will be *(specify what the item will be, where the sponsor's logo will be placed, color, where your logo will be placed)*.

*(The name of your library, Friends group and/or Foundation)* shall provide you with:

- Named and logo recognition in the following form in all promotional materials prepared regarding the Item:

    *(Name of sponsor)* named as the sponsor

    Sponsored by *(name of sponsor)*

    Supported through the generosity of our sponsor, *(name of sponsor)*

- Named and logo sponsor recognition in *(the name of your library, Friends group, and/or Foundation)* newsletter;

- The opportunity to provide copy to be used in recognition in *(the name of your library, Friends group, and/or Foundation)* newsletter;

- Named and logo sponsor recognition on the *(the name of your library, Friends group, and/or Foundation)* website and in *(#)* blast e-mail to *(# mailed to)* each 6-month period of the agreement.
- The opportunity to publicize and market the sponsorship in "sponsor" communications (written or in-store promotion), where the Item is not exposed to "ambush marketing," i.e., other sponsorships or projects executed by "sponsor" or *(the name of your library, Friends group, and/or Foundation)* may only be mentioned when clearly delineated as efforts separate from the sponsorship of the Item.
- Language to be used in *"sponsor"* communications regarding sponsorship;
- The opportunity to proof copy in which *"sponsor"* is referenced other than listing, prior to release; and
- The opportunity to investigate further collaborative activities to leverage the sponsorship.
- Both we and you reserve the right to terminate this agreement with seven (7) days' written notice in any instance in which the actions or behavior of the other party or its officers presents, by association or otherwise, a substantial risk to the reputation or functioning of the other. In either of the above instances, *(the name of your library, Friends group, and/or Foundation)* only obligation shall be to return to you the amount of the Sponsorship Fee paid, less any direct out-of-pocket expenses that are incurred in furtherance of this Agreement prior to the date of the notice of termination.

Upon receipt of this agreement with your signature, we grant you the right to be the exclusive official sponsor of the Items. This sponsorship fee associated with this agreement shall be payable to *(the name of your library, Friends group, and/or Foundation)* under the following terms, for which you shall receive invoices at least 30 days in advance:

| | | |
|---|---|---|
| 1st Payment: | On or before (date) | $ |
| 2nd Payment: | On or before (date) | $ |
| Total Fee: | | $ |

If this accurately sets forth our Agreement, please sign below and return a copy to me. I will return a fully executed copy to you upon receipt.

**REPRESENTING (SPONSOR ORGANIZATION):**

Print Name, Title:

Signature, Date:

**REPRESENTING (LIBRARY OR FRIENDS GROUP):**

Print Name, Title:

Signature, Date:

# Grant Project Concept Worksheet

Project Name:

Project Concept:

Project Director (responsible for implementation, oversight, and reports):

## PRELIMINARY BUDGET

| Item | Time /Cost | In-Kind | Year 1 Total | Year 2 Total (if this is two-year project) | Total |
|---|---|---|---|---|---|
| Staff Costs (hours to be replaced /released) | Project leader? Creative time? Meeting time? Training time? | Don't forget management, IT, accounting | | | |
| Partner Organization Staff Costs | | | | | |
| Outside Expertise (planning consultants, trainers, advisors) | Stipend? Hourly? Flat rate contract? | | | | |
| Support Materials | Equipment or collection | | | | |
| Supplies | Things that get used up (giveaways, printed materials) | | | | |
| Evaluation (10-15% of total) | Contract? Cost to create measurement tools, conduct, and write final. | | | | |
| PR (10-15% of total) | Postcards, flyers, ads? | | | | |
| Total Estimated Budget | | | | | |

Other Staff involved / affected (project team, IT, webmaster, collections, PR):

Concept and Budget Approved by:

Library Branch Supervisor (if branch-specific):

Library Director or _____ (necessary for all):

## PROSPECTIVE FUNDERS

| Name | Amount to Ask for | Fit/Rationale | LOI or Proposal (date)? |
|------|-------------------|---------------|--------------------------|
|      |                   |               |                          |
|      |                   |               |                          |
|      |                   |               |                          |

## IMPLEMENTATION STEPS AND SCHEDULE

|                          | Who Is Responsible? | Date Due |
|--------------------------|---------------------|----------|
| Contact potential funder |                     |          |
| Goal statement           |                     |          |
| Partner recruitment      |                     |          |
| Project description      |                     |          |
| Project timetable        |                     |          |
| Budget                   |                     |          |
| 1st draft write and route |                    |          |
| Outside reader           |                     |          |
| Final write and route    |                     |          |
| Signatures or e-rules    |                     |          |
| Supporting docs or letters |                   |          |
| Mail/send proposal       |                     |          |

# Template for a Letter of Support

(Print on letter writer's letterhead or personal stationery.)

Date:

Name of contact at funding organization:

Funding organization's name:

Funding organization's address:

Re: Request for support for
*(the name of your library, Friends group, and/or Foundation)*

Dear *(name of contact at foundation)*,

I am pleased to support the application of *(the name of your library, Friends group, and/or Foundation)* for funding of $ *(amount)* in *(specify project or general operating)* funds.

I have been associated with *(the name of your library, Friends group, and/or Foundation)* since *(year)*, as a *(board member/volunteer/collaborator on behalf of my organization)*. I have worked specifically with *(name of library director, project manager, or key project personnel)* and am impressed with their vision for the project for which this application requests support.

(Add 1–4 sentences describing the project and the letter writer's role in it, if any.)

I encourage you to give full consideration to this grant proposal, as I am confident *(the name of your library, Friends group, and/or Foundation)* will *(state a prime benefit if the project or organization is funded)* with the funding requested.

Sincerely,

*Name*
*Title*
*Name of organization the writer works for or represents, or use the term "Community Volunteer" when appropriate*

### Proposal Requesting Funding for Summer Reading Program

#### 1. ORGANIZATION INFORMATION

The mission of The Friends of the ___ Public Library is to expand the ___ Library's capacity to serve ___'s many communities. The Friends accomplishes this by providing private funding to enhance Library services; advocating for strong public funding of the Library; and increasing use of the Library through public awareness and cultural programming.

The Friends is a nonprofit organization established in ___. Engaging its first paid staff member in ___, The Friends has grown to ___ full-time and ___ part-time professional staff, as well ___ actively engaged board members and more than ___ highly involved volunteers who assist the organization on programs such as ___. Membership in (year) was ___ households, with an additional ___ business and foundation supporters.

The Friends and the Library have a history of successful partnerships to serve the people of ___. Special programs initiated at the Library with The Friends include Homework Help programming with online assistance for students, job skills and application assistance as part of Workforce Development, a Small Business Resource Center, and outreach to families and community partners to support literacy development in children under the age of four. In (year), items were checked out from the Library over ___ times. Library staff answered ___ information requests by the over ___ library visitors.

The Friends is the only nonprofit focused on supporting the ___ Library. The Friends conducts fund-raising activities for the Library in order to support new initiatives and special activities. In (year), The Friends assisted the Library in securing funding in excess of $___ for two new projects: one to provide certification in digital literacy for job seekers, and another to create a technology project-based learning lab for teens. All programs and services provided by The Friends and the Library are open to all members of the community, without regard for ethnicity, income, age, or other considerations.

Second, The Friends annually conducts a grassroots advocacy effort to maintain or increase public city funding for the Library. Third, The Friends, in close collaboration with the Library, conducts public relations and awareness activities so that the Library is better known and understood as a resource in the community.

Finally, The Friends conducts almost all arts, humanities, civic, and cultural programs for adults at the Library, in addition to funding some of the Youth Services area's programming for children. Attendance at The Friends programs was over ___ at more than ___ programs in (year). These included author readings, discussion groups, film screenings, and more. Twenty-eight community organizations served as partners to one or more programs. All programs by The Friends are free to the public.

## 2. SITUATION OR NEED

In (city), students can do better. In (year), only 56% of students met the level of "proficient" on the (state) Comprehensive Assessment reading test.

Challenges to (city) students include race, ethnicity, and economic status, each of which demonstrates a gap in performance. According to the (city) School District Data Center, 76% of all students are students of color. On the (test name) reading test, students of color of any background were at least 30% less able to show proficiency than their white peers. Low-income students, as indicated by eligibility for free or reduced-price lunch, comprise 71% of the student body in (city). Only 46% of low-income students tested proficient in reading.

Based on 20 years of tracking and study, the National Research Council concluded, "Academic success, as defined by high school graduation, can be predicted with reasonable accuracy by knowing someone's reading skill at the end of 3rd grade. A person who is not at least a modestly skilled reader by that time is unlikely to graduate from high school" (*Preventing Reading Difficulties in Young Children,* National Research Council, 1998).

The ability to read is a key indicator of a child's future successes in life. The foundations of reading skills begin at birth. Children learn about language through talking, listening, singing, storytelling, and reading—things that help them understand the sounds that make up language. It is never too early to prepare children for success as readers.

One area in which school-year learning can be supported is summer reading. Libraries play a key role in supporting families, caregivers, schools, and students themselves in doing better in their reading pursuits. A study published in 2010 by Dominican University, which included pre- and post-testing of students, found that "students who participated in the public library summer reading program had better reading skills at the end of third grade and scored higher on the standards test than the students who did not participate" (*Public Library Summer Reading Programs Close the Reading Gap,* Dominican University, 2010).

Students lose what they have learned if they do not practice over the summer. For each month of the summer they do not keep reading, it is as if they missed the last month of the school year. Summer losses in achievement add up year by year and "seem to be the major reason why the academic gap between low- and high-income children grows throughout the elementary school years" (Peter Johnson, *Building Effective Programs for Summer Learning,* U.S. Department of Education, 2000).

This is a traditional role for the ___ Library, and remains at the core of its mission. The Library's mission was revised in 2011 via strategic planning with the public and is now "to connect people in (city) with the imperative and the joy of learning."

The Friends recognizes the need for a robust program to allow the Library to serve a diverse community and has been committed to fund-raising for the Summer Reading Program for over a decade.

## 3. SOLUTION OR ACTIVITIES

The Summer Reading Program (SRP) will offer events at each library facility that will attract children from infants to third graders. These events will take a range of formats, including storytelling, performances by jugglers, musicians, or puppeteers, and presentations from community organizations like ___. According to a 2001 study by Celano and Neuman, literacy-related activities and events enrich reading experiences, encouraging children to read by themselves. Each performer or presenter will make reference to learning from books or at the Library. Each event will be followed by a time when Librarians and other library staff make a special effort to assist families and caregivers in finding age-appropriate materials for their readers to check out.

Students of all ages will be encouraged to read with the time-recording component of the Summer Reading Program. The National Reading Panel found that increasing the time that children spend reading is the single most powerful strategy for improving literacy skills in fluency, vocabulary, and comprehension. Students are asked to register to participate in the time-recording component by signing their name and setting a goal of how many hours they will read. They are given a form where they can write down the items they are reading as well as keep track of their time by filling in clocks in increments. When a student has read ten hours, they bring their record in and choose a book to add to their personal library. They can choose another book when they reach twenty hours. The selection of books to choose from is recommended by a teen advisory council and library staff. Some branches offer to place readers' names on a "wall of fame" if they go on to read more.

In a study funded by the Institute of Museum and Library Services (IMLS) in 2006–2009, "parents of children enrolled in the public library summer reading program reported that their children spent more time reading over the summer and read more books, were well-prepared for school in the fall, and read more confidently" (*Public Library Summer Reading Programs Close the Reading Gap*, Dominican University, 2010). The Nellie Mae Education Foundation notes that preliminary studies "suggest that providing books to low-income children and encouraging them to read is a relatively cost-effective and replicable approach for supporting children's reading skills over the summer" (Miller, *The Learning Season*, 2007).

In 2009 a community member provided funds to allow teens to "earn" away their fines by reading in the library. In 2011, teens who read at least 15 hours were eligible to receive a book, and those who read 30 hours could win an iPod in a drawing. Staff reported that teens would be invited to join SRP, would often decline, then see a poster that promoted the iPod incentive and come back to join.

In 2012 the Library started a new partnership with the (city) Parks and Recreation Department in order to reach youth who do not visit the Library. Eleven recreation centers offered students places to read and bookshelves where children found books to take home. Parks and Recreation staff worked with Library staff to model "reading for fun" as well as referred youth and families to specific Library facilities to visit. In 2013 this opportunity will expand to 15 recreation centers. Attendance at programs was not calculated, but participation in reading time increased significantly.

*Goals and Objectives*

The 2013 Summer Reading Program has three overall goals in regard to the situation above.

1. To engage young children (and their caregivers) in activities that support their literacy development.

2. To encourage students of all ages to read over the summer.

3. To reach out to more children who may not identify the Library as a place for positive experiences.

These goals will be met in the following ways:

Children, including pre-readers, will be attracted to the library for events.

Students will be supported in reading activities, and will be motivated by eligibility for incentives regardless of reading ability.

The Library will continue to partner with Parks and Recreation to reach more children.

*Timeline*

Planning and scheduling for the 2013 SRP will begin in December 2012. Promotion begins in mid-April, with Library staff connecting to public and private school staff. There is a kick-off event shortly after the ___ Public Schools release for summer, typically mid-June. Events will occur from mid-June to the end of August, scheduled such that a family in any neighborhood has the opportunity to attend something nearby whether they are free in the morning, afternoon, or evening. Each branch may offer additional events using library and community talent. Students must turn in their reading records for books before the end of August.

*Personnel*

The project will be administered by ___, Youth Services Supervisor at the ___ Library. SRP is planned and coordinated by a council of library youth services staff under the leadership of ___, working with Parks and Recreation staff. All library staffing costs are provided in-kind by the ___ Library. ___, Director of Institutional Relations at The Friends, will facilitate evaluation.

**4. MEASUREMENT AND EVALUATION**

Improved evaluation of the SRP has been a goal of the Library and The Friends for several years. Improvement has been achieved in accuracy regarding both reading time spent by youth and attendance at programs. Yet the intensity of programs with an average attendance of nearly 100 demands that library staff focus on customer service. Attendance at the SRP performances is recorded across the system and individually by branch, and analyzed to determine what times of day and which performers are best received. The 2013 goal is to achieve a participation level of at least 6,000 youth in the reading incentives component (an increase of 10%) and a cumulative attendance of at least 8,000 at the library programs (an increase of 18%). Evaluation analysis and data collection will occur during September and October, with results reported to all Library staff and stakeholders in the fall. In 2013, students will be asked to fill out a survey about the Summer Reading Program, to be accessed via the Library website.

## 5. BUDGET AND BUDGET NARRATIVE

### PROJECT BUDGET

| Item | Expense | Total |
|------|---------|-------|
| 1. Performances at Libraries | $ 21,250 | $ 21,250 |
| 2. Programs at Libraries by Library staff | In-kind | $ 8,000 |
| 3. Books awarded to readers | $ 6,500 | $ 6,500 |
| 4. Printing of calendar | $ 7,500 | $ 7,500 |
| 5. Supplies | $ 2,500 | $ 2,500 |
| 6. Design and PR | In-kind | $ 7,000 |
| 7. Evaluation | 50% In-kind ($500) | $ 1,000 |
| TOTAL | $38,250 | $53,750 |

1. 85 performances by professionals, paid at a standard rate of $250 per performance

2. 40 programs developed and executed by Library staff at a flat rate of $200 per program. This in-kind amount represents event time only. Administration of the entire Summer Reading Program, including planning, coordination, and management, are also provided in-kind by Library staff. The value of that in-kind time is approximately $65,000.

3. Library vendor agreements allow for mass purchases at significant discounts. Goal to distribute 6,000 books.

4. 35,000 four-color tri-fold calendar for families to hang at home.

5. Reading records, signage, pens, postage, stickers.

6. In-kind time provided by Library staff on calendar, reading records, signage, website updates: 70 hours at $100 per hour.

7. Development, mailing, and tabulation of surveys targeting area child care providers: 5 hours at $100 per hour. In-kind staff time to distribute and collect surveys on-site; 10 hours at $50 per hour.

# Sample Grant Proposal Cover Letter

(Your Library, Friends group, or Foundation's letterhead)

Date:

Contact name, organization:

Address:

Dear ___ ,

On behalf of the Board of Trustees of *The Friends of the ___ Library*, I write today to thank you for the ___ Foundation's past support, and to ask you to consider a gift of $3,500 to support the Summer Reading Program in 2013.

If children don't keep reading over the summer, they lose what they learned in the spring. "Studies have shown that successful summer programs get children excited about learning and increase their motivation to pursue knowledge in the months and years ahead" (Miller, *The Learning Season,* 2007).

The Summer Reading Program (SRP) takes a three-pronged approach to give children positive reading and library experiences:

> For pre-school children and beginning readers the Library offers SRP events from mid-June through August. In 2012 there were 75 free performances of storytelling, music, magic, and science activities, with attendance of nearly 7,000!

> Youth register and agree to record the time they spend reading. When they have read ten and twenty hours, they return to the library for a prize. All prizes awarded are books, chosen by librarians with assistance from a teen advisory group. Over 4,500 books were given away to students during summer 2012.

> 726 teens participated—three times more than last year.

> Our partners at Parks and Recreation also awarded over 225 books.

Enclosed are additional materials on the program, as well as details on the work of The Friends. I hope you will agree this program deserves your continued support. *Your contribution is very important to the reading success of the children in our community.*

Thank you for your generous consideration.

Sincerely,

*Your name*
*Title*

*Is your library or its fund-raising organization ready for a capital campaign?* Answer the following questions with a score ranging from 1–10, with 1 representing "not ready" and 10 representing "ready." The stronger you agree with the statements in the left column, the higher you should score yourself. Enter your score in the right column. After you have finished, total your numbers for your final score.

| "ARE WE READY?" INDICATOR | SCORE RANGE | YOUR LIBRARY'S SCORE |
|---|---|---|
| We have commitment from key participants (library trustees, fund-raising organization board and staff, library director). | 1-10 | |
| We have a sound plan that is the result of careful strategic planning and an understanding of our community's needs. | 1-10 | |
| We have a case statement that clearly articulates the needs and opportunities to which we want to respond. | 1-10 | |
| We have a strong history of private fund-raising support. | 1-10 | |
| We have individuals or organizations who can make large lead gifts. | 1-10 | |
| We have the funds to cover the costs of a capital campaign. | 1-10 | |
| We have capable staff with the time and skills needed for a capital campaign. | 1-10 | |
| We have well-organized, dedicated volunteers we can call on for help. | 1-10 | |
| We have a system of communication in place. | 1-10 | |
| We have a system of record keeping in place. | 1-10 | |
| | TOTAL | |

If your score is less than 75, your library is *not ready* to begin a capital campaign.

# Sample Gift Table

One of the handiest tools for any capital campaign is a gift table. It serves several purposes. First and foremost, it tells you how many gifts of various sizes are needed if you are to reach your goal. It also provides a sobering reality check: can you really accomplish this? A gift table helps gauge your campaign's progress and can help with your evaluation when it's ended.

You can construct your own gift table using the following general guidelines:

- The lead gift, the single largest gift needed, should be about 15–20 percent of your goal.
- Work down the table in increments that make sense for your library's potential givers, with each gift amount approximately half the number above it. (Mathematical rule: If you halve the size of the gift as you move through each line of the table, double the number of givers needed at that giving level. Thus, as the size of the gift decreases, the number of donors needed will increase.)
- When you are finished, the total should equal your campaign goal.

A word of caution. Although it is tempting to follow the simple mathematical rule above, the fact is that fund-raising is not simply science. It is also art. Thus, the approach you should take is one that tweaks the rule according to your library's community and the number of potential large givers to whom you have access. The following sample gift table illustrates the size and number of gifts needed for a $2 million capital campaign. It incorporates both science and art in its calculations.

### SAMPLE $2 MILLION GIFT TABLE

| Gift Size | # of Gifts Required | To Produce | Cumulative Total |
|---|---|---|---|
| $400,000 | 1 | $400,000 | $  400,000 |
| $150,000 | 2 | $300,000 | $  700,000 |
| $ 75,000 | 4 | $300,000 | $ 1,000,000 |
| $ 50,000 | 8 | $400,000 | $ 1,400,000 |
| $ 25,000 | 14 | $350,000 | $ 1,750,000 |
| $ 10,000 | 12 | $ 120,000 | $ 1,870,000 |
| $  2,500 | 20 | $ 50,000 | $ 1,920,000 |
| $  1,000 | 50 | $ 50,000 | $ 1,970,000 |
| Less than $10,000 | Many | $ 30,000 | $2,000,000 |

It is the policy of the Library from time to time to recognize the generosity of an individual(s) and/or corporation(s), foundation, and/or other donor(s) by choosing to create a specific naming designation for a library program, collection, facility, or portion of a facility.

The *(governing board)* of *(your library's name here)* has the sole right to name or rename library programs, collections, or facilities. They may recommend naming opportunities to the *(governing board)* for consideration. While the *(governing board)* is grateful for and encourages donations from all individuals, businesses, and organizations, the *(governing board)* has the right to decline any gift to the Library and/or reject naming proposals.

Meeting rooms, reading lounges, special use areas, equipment, gardens, walkways, and other interior and exterior spaces and facilities may be named or renamed by the *(governing board)* to recognize a donor. Appropriate contributions for such naming opportunities will be at the discretion of the *(governing board)* and will be determined by square footage cost, actual cost of equipment, ongoing operating cost, etc., depending on the specific area or item.

Endowment proposals such as those for programs and collections may also include naming rights. Programs and collections may be named or renamed by the *(governing board)* to recognize a donor. Appropriate contributions for such naming opportunities will be at the discretion of the *(governing board)* and will be determined by cost of materials, staff, ongoing operating costs, etc., depending on the specific program or collection.

The *(governing board)* may name or rename library buildings. The *(governing board)* will review, consider, and approve or decline a proposal that a library building bear a designated name only when a prospective donor wishes to make a substantial gift to the Library through its 501(c)(3) Foundation or Friends group.

For contributions toward an existing building, a substantial gift is defined as at least 25 percent of the current assessed value of the facility, or a number agreed upon by the *(governing board)*.

For contributions toward new construction or significant renovation of an existing building, a substantial gift is defined as at least 25 percent of the total project cost, or a number agreed upon by the *(governing board)*.

The name of the neighborhood in which the library building resides will be included in a facility's name unless otherwise agreed upon by the *(governing board)*.

The *(governing board)* may choose to grant naming rights for buildings and other spaces that are a part of the Library's tax-supported construction schedule if a donor contributes the equivalent sum detailed above through the Library's 501(c)(3) Foundation or Friends group.

The *(governing board)* reserves the right to terminate or alter a naming designation under unusual or extraordinary circumstances.

If a distinctively named library facility is relocated, substantially remodeled, or converted to use other than its original use, the facility may be renamed to reflect the association of new donors or community interests related to the changing facility. In such instances, the original name shall be honored in an appropriate manner.

(Date)

# Checklist for a Great Capital Campaign Chair

This checklist is a tool designed to help you objectively compare and evaluate potential capital campaign chairs. Feel free to add additional specific criteria of your own.

Name of Individual: _____

- [ ] Is a highly visible, well-respected community leader
- [ ] Is a business owner or leader, or has connections to businesses in your community
- [ ] Leads an organization with a mission that is compatible with that of your library
- [ ] Is not already on your library's or its fund-raising organization's board
- [ ] Knows something about your library and its needs, or is enthusiastic to learn them
- [ ] Is comfortable and effective when speaking in public
- [ ] Possesses both "affluence" and "influence"—the ability to make a major gift and to persuade others to do the same
- [ ] Has the time to lead your effort
- [ ] Is reliable and can be counted upon to remain with the campaign throughout its duration
- [ ] Is a "team player," good listener, and easy person to work with
- [ ] Can focus on the big picture and delegate tasks, letting staff and volunteers handle the details
- [ ] Can bring other capable workers on board to champion the campaign
- [ ] Has not recently chaired another major capital campaign
- [ ] Can meet deadlines

APPENDIX B

# Fund-Raising
# Gallery

# Fund-Raising Gallery Contents

James V. Brown Library
**Annual Fund**
EDUCATION•ECONOMY•ART•HEALTH

James V. Brown Library
19 East Fourth Street
Williamsport, PA 17701
www.jvbrown.edu

When you include the library in your charitable giving program you do much more than sustain a century old institution.

**When you support the library you support the future of education.**

- The United States ranks seventeenth in literacy in the developed world

- If 50 first-graders have trouble reading 44 of them will have reading problems in the fourth grade.

**When you support the library you support the future of the economy.**

- Employers rank reading and writing as top deficiencies in new hires. 38% of employers find high school graduates "deficient" in reading comprehension. 63% rate this basic skill "very important."

- Good readers generally have more financially rewarding jobs. Proficient readers are 2.5 times as likely as basic readers to be earning $850 or more a week.

**When you support the library you support the future of the arts.**

- Good readers play a crucial role in enriching our cultural and civic life. Literary readers are more than 3 times as likely as non-readers to visit museums, attend plays or concerts, and create artworks of their own. They are also more likely to play sports, attend sporting events, or participate in outdoor activities.

**When you support the library you support the future of healthcare.**

- Nothing – not age, income, employment status, education level or racial and ethnic group – affects health status more than literacy skills.

*Thank you for your support!*
*Charitable donations made to the James V. Brown Library are tax deductible.*

Learn    Explore    Grow

234

## I want to support the James V. Brown Library

# Annual Fund

Name _____

Address _____

City _____

State _____ Zip _____

Phone _____

### Benefactor Level Gift
- ☐ $1000  (or $83 per month)
- ☐ $ 500  (or $42 per month)
- ☐ $ 250  (or $20 per month)
- ☐ $ 100  (or $8.33 per month)

### PAYMENT OPTIONS
- ☐ I am enclosing payment (check made payable to the James V. Brown Library)
- ☐ I wish to pay by credit card
  ☐ Visa ☐ MasterCard ☐ American Express
  CC# _____
  Signature _____
  Expiration Date _____
- ☐ Please bill me quarterly
- ☐ Please charge my credit card monthly
- ☐ I have included the Brown Library in my estate plans

Please mail reply card along with payment in the enclosed envelope to the James V. Brown Library, 19 East Fourth Street, Williamsport, PA 17701

## Why Libraries?

*Every day your mailbox brings requests from worthy organizations. Why should the library be a charitable giving priority for you?*

**Because the need for library services has never been greater.**

In this recession the James V. Brown Library is both a bargain and a boon to those hit hard by current conditions. More than a thousand people come through our doors every day. More books and other materials are being borrowed than last year. The library's public access computers and wireless Internet capability are being used to research job opportunities, apply for government benefits and keep connected to the world.

**Library services continue to be threatened by a reduction in state funding caused by the current economic crisis.**

The library is funded by Lycoming County government, the state of Pennsylvania, its own earned income efforts, grants, and individual donors. Over the last few years the library has seen a loss of **33%** in state funding. It is essential for us to increase our local, public and private support to continue to transform lives in our community.

With the Internet, bookstores, preschool programs and enrollment in kindergarten at an increasingly earlier age, do we still need libraries?

The evidence suggests that far from being obsolete libraries are more important than ever.

Nothing contributes more to a child's ability to succeed in school than exposure to books and reading beginning at birth and no organization can provide and nurture that exposure the way libraries can and do. And the impact continues during the elementary school years.

Data from across the country released by the National Center for Education Statistics provides evidence of a strong link – between the amount of children's materials circulated by public libraries and fourth grade reading scores on the same agency's National Assessment of Educational Progress.

For adults who did not succeed in the classroom Brown's literacy programs offer the adult and family literacy programs that give learners a second chance at achieving the skills they need to succeed.

**You** can help keep the library doors open, buy books for children, teens and adults and support GED and English as a Second Language classes offered through our literacy programs.

*This man remembered you in his will.*

*Please support the James V. Brown Library's Annual Fund.*

**THE FRIENDS OF THE SAINT PAUL PUBLIC LIBRARY**

*Libraries are of whatever caliber they are because of what the community wishes them to be.*
— Alex Haley

Date

«Addressee»
«Address_Lines»
«City», «State»  «ZIP_Code»

Dear «Salutation»,

Due to recent cuts in Local Government Aid from the State of Minnesota to the City of Saint Paul, the Saint Paul Public Library is being forced to drastically slash its current budget for books and other resources. We have all read the headlines: in times of economic difficulty people are using the libraries more. Usage is up, more people are coming to the library and overall demand for library materials and resources increases daily. Even the most generous budget could not cover the current need.

In response to these unprecedented and dramatic cuts, The Friends of the Saint Paul Public Library is launching – for the first time – a citywide campaign to raise money for the purchase of books and other resources for the Library. It is time to **Stock the Stacks!** The City of Saint Paul deserves a public library of the highest caliber. You can help guarantee the continued

vitality and quality of your community library. In these trying times, it is all about *your* support, as a member of this community, for the Library—an essential institution in the City of Saint Paul.

Please take a moment to send a gift of $50, $100, or whatever amount *you* can to help **Stock the Stacks**. Your gift is urgently needed and the results of this campaign will go directly to the purchase of materials. Enclosed is a commemorative bookplate for you to fill in and return with your donation. We will make sure that your bookplate is affixed inside a book purchased with your gift. Please give generously.

Best Regards,

George Latimer
Board Chair

Peter Pearson
President

Encl.

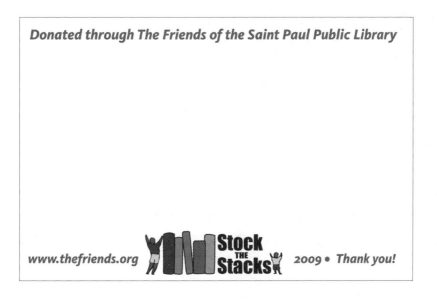

The Friends of the Saint Paul Public Library recognizes that our library is a transformational force in the lives of the residents of Saint Paul.  You can help guarantee the continued vitality and quality of your community library.

**The Saint Paul Public Library:**

* **Serves children from birth to school-age and beyond** by providing interactive Storytimes, the Summer Reading Program, Homework Help, and college access centers.
* **Bridges the digital divide** by providing all residents of the city with free access to the Internet.
* Helps people **work on resumes, find jobs** and learn how to **save money**.
* Offers **mortgage foreclosure prevention counseling**.
* **Enhances quality of life** and **promotes the cultural environment** in the communities the library serves.
* **Promotes individual well-being** and helps people become **more productive in their jobs and in their personal lives**.
* **Spurs economic development** and serves as a catalyst for public- and private-sector investment.

THE
**FRIENDS**
OF THE **SAINT PAUL**
**PUBLIC LIBRARY**

**The Saint Paul Public Library plays a key role in the educational and cultural survival of the City.**
*You can play a key role in supporting the Saint Paul Public Library.*

In response to unprecedented cuts in the city budget, The Friends of the Saint Paul Public Library is launching a citywide campaign to raise money for the library's collection. The results of this campaign will be used to purchase books and electronic materials for the Saint Paul Public Library.

---

***Please send your gift today!*** Fill in the enclosed bookplate with your name, the name of someone you wish to honor or remember, or some other message, and return it with this card in the envelope provided.  We'll make sure your bookplate is affixed inside a book purchased with your gift.

**Yes!** I want to make a tax-deductible gift of:   ___$1,000  ___$500  ___$250  ___$100  ___$50  ___$25   Other:_____

Name(s)_____

Address _____ City_____ State_____ Zip_____

Email_____ Phone_____

❏ My check is enclosed *(payable to* The Friends of the Saint Paul Public Library*)*

❏ Please charge my:   ___Visa  ___MasterCard  ___American Express  ___Discover

   Credit card number _____Expiration date_____

   Signature _____

❏ I prefer that my gift remain anonymous.

❏ Please send me library news and information about the activities of The Friends of the Saint Paul Public Library.

---

**325 Cedar Street, Suite 555 • Saint Paul, MN 55101-1055 • www.thefriends.org • (651) 222-3242 • Fax (651) 222-1988 • friends@thefriends.org**

*The Friends of the St. Paul Public Library is a not-for-profit 501(c)(3) organization. Your gift is fully tax deductible as allowable by law.*

*"At the moment that we persuade a child, any child, to cross that threshold, that magic threshold into a library, we change their lives forever, for the better."*
— President Barack Obama

June 8, 2011

Dear Friend,

The Friends of the Saint Paul Public Library is proud to celebrate 52 years of summer reading. Since 1960, The Friends—along with other sponsors—have had the privilege of funding summer reading programs (SRP). These programs are shown to be an antidote for learning loss. Instead of losing knowledge and skills during the summer months, kids who participate in library reading programs actually show gains. They accelerate learning while having active fun over the summer!

Again this year, the youth and teens who take part in SRP will receive free books for reaching their reading goals. What could be better than book incentives for reading books? We're rewarding reading with more ways to read – a wonderful cycle that promotes and rewards the love of reading.

The Friends recently launched a special campaign – called *XLR8 Summer Reading!* – dedicated to supporting this annual program.  We invite you to *join your children in attending the wide variety of programs* at your local library this summer while having the satisfaction of knowing you have done your part to *help other children participate, as well.* Visit www.sppl.org for more information and a complete schedule of SRP events.

**Please donate to The Friends' *XLR8 Summer Reading* campaign and know that the dollars you send will support the Summer Reading Program. It takes all of us to put together the summer of fun and reading, and we need your help.**

Visit our website at www.thefriends.org to make a secure online donation or use the enclosed return envelope.  Make your tax-deductible gift today and help Saint Paul's children activate and accelerate their reading and learning all summer long!

Best Wishes,

*Peter D. Pearson*

Peter Pearson
President

P.S. Summer reading can literally change a child's life for the better, *forever.* Be part of this change and send a donation today! *Thank you!*

325 Cedar Street, Suite 555 • Saint Paul, MN 55101-1055 • www.thefriends.org
**(651) 222-3242** • Fax (651) 222-1988 • friends@thefriends.org

Adopt-A-Summer-Reader

2011 One World, Many Stories @ Your Library

☐ YES

I want to adopt a Summer Reader!

Adopt 5 Readers ............ $ 50.00
Adopt 10 Readers .......... $100.00
Adopt 15 Readers .......... $150.00
Adopt 20 Readers .......... $200.00
Other ..................... $ _____

For just 27¢ a day you can help 10 children go back to school next fall ready to learn new lessons.

Please list your name as you would like it to appear on our website and provide a phone number should we need to contact you with questions.

Check enclosed $ _____     Pay by Credit Card:    MasterCard        Visa        American Express

Name (as it appears on card) _____

Expiration Date _____ Card Number _____     Amount $ _____

Security Code _____ (last 3 digits on signature line)    THANK YOU!

Contributions to the library are tax deductible, good for the soul and greatly appreciated!
Please mail contribution to the James V. Brown Library, 19 East Fourth Street, Williamsport, PA  17701

"*The throwing wide of the doors of the James V. Brown Memorial Library to the public, on Tuesday morning June 18th, at 9 o'clock, will be one of the most significant in the annals of Williamsport. For the first time in the history of the city the public will be offered opportunities for educational development, through the medium of the best books obtainable. The thousands of volumes in the James V. Brown Library furnish information on every subject worth knowing about, and all are at the disposal of those who would read and learn.*" From the Pennsylvania Grit, June 16, 1907

Indeed, by the noon hour on **Tuesday, June 18, 1907**, 150 books had been borrowed, and when the Children's Room opened at 2:00 P.M., scores of children were waiting to rush in!

The Brown Library was a bequest to the city from lumber baron and philanthropist **James VanDuzee Brown** who died on December 8, 1904, at age 78. Already a widower with no children, Brown had dreamt for years of giving Williamsport a free, public library. The idea for the library was suggested by his late wife, Carile Brown.

**James V. Brown** came from a large family in New York state, and was a descendant of the family that founded Brown University in Providence, Rhode Island. Arriving in Williamsport in 1859, he worked in the printing and flour mill trades, then went into lumbering where he made his fortune as a partner in the Brown, Early & Company Lumber Mill.

Mr. Brown was a prominent city leader with an impressive resume, including his service as: president of the Williamsport Water Company, where he masterminded the development of the city's water system; president of the Citizen Gas Company, an original stockholder of the Market Street Bridge (it was a privately owned toll bridge), a controlling stockholder of the Gazette Bulletin newspaper, the Central PA Telephone Company, and organizer of First National Bank.

# Book Endowment

## This man cared enough to endow a library

*James Vanduzee Brown*

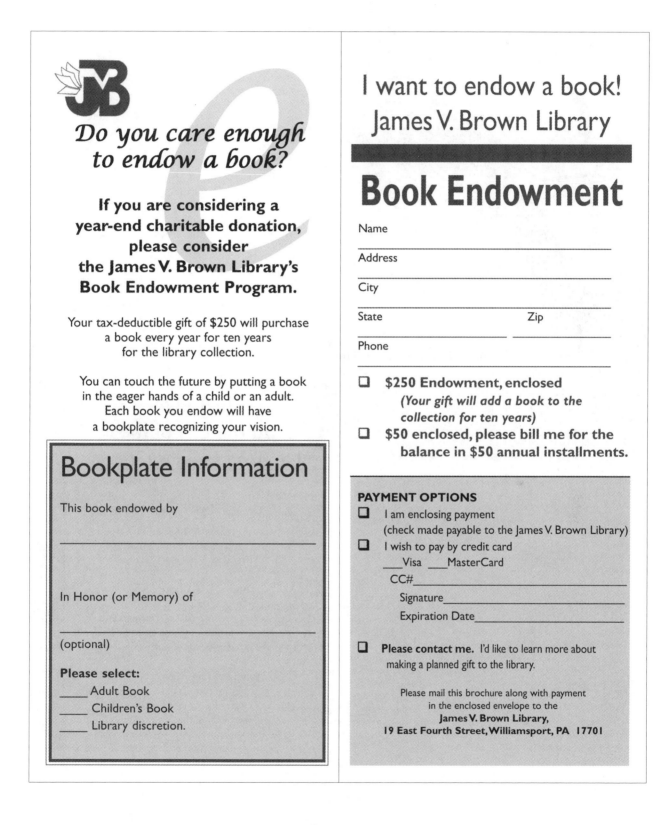

Do you care enough
to endow a book?

If you are considering a
year-end charitable donation,
please consider
the James V. Brown Library's
Book Endowment Program.

Your tax-deductible gift of $250 will purchase
a book every year for ten years
for the library collection.

You can touch the future by putting a book
in the eager hands of a child or an adult.
Each book you endow will have
a bookplate recognizing your vision.

## Bookplate Information

This book endowed by

_____

In Honor (or Memory) of

_____

(optional)

**Please select:**

_____ Adult Book

_____ Children's Book

_____ Library discretion.

I want to endow a book!
James V. Brown Library

# Book Endowment

Name

_____

Address

_____

City

_____

State                          Zip

_____   _____

Phone

_____

☐  **$250 Endowment, enclosed**
      *(Your gift will add a book to the
      collection for ten years)*

☐  **$50 enclosed, please bill me for the
      balance in $50 annual installments.**

**PAYMENT OPTIONS**

☐  I am enclosing payment
      (check made payable to the James V. Brown Library)

☐  I wish to pay by credit card
      ___Visa ____MasterCard
      CC#_____
      Signature_____
      Expiration Date_____

☐  **Please contact me.**  I'd like to learn more about
      making a planned gift to the library.

Please mail this brochure along with payment
in the enclosed envelope to the
**James V. Brown Library,
19 East Fourth Street, Williamsport, PA  17701**

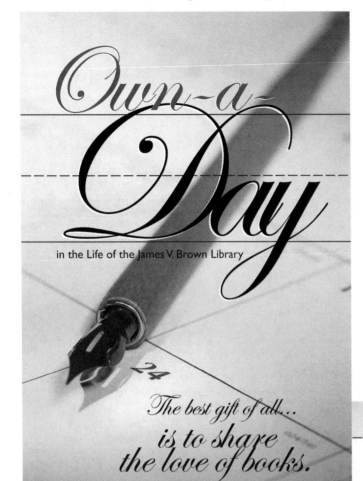

## Own-a-Day
## in the Life of the
## James V. Brown Library

When you sponsor a day of library service
your investment of $100 touches 1000 lives.

Every day an average of 1000 children, teens,
adults and seniors use the services
of the James V. Brown Library.

**Choose your favorite day –**
**sponsor your own or a loved one's birthday**
**or practice a random act of kindness and**
**let us choose your day - and you help the library**
**meet the growing needs of our community.**

On "Your Day" your name or the name
of someone you care about will be on every receipt
given to our readers as they checkout items
as a special thank you.
Our ongoing calendar will be a
yearlong recognition of your gift and
an inspiration to others to also sponsor a day.

If we reach 300 sponsors we will have $30,000
to invest in books and other circulated items.

www.foundation.spl.org    206.386.4130

# JOIN OUR

## *Books for Branches*

# Campaign today!

## Help provide needed books
### for The Seattle Public Library branches.

- Last year more than 7 million books and materials were checked out of the Library — nearly 50% more than in 2000.

- Every day more than 10,000 people visit the Library's website to reserve books, get information about upcoming programs or search our online databases.

- Your gifts support weekly early literacy activities for pre-school children in every Library branch, an online homework help service for teens, book groups for seniors and free public presentations by leading authors and artists.

- Your support provides information resources to help the disadvantaged, disabled and needy in our community.

- In 2005, the Library was able to purchase the equivalent of 67,000 additional items for the collection thanks to donors who gave gifts both large and small.

## To keep The Seattle Public Library growing and thriving,

please join the
Books for Branches
Campaign by

## sending your gift
## today!

The
Seattle
Public
Library
Foundation

## Join the *Books for Branches* Campaign Today!

☐ **YES!** I want to help purchase needed books and materials for The Seattle Public Library. Here is my Books for Branches gift of:

☐ $35 to purchase 2 children's picture books
☐ $50 for 2 books that will be checked out by 100 people.
☐ $100 for 4 books that will be checked out by 200 people.
☐ $500 for an entire shelf of 20 books.
☐ $ _____ to help as much as possible.

☐ Enclosed is my check.
or
☐ I'd like to make my gift by credit card.
(I've included my credit card information on back)

**Use my gift for:**
☐ Books for library shelves all over the city.
☐ Books for the _____ Branch.

(Name)
(Address 1)
(Address 2)
(City, State, ZIP)
(BARCODE)

(Cons Code)   (Appeal Code)

Phone ____ (laser if available) ____
E-mail ____ (laser if available) ____

*Help provide needed books for The Seattle Public Library branches.*

The Seattle Public Library Foundation

*Thank you for caring!*   Your gift to The Seattle Public Library Foundation is tax deductible as allowed by law.   1000 Fourth Avenue, Seattle, WA 98104

---

The Seattle Public Library Foundation

(Date)

(Name)
(Address 1)
(Address 2)
(City, State, ZIP)

Dear (Salutation),

A friend of the Library recently shared with me her favorite "library memory" . . .

*For me, it was always about Saturday mornings. My big sister and I would go down to our neighborhood library branch . . . which was an incredible adventure to me all on its own.*

*Then she and I would comb the shelves for* Dr. Seuss, The Bobbsey Twins, A Wrinkle in Time *and countless other classics. And I'd collect as many books as I was allowed to check out. I was SO proud I had my very own library card. It was like having a magic ticket to the end of the universe!*

All of us who love the Library have our own special library memories. And now, **you can give these special memories to *hundreds* of children this year by making a gift to purchase books for your Seattle Public Library branch.**

Every library is special, of course. But we believe The Seattle Public Library system is a real treasure and vital resource for the community. <FOR DONORS> Your past support demonstrates your commitment to our Library and I couldn't be more grateful.

That's why I'm writing today. Because right now we need your help to create great library memories for a new generation of readers by providing more books and materials for our libraries.

With the effort to rebuild and expand all of our neighborhood branches, every library in our system has become more popular. Naturally, I'm thrilled about that. I'm especially excited that since 2000 the circulation of Library materials has grown by nearly 50%. We were already busy, so this is huge!

But our budget for books hasn't kept pace with the demand. We want to have a rich collection of library materials for *everyone* who is looking for that special book . . . or researching information about a new job . . . or trying to understand the political situation in Iraq. It's especially important for children who are beginning to create their own special library memories.

With your help, we'll be able to carry many more of the books and resources people are requesting.

With your help, people will have a shorter wait for the materials they need.

With your help, kids in our community will have a larger selection of reading and research

1000 Fourth Avenue, Seattle, WA 98104   **P** 206-386-4130   **F** 206-386-4132   **W** www.foundation.spl.org

## For credit card payment

TYPE OF CARD    ☐ VISA        ☐ MasterCard        ☐ AmEx

Credit card number    _____    Expiration date    _____

Cardholder's name    _____

Cardholder's signature  _____
                        (required for credit card use only)

The Seattle Public Library Foundation is committed to safeguarding donor information.
We do not rent, sell or trade it with any outside company or organization.

**CHARITY NAVIGATOR**
★ ★ ★ ★
Four Star Charity

---

materials to develop their academic skills.

That's why I want you to take a minute to think about your favorite Library memory. And remember why giving to The Seattle Public Library is so important.

Then join us in **our exciting new Books for Branches Campaign** by sending your gift with the response card and envelope I'm enclosing. Public funding just can't cover the needs all our library branches have for new books.

- A gift of just $35 buys two children's picture books — each will be checked out by at least 50 children before they're loved to death.

- Just $100 will buy 4 new books, each of which will be checked out by an average of 50 people — so 200 lives will be touched!

- Just $500 buys an entire shelf full of 20 books! What an enormous impact that would make on our community — touching 1000 lives.

It's up to you to help make great Library memories for the next generation. Someone provided the books that gave you such wonderful memories. Now it's your turn. **Join our Books for Branches Campaign today.**

I look forward to hearing from you! Please respond today with the most generous gift possible, and thank you for your support.

Sincerely,

Deborah L. Jacobs
City Librarian

P.S.    You can give special library memories and a world of opportunity to children in our community. Please be as generous as you can today. Join the Books for Branches Campaign to help your Seattle Public Library buy the books and materials our library branches so desperately need.

# Thank you for making the

## *Books for Branches*

## Campaign a success!

More than 2,450 people gave a total of $140,000 to help us fill the shelves in all our libraries with new books and materials.

The funds raised from this special campaign put more than 5,000 new materials in circulation for patrons of all ages.

Many of these new books will be marked with a bookplate designating them as gifts from "people in the community who love libraries."

This book purchased with donations from people in our community who love libraries.

The Seattle Public Library Foundation

**The Seattle Public Library Foundation**

**It's not too late to help keep The Seattle Public Library growing and thriving,**

## become a donor
## today!

www.foundation.spl.org • (206) 386-4130

*Love
Your
Library?*

## How can I give back to Bayport Public Library?

Patrons frequently ask how they can support Bayport Public Library. This brochure is designed to provide answers. Inside you will find facts about the function and funding of Bayport Public Library and the Bayport Public Library Foundation. This information will clarify why *making your donation to the Foundation will ensure that the library receives the most benefit from your gift.*

## How will my donation be used if I give it to the BPL Foundation?

Foundation funds are used to support the library by:

- adding to the collection;
- updating technology;
- funding programs and activities;
- enhancing the library building;
- and adding to the endowment fund.

## How can I include Bayport Public Library in my estate planning?

Once you decide to make a bequest to the library, the following language is appropriate for inclusion in your will:

*I give to the Bayport Public Library Foundation, 582 North Fourth Street, Bayport, Minnesota 55003, _____ percent of my residuary estate (or, the sum of $ _____, or a description of property, securities, etc.) for its endowment fund.*

*Thank you
for
your interest
in
Bayport
Public Library.*

## Bayport Public Library

Bayport Public Library was established by city ordinance. It is governed by a volunteer five-member Board of Directors.

As a public library, BPL is subject to Minnesota statute, which states that **the library cannot receive more than 50 percent of its funding from private sources (donations).** At least 50 percent of its funding must come from tax dollars.

Because of this limitation, the best way to support Bayport Public Library is to make your contribution to the Foundation.

~~~~~~~~~~~~~~~~~~~~~

## Bayport Public Library Foundation

The Bayport Public Library Foundation was established in 1990 as a non-profit corporation in accordance with Federal and Minnesota statutes. Foundation Articles of Incorporation state:

- "(Bayport Public Library Foundation) is organized and shall be operated **exclusively** to provide financial support to the Bayport Public Library."

- "…the purpose of this corporation shall be to provide for services and facilities over and above what the traditional tax base funding of the Bayport Public Library has provided."

**Contributions made to the Foundation are not subject to the 50 percent limitation.**

The BPL Foundation is governed by a volunteer Board of Directors. Administrative costs are approximately 3.5 percent of the Foundation's annual expenses and include printing, postage and bookkeeping.

Foundation support makes it possible for Bayport Public Library to go beyond what the regular budget can accomplish and is the key to continuing the role of our library as a true community center.

~~~~~~~~~~~~~~~~~~~~~

## Bayport Public Library and Bayport Public Library Foundation
### Working together to deliver an exceptional library experience

---

### THE BAYPORT PUBLIC LIBRARY FOUNDATION THANKS YOU

I/We would like to contribute $ _____

In memory / honor of _____

**GIFT SELECTION**

___ Donation to General Fund        $ _____

___ Donation to Endowment Fund      $ _____

___ Annual Associate Membership     $ _____
    ($10 Individual/ $15 Family)

                        TOTAL $ _____

NAME(S): _____

ADDRESS: _____

CITY: _____    STATE: _____    ZIP _____

EMAIL: _____

PHONE: _____

___ I /We would like this donation to be anonymous.

___ Employer's matching gift form(s) enclosed.

___ Please contact me about including the Bayport Public Library Foundation in my estate planning.

___ I would like to discuss giving options further; please contact me.

Please return this form to:
   Bayport Public Library Foundation
   582 N. 4th St., Bayport, MN  55003
                        651-275-4416

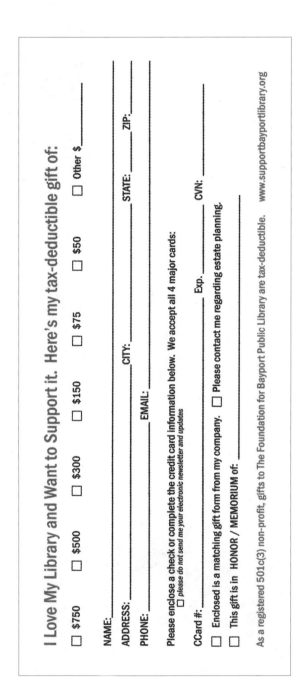

I Love My Library and Want to Support it.  Here's my tax-deductible gift of:

☐ $750    ☐ $500    ☐ $300    ☐ $150    ☐ $75    ☐ $50    ☐ Other $ _____

NAME: _____

ADDRESS: _____    CITY: _____    STATE: _____    ZIP: _____

PHONE: _____    EMAIL: _____

Please enclose a check or complete the credit card information below.  We accept all 4 major cards:
   ☐ please do not send me your electronic newsletter and updates

CCard #: _____    Exp. _____    CVN: _____

☐  Enclosed is a matching gift form from my company.    ☐ Please contact me regarding estate planning.

☐  This gift is in  HONOR / MEMORIUM of: _____

As a registered 501c(3) non-profit, gifts to The Foundation for Bayport Public Library are tax-deductible.    www.supportbayportlibrary.org

Make a great library better.
Support the RCPL Foundation.

Richland County
Public Library
Foundation

The Richland County Public Library touches tens of thousands of families in the Midlands and beyond. RCPL serves everyone in our community, regardless of age or background, and provides free access to quality information and resources that enhance their lives, both personally and professionally.

With more than *1.1 million books* and another *90,000 nonprint resources*, RCPL has something for everyone, regardless of their age or background. That's why *70 percent of the people in Richland County have library cards*, using its resources to enhance their lives and prepare for their futures.

Richland County Public Library Foundation
1431 Assembly St., Box 8
Columbia, SC 29201
|p| 803.929.3424
|f| 803.929.3448

Make your gift online at www.myRCPL.com.

6/09 - 10,000

## Who We Are

RCPL receives operational funding from property taxes, but public funding alone does not make a great public library. Private support of individuals and businesses has made RCPL a leader among libraries in the Southeast, across the United States and internationally.

Innovative programs and services, outstanding staff, a strong Friends of RCPL organization and a community that eagerly supports its public library helped RCPL become the 2001 National Library of the Year. RCPL is one of the most important cultural and educational resources in our region. The RCPL Foundation works to increase financial support so the library can broaden and diversify its ability to serve the citizens of Richland County.

By securing significant private support through annual giving and other efforts, the Foundation will help take the library to levels of unsurpassed excellence.

## What We Do

Philanthropic giving has enabled RCPL to:

- Establish the Walker Local History Room at the Main Library, which includes historical material focusing on Columbia and the Midlands area.
- Establish the Columbia Academy Children's Room and Bristow-Marchant Storytime Room at the Main Library to inspire young readers to be life-long learners.
- Establish the Cunningham-Monteith Large Print Center to ensure equal access to people with physical disabilities.

With library usage up more than 25 percent and continuing to rise, it is critical for the Foundation to increase private support for the library—the one public institution serving people of all ages and backgrounds. Only by leveraging its public funding with private support will RCPL be able to continue to ensure its high quality services for future generations.

## How You Can Contribute

Constant innovation and improvement are at the very core of what has made RCPL one of the nation's finest libraries. Please consider supporting RCPL through the RCPL Foundation.

To maintain the high level of services citizens have come to expect and demand from the library, public funding will not be enough.

## I would like to contribute to the RCPL Foundation.

Name ...........................................................

Company .....................................................

Address ......................................................

City ....................... State ......... Zip ...........

Phone .........................................................

E-mail .........................................................

Gift amount $ ..............................................

☐ My check is enclosed (made payable to RCPL Foundation).

☐ Please charge my VISA/MASTERCARD

Number ......................................................

Exp .......... Signature .................................

### This gift is made –

☐ In memory of ...........................................

☐ In honor of ..............................................

### Send notification of this gift to:

Name ...........................................................

Address ......................................................

City ....................... State ......... Zip ...........

Relationship ...............................................

Please complete and return to –

**RCPL Foundation**
**1431 Assembly St.**
**Columbia, SC 29201**

You may also make your gift online at **www.myRCPL.com**.

For more information or to discuss including the RCPL Foundation in your estate plans, please contact the Development Manager at 803.929.3424.

*The Richland County Public Library Foundation is a 501(c)(3) nonprofit organization, and your contribution is tax deductible to the fullest extent allowed by law.*

## YOUR LIBRARY AT A GLANCE: BOOKS AND SERVICES

| | |
|---|---|
| Items in collection | 1,158,603 |
| Items loaned | 3,394,664 |
| Visitors system-wide | 2,785,784 |
| Information inquiries to staff | 448,422 |

## COMPUTERS AND TECHNOLOGY

| | |
|---|---|
| Public access computers | 312 |
| Users of library computers | 623,482 |
| Online visits | 1,573,314 |

## PROGRAMS

| | |
|---|---|
| Programs for children & teens | 2,624 |
| Children & teens attending programs | 74,842 |
| Homework Center student visits | 21,348 |
| Summer Reading Program participants | 6,363 |
| Summer Reading Program attendees | 13,466 |
| Programs for adults | 1,181 |
| Adults attending programs | 18,822 |

**THE FRIENDS OF THE SAINT PAUL PUBLIC LIBRARY**

325 Cedar Street, Suite 555
Saint Paul, MN 55101
651-222-3242

**www.thefriends.org**

*Statistics shown are from 2008, the latest year for which we have data.*

**An important economic development tool for the City of Saint Paul, the Saint Paul Public Library:**

- Bridges the digital divide by providing all residents of the city with **access to the Internet,** and offers **free computer training** to seniors and other adults.

- Offers adults access to **job and career assistance,** as well as a myriad of helpful online databases and information.

- Helps you **"Make Economic Cent$"** by offering free information on starting, marketing, financing and sustaining small businesses in difficult economic times.

- **Supports sustainable home ownership** by providing market and finance information and mortgage foreclosure prevention counseling.

- **Collaborates** with other City departments and nonprofit organizations to provide **educational and cultural programs.**

**Your support is critically important to Saint Paul's children:**

- **1.3 million children's items were checked out of the library last year** – more than 25 items for every child in the City of Saint Paul.

Key to the education of our city's children from birth to school-age and beyond, the Library provides **storytimes,** the **Summer Reading Program, Homework Help,** and **access to college centers.** This comprehensive service to youth, families and adults happens 12 months a year, in the morning, afternoons, evenings and on weekends, and *anytime* at **www.sppl.org.**

*When you give to The Friends, you're making your library stronger, and contributing to the stability, prosperity and quality of life in Saint Paul.*

## Thank You!

How is the Saint Paul Public Library the *PLACE* for you?
For your family?
For your community?

*The Work Place*
A wide variety of job, career and small business programs and services are available at the SPPL.

*The Study Place*
Homework Centers offer computers, printers, references and supplies for students of all ages.

*The Reading Place*
The Friends provides extensive support for children's programs at the SPPL.

*The Movie Place*
Besides having access to a variety of DVDs and videos, the SPPL is the place to go see movies.

*The Arts Place*
The SPPL offers popular classes, discussion and performances by our favorite local artists.

*The Research Place*
The SPPL is the place to do all your research with new online tools as well as the old-fashioned way.

*The Story Place*
The SPPL offers more than 250 free storytimes each year at every branch in the system.

*The Training Place*
The SPPL offers trainings, including computer classes, GED, College Prep, ESL and more.

**Please ensure the future of the Saint Paul Public Library through a gift to The Friends today.  Thank You!**

*The Friends is a 501(c)(3) nonprofit organization.  For income tax purposes, your gift is tax-deductible to the full extent of the law.*

# Yes!  I'm pleased to support the work of The Friends.

**Enclosed is my tax deductible gift of:**

- ❏ $1,000
- ❏ $500
- ❏ $250
- ❏ $100
- ❏ $50
- ❏ $25
- ❏ Other: $_____

_____
Name (s)

_____
Address

_____
City                          State        Zip

_____
Phone
May we send your receipt electronically?  ❏ Yes  ❏ No

_____
Email

❏ My check is enclosed (*made payable to* **FSPPL**)

Please charge my credit card:
❏ Visa   ❏ MasterCard   ❏ American Express   ❏ Discover

_____
Credit card number

_____
Expiration date                          CVV code

_____
Signature

❏ I prefer that my gift remain anonymous.

THE **FRIENDS** OF THE **SAINT PAUL** **PUBLIC LIBRARY**

*Please return to:*
The Friends of the
Saint Paul Public Library
325 Cedar Street, Suite 555
Saint Paul, MN  55101

**For more information, call 651-222-3242, email friends@thefriends.org, or visit www.thefriends.org**

## The Friends of the Saint Paul Public Library

Started in 1945, The Friends of the Saint Paul Public Library is a nonprofit, community membership organization dedicated to supporting the Saint Paul Public Library. We believe that ours is the best Library system of its size in the country, and that it deserves an engaged organization that represents the community's interests on Library issues.

The Friends has an active board of directors, vital civic and corporate partners, more than 3,000 members, and we're growing each year. We are proud that our group has been honored as one of the nation's premier Friends organizations.

Your membership helps to strengthen the Saint Paul Public Library and ensure the continued growth and improvement of Library services. The Friends support a variety of Library initiatives, including:

- **Purchase of thousands of new books and materials for the Library's collection**
- **More than 50 years of children's Summer Reading Programs**
- **Free help with schoolwork in six Homework Centers and online**
- **Award-winning literary and cultural events.**

### Our Mission

- **Increase the use of the Library through cultural programming and public awareness activities;**
- **Advocate for strong public funding of the Library; and**
- **Provide private funding to enhance Library services.**

Through this work, The Friends serves as a national model for its unique and comprehensive support of the Saint Paul Public Library.

### Become a Friend

The Saint Paul Public Library had 4,359,098 visitors last year, checking out an average of 9,300 items per day. Your annual membership and involvement help to sustain this record of excellence.

Thanks to strong public support, the Saint Paul Public Library stands at the forefront of our nation's public libraries. The important work we do advocating on behalf of the Library depends upon a large and vocal membership base. As a member of The Friends, your voice will be heard on Library issues – and together our voices become louder as our membership grows.

### Enjoy the Benefits of Membership

All Friends members receive:

- **Friendly Connections,** our online and print member newsletter, keeping you updated on Friends' activities, Library programs, and other happenings.
- **Events and Classes** - the Library's bimonthly program calendar, mailed directly to your home.
- **An official membership card** which offers special discounts at the Minnesota Book Awards, select Saint Paul cultural venues and local bookstores.
- **Invitations** to special events and programs.
- **The sense of fulfillment and civic pride** that come with supporting an important and vital community institution.
- **The knowledge that your gift makes a real difference to the Saint Paul Public Library.**

## Supporting Your Library Has Never Been Easier!

You can renew your membership or purchase a gift membership online by scanning this QR code or visit: **www.thefriends.org**

# JOIN THE FRIENDS

*Your membership is vital to the strength of your library and your community.*

## THE FRIENDS OF THE SAINT PAUL PUBLIC LIBRARY

325 Cedar Street, Suite 555
Saint Paul, MN 55101-1055
**www.thefriends.org**

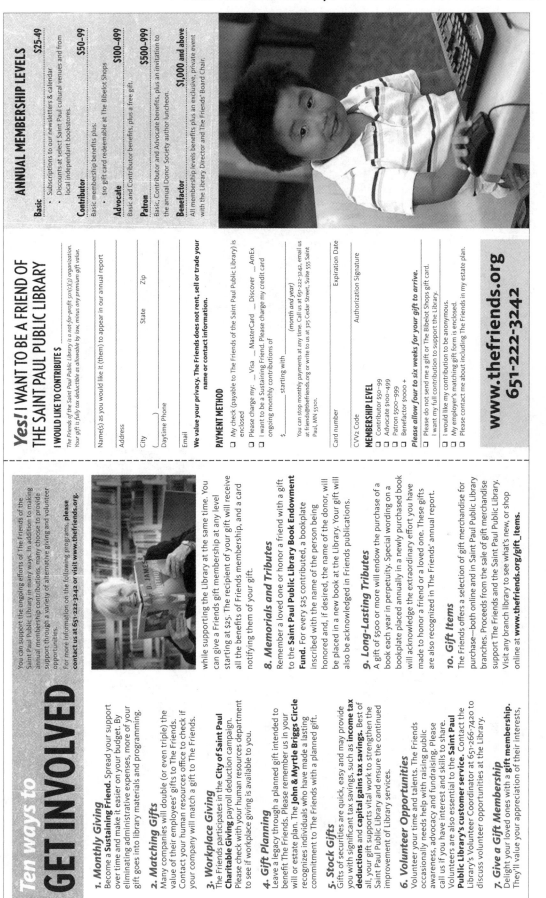

## ANNUAL MEMBERSHIP LEVELS

**Basic**  $25-49
- Subscriptions to our newsletters & calendar
- Discounts at select Saint Paul cultural venues and from local independant bookstores.

**Contributor**  $50-99
Basic membership benefits plus:
- $10 gift card redeemable at The Bibelot Shops

**Advocate**  $100-499
Basic and Contributor benefits, plus a free gift.

**Patron**  $500-999
Basic, Contributor and Advocate benefits, plus an invitation to the annual Donor Society author luncheon.

**Benefactor**  $1,000 and above
All membership levels benefits plus an exclusive, private event with the Library Director and The Friends' Board Chair.

# Ten ways to
# GET INVOLVED

You can support the ongoing efforts of the Friends of the Saint Paul Public Library in many ways. In addition to making annual membership contributions, many choose to provide support through a variety of alternative giving and volunteer opportunities.

For more information on the following programs, **please contact us at 651-222-3242 or visit www.thefriends.org.**

### 1. Monthly Giving
Become a **Sustaining Friend.** Spread your support over time and make it easier on your budget. By eliminating administrative expenses, more of your gift goes into library materials and programming.

### 2. Matching Gifts
Many companies will double (or even triple) the value of their employees' gifts to The Friends. Contact your human resources office to check if your company will match a gift to The Friends.

### 3. Workplace Giving
The Friends participates in the **City of Saint Paul Charitable Giving** payroll deduction campaign. Please check with your human resources department to see if workplace giving is available to you.

### 4. Gift Planning
Leave a legacy through a planned gift intended to benefit The Friends. Please remember us in your will or estate plan. The **John & Myrtle Briggs Circle** recognizes individuals who have made a lasting commitment to The Friends with a planned gift.

### 5. Stock Gifts
Gifts of securities are quick, easy and may provide you with significant tax savings, such as **income tax deductions** and **capital gains tax savings.** Best of all, your gift supports vital work to strengthen the Saint Paul Public Library and ensure the continued improvement of library services.

### 6. Volunteer Opportunities
Volunteer your time and talents. The Friends occasionally needs help with raising public awareness, advocacy and fundraising. Please call us if you have interest and skills to share. Volunteers are also essential to the **Saint Paul Public Library's customer service.** Contact the Library's Volunteer Coordinator at 651-266-7420 to discuss volunteer opportunities at the Library.

### 7. Give a Gift Membership
Delight your loved ones with a **gift membership.** They'll value your appreciation of their interests, while supporting the Library at the same time. You can give a Friends gift membership at any level starting at $25. The recipient of your gift will receive all the benefits of Friends membership, and a card notifying them of your gift.

### 8. Memorials and Tributes
Remember a loved one or honor a friend with a gift to the **Saint Paul Public Library Book Endowment Fund.** For every $25 contributed, a bookplate inscribed with the name of the person being honored and, if desired, the name of the donor, will be placed in a new book at the Library. Your gift will also be acknowledged in Friends publications.

### 9. Long-Lasting Tributes
A gift of $500 or more will endow the purchase of a book each year in perpetuity. Special wording on a bookplate placed annually in a newly purchased book will acknowledge the extraordinary effort you have made to honor a friend or a loved one. These gifts are also recognized in The Friends' annual report.

### 10. Gift Items
The Friends offers a selection of gift merchandise for purchase—both online and in Saint Paul Public Library branches. Proceeds from the sale of gift merchandise support The Friends and the Saint Paul Public Library. Visit any branch library to see what's new, or shop online at **www.thefriends.org/gift_items.**

## Yes! I WANT TO BE A FRIEND OF THE SAINT PAUL PUBLIC LIBRARY

**I WOULD LIKE TO CONTRIBUTE $**
*The Friends of the Saint Paul Public Library is a not-for-profit 501(c)(3) organization. Your gift is fully tax deductible as allowable by law, minus any premium gift value.*

Name(s) as you would like it (them) to appear in our annual report

Address

City                State        Zip

(     ) Daytime Phone

Email

**We value your privacy. The Friends does not rent, sell or trade your name or contact information.**

**PAYMENT METHOD**
☐ My check (payable to The Friends of the Saint Paul Public Library) is enclosed
☐ Please charge my: __Visa __MasterCard __Discover __AmEx
☐ I want to be a Sustaining Friend. Please charge my credit card ongoing monthly contributions of
$_____ starting with _____ *(month and year)*
You can stop monthly payments at any time. Call us at 651-222-3242, email us at friends@thefriends.org or write to us at 325 Cedar Street, Suite 555 Saint Paul, MN 55101.

Card number _____ Expiration Date _____

CVV2 Code _____  Authorization Signature _____

**MEMBERSHIP LEVEL**
☐ Contributor $50-99
☐ Advocate $100-499
☐ Patron $500-999
☐ Benefactor $1000 +

***Please allow four to six weeks for your gift to arrive.***
☐ Please do not send me a gift or The Bibelot Shops gift card. I want my full contribution to support the Library.
☐ I would like my contribution to be anonymous.
☐ My employer's matching gift form is enclosed.
☐ Please contact me about including The Friends in my estate plan.

## www.thefriends.org
## 651-222-3242

The Library needs your support, *now more than ever.* You can help by becoming a Friend of the Saint Paul Public Library.

Our mission is to expand the Library's capacity to serve, without exception, Saint Paul's many communities. The Friends does this by providing **private funding** to enhance Library services; **advocating** for strong public funding of the Library; and increasing use of the Library through **cultural programming and public awareness activities.**

**SPPL staff and volunteers qualify for a FREE BASIC MEMBERSHIP in The Friends.**

A large Friends membership advances advocacy for strong public funding of the Library. If you have not done so already, **please help by joining The Friends today.** Use The Friends' regular membership brochure to register for your free membership. Just write "SPPL Staff" or "SPPL Volunteer" over the payment method or, if you wish to make an additional contribution and join at a higher level, we'll send you the premium gift(s) you designate.

*NOTE: As a member of The Friends you'll receive special discounts from Park Square Theatre, local independent bookstores, the Minnesota Book Awards and other local cultural attractions. Members above the basic level also receive special gifts, including a $10 gift card, courtesy of The Bibelot Shops. Our brochure describes membership levels and the available gift items.*

**651-222-3242 ● www.thefriends.org**

THE **FRIENDS** OF THE SAINT PAUL PUBLIC LIBRARY

*Associate*

*with*

*The Best*

*Bayport*
*Public*
*Library*

"A library is not a luxury,
but one of the necessities of life."
*Henry Ward Beecher*

Associates of the Bayport Public Library Foundation
582 North Fourth Street
Bayport, Minnesota 55003

*Bayport Public Library Hours*
Monday:  12 noon to 8 p.m.
Tuesday:  10 a.m. to 6 p.m.
Wednesday and Thursday:  12 noon to 8 p.m.
Friday:  10 a.m. to 4 p.m.
Saturday:  12 noon to 2 p.m.*
Sunday:  Closed
* Closed Saturdays Memorial Day
through Labor Day

*Did you know?*
That some of your neighbors are —

• redoing their résumés
• listening to CD's
• looking up medical facts
• checking out videos
• traveling with tapes
• participating in
  children's programs
• reading latest books,
  magazines and papers
• learning with children's
  computer software

"If we didn't have libraries,
many people thirsty for knowledge would dehydrate."
*Megan Jo Tetrick, age 12*

♻ *Printed on recycled stock*

# Associates of the Bayport Public Library Foundation

582 North Fourth Street
Bayport, Minnesota 55003

## What is it?

The purpose of the Associates' Program is to support the library. For over 90 years, the Bayport Public Library has served the community. This program offers you an opportunity to give something back. By becoming an Associate, you can be actively involved in the future of the Library.

The Associates' Program is a part of the Bayport Public Library Foundation. Founded in 1990, the Foundation provides supplemental assistance for programs and services of the library.

## Why do we need it?

For the past several years, income from local property tax dollars has not been sufficient to pay 100 percent of the Library's operating budget. In 1996, about two-thirds of the budget was funded by local property tax. The remaining one-third was generated through donations and miscellaneous revenues.

The Library Foundation is a critical element in helping to attract additional funding to the Library. The Associates' Program allows broader participation by the community and everyone who uses the Library.

## Who can join

Anyone with an interest in maintaining the quality of services and programs of the Bayport Public Library may become a Library Associate.

## How to join

Use the enclosed envelope to indicate your membership status.

## Membership benefits

As a Bayport Public Library Associate you will:

- Demonstrate concern for your community
- Receive a newsletter
- Participate in special events
- Receive an invitation to attend the Foundation's annual meeting in May

"Whatever the costs of our libraries, the price is cheap compared to that of an ignorant nation."
Walter Cronkite

# When the going gets tough, the tough get going... to the library!

In this challenging economy there is no better resource for learning and entertainment than the Saint Paul Public Library.  While it continues to be your favorite place for books, movies and music, it has evolved into THE place for early literacy, homework help, technology training and workforce development.

**The Library needs your support to ensure that the best resources are available at our libraries for everyone in Saint Paul to learn and grow.**

*Thanks to contributions like yours, the Saint Paul Public Library will continue to thrive!*

www.thefriends.org          www.sppl.org

**HONOR SOMEONE EXTRAORDINARY! CELEBRATE A SPECIAL EVENT! AND HELP BUY LIBRARY BOOKS...**

*Donations to The Friends of the Saint Paul Public Library in honor of someone special or to mark a signature event such as a birthday, graduation, anniversary or wedding, are added to the Book Endowment Fund. Income from the Endowment helps purchase thousands of Library books and other materials every year.*

**THE FRIENDS** OF THE SAINT PAUL PUBLIC LIBRARY

SEE INSIDE FOR DETAILS ON MAKING A TRIBUTE GIFT TO SUPPORT THE LIBRARY

For more information, contact:

**THE FRIENDS** OF THE SAINT PAUL PUBLIC LIBRARY

325 Cedar Street, Suite 555 • Saint Paul, MN 55101-1055
651-222-3242 • friends@thefriends.org • www.thefriends.org

**CELEBRATE AND HONOR SOMEONE IMPORTANT TO YOU WITH A GIFT TO THE BOOK ENDOWMENT FUND**

Please return completed form and payment to:
**The Friends of the Saint Paul Public Library**
**325 Cedar Street, Suite 555**
**Saint Paul, MN 55101-1055**
**Phone: 651-222-3242**
**Email: friends@thefriends.org**
**Web: www.thefriends.org**

Memorial gifts may also be made with a credit card by phone (651-222-3242) from 9 a.m. to 5 p.m., Monday through Friday, or online anytime (www.thefriends.org >> support the library >> tributes). For online gifts, please include your email address so you can be contacted for additional information, if needed.

*C*elebrate a birthday, anniversary, wedding or graduation. Honor someone special in your life, or someone who has done something special for you. Tribute gifts are an excellent way to recognize someone special or to mark a noteworthy event, as well as to help buy new books for Library patrons. Tribute donations are also recognized with the placement of a bookplate in a Library book, and listings in Friends publications.

There are two types of honor gifts through the Book Endowment Fund:

## ONE-TIME TRIBUTES

With one-time tribute gifts, for every $25 donated, one bookplate inscribed with the name of the person being honored, and if desired, the name of the donor, is placed in a newly purchased book at the Library.

## LONG-LASTING TRIBUTES

Gifts of $500 or more endow the purchase of a book each year in perpetuity. For every $500 donated, special wording on a bookplate – acknowledging the extraordinary effort you have made to honor a friend or relative – is placed annually in a newly purchased Library book.

*Gifts to help buy Library books through the Book Endowment Fund may also be made to remember a departed loved one. To receive a "Memorial" brochure, or for additional information about The Friends' Book Endowment Fund and honor/memorial gifts in support of the Saint Paul Public Library, please contact The Friends' office at 651-222-3242 or friends@thefriends.org.*

*Honor someone important to you with a gift to the Book Endowment Fund*

Tribute gifts to The Friends of the Saint Paul Public Library are added to a Book Endowment Fund. Income from this Fund is used solely to buy books and materials at the Saint Paul Public Library, and every year, thousands of new Library books are purchased.

## GIFT DETAILS

PLEASE COMPLETE THE FOLLOWING:

This gift is in honor of: _____

If the gift is in honor of a special event or occasion, please tell us how you would like the event recognized on the bookplate (for example, "In honor of Grandma's 75th birthday," or "In celebration of the college graduation of our nephew Mark"): _____

☐ This is a one-time gift of $_____
   *(One bookplate is placed in a Library book for each $25 donated)*

☐ This is a gift in perpetuity of $_____
   *($500 minimum – One bookplate is placed in a Library book every year in perpetuity for every $500 donated)*

Donor Name(s): _____

Address: _____

City _____ State _____ Zip _____

Donor Daytime Phone: (____) _____

Donor Email: _____

Please include my name as listed above as a donor on the bookplate(s):
☐ Yes   ☐ No

Please include my name as a memorial donor in Friends publications:
☐ Yes   ☐ No

We are pleased to notify other family or friends of your tribute. If you would like the honoree or someone else notified, please complete the following:

Recipient Name: _____

Address: _____

City _____ State _____ Zip _____

☐ My check (payable to The Friends of the Saint Paul Public Library) is enclosed

☐ Please charge my: __ Visa __ MasterCard __ Discover __ AmEx

Name on card: _____

Card number: _____

Expiration date: _____ CVV _____

Signature: _____

*Your generous contribution in honor of a friend or relative is tax deductible to the full extent allowed by law. A receipt for your gift will be mailed to you.*

**THANK YOU for supporting the Saint Paul Public Library.**

325 Cedar Street, Suite 555 • Saint Paul, MN 55101-1055
(651) 222-3242 • Fax (651) 222-1988 • friends@thefriends.org • **www.thefriends.org**

All you need is love...

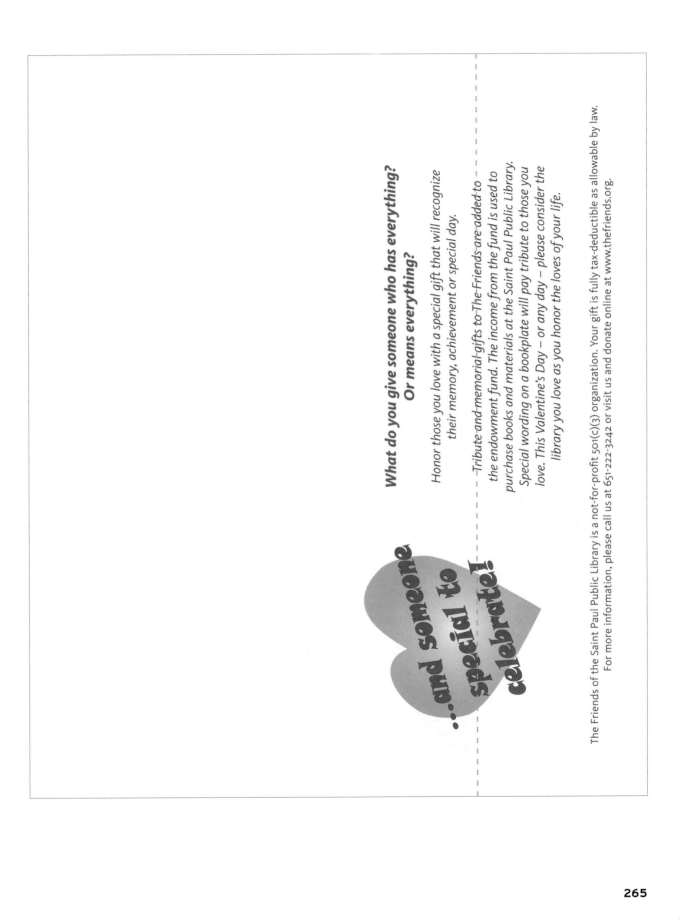

**What do you give someone who has everything?
Or means everything?**

*Honor those you love with a special gift that will recognize their memory, achievement or special day.*

*Tribute and memorial gifts to The Friends are added to the endowment fund. The income from the fund is used to purchase books and materials at the Saint Paul Public Library. Special wording on a bookplate will pay tribute to those you love. This Valentine's Day – or any day – please consider the library you love as you honor the loves of your life.*

. . . and someone special to celebrate!

The Friends of the Saint Paul Public Library is a not-for-profit 501(c)(3) organization. Your gift is fully tax-deductible as allowable by law. For more information, please call us at 651-222-3242 or visit us and donate online at www.thefriends.org.

THE FRIENDS OF THE SAINT PAUL PUBLIC LIBRARY

325 Cedar Street, Suite 555
Saint Paul, MN 55101-1088
www.thefriends.org

What do you give
the person who
has everything?
– Or means
everything?

REMEMBER A LOVED ONE AND HELP BUY LIBRARY BOOKS

Donations to The Friends of the Saint Paul Public Library in memory of someone special are added to the Book Endowment Fund. Income from the Endowment helps purchase thousands of Library books and other materials every year.

SEE INSIDE FOR DETAILS ON MAKING A MEMORIAL GIFT TO SUPPORT THE LIBRARY

THE FRIENDS OF THE SAINT PAUL PUBLIC LIBRARY

For more information, contact:

THE FRIENDS OF THE SAINT PAUL PUBLIC LIBRARY

325 Cedar Street, Suite 555 • Saint Paul, MN  55101-1055
651-222-3242 • friends@thefriends.org • www.thefriends.org

CELEBRATE THE MEMORY OF SOMEONE IMPORTANT TO YOU WITH A GIFT TO THE BOOK ENDOWMENT FUND

Please return completed form and payment to:

**The Friends of the Saint Paul Public Library**
**325 Cedar Street, Suite 555**
**Saint Paul, MN  55101-1055**
**Phone: 651-222-3242**
**Email: friends@thefriends.org**
**Web: www.thefriends.org**

Memorial gifts may also be made with a credit card by phone (651-222-3242) from 9 a.m. to 5 p.m., Monday through Friday, or online anytime (www.thefriends.org >> support the library >> memorials). For online gifts, please include your email address so you can be contacted for additional information, if needed.

*R**emember a loved one** with a gift to support book purchases at the Saint Paul Public Library. Memorial gifts are an excellent way to pay tribute to a departed relative or friend, as well as to help buy new books for Library patrons. Memorial donations are also recognized with the placement of a bookplate in a Library book, and listings in Friends publications.

There are two types of memorial gifts through the Book Endowment Fund:

## ONE-TIME MEMORIALS

With one-time memorial gifts, for every $25 donated, one bookplate inscribed with the name of the person being remembered, and if desired, the name of the donor, is placed in a newly purchased book at the Library.

## LONG-LASTING MEMORIALS

Gifts of $500 or more endow the purchase of a book each year in perpetuity. For every $500 donated, special wording on a bookplate – acknowledging the extraordinary effort you have made to commemorate a loved one – is placed annually in a newly purchased Library book.

*Gifts to help buy Library books through the Book Endowment Fund may also be made to pay tribute to someone special, or to mark a noteworthy occasion such as an anniversary, birthday, wedding or graduation. To receive a "Tribute" brochure, or for additional information about The Friends' Book Endowment Fund or larger memorial/tribute gifts in support of the Saint Paul Public Library, please contact The Friends' office at 651-222-3242 or friends@thefriends.org.*

*Celebrate the memory of someone important to you with a gift to the Book Endowment Fund.*

Memorial gifts to The Friends of the Saint Paul Public Library are added to a Book Endowment Fund. Income from this Fund is used to buy books and materials at the Saint Paul Public Library, and every year, thousands of new Library books are purchased through this endowment.

## GIFT DETAILS

PLEASE COMPLETE THE FOLLOWING:

This gift is in memory of:

_____

☐ This is a one-time gift of $_____
 *(One bookplate is placed in a Library book for each $25 donated)*

☐ This is a gift in perpetuity of $_____
 *($500 minimum – One bookplate is placed in a Library book every year in perpetuity for every $500 donated)*

Donor Name(s): _____

Address: _____

City _____ State _____ Zip _____

Donor Daytime Phone: ( )_____

Donor Email: _____

Please include my name as listed above as a donor on the bookplate(s):

☐ Yes   ☐ No

Please include my name as a memorial donor in Friends publications:

☐ Yes   ☐ No

We are pleased to notify other family or friends of your memorial. If you would like someone notified, please complete the following:

Recipient Name: _____

Address: _____

City _____ State _____ Zip _____

☐ My check (payable to The Friends of the Saint Paul Public Library) is enclosed

☐ Please charge my:  __ Visa  __ MasterCard  __ Discover  __ AmEx

Name on card: _____

Card number: _____

Expiration date: _____ CVV _____

Signature: _____

Your generous memorial contribution is tax deductible to the full extent allowed by law.  A receipt for your gift will be mailed to you.

*THANK YOU for supporting the Saint Paul Public Library.*

# Are you ready for the next step?

Please complete the form below and send it to us. We would be delighted to discuss the various options that are available and the wide variety of ways you can make a lasting gift to The Friends to help support the Saint Paul Public Library. We will call you to discuss your giving plan. Thank you!

Name(s) _____

Address _____

City/State/Zip _____

Phone_____

Email_____

❏ Please send me information about including The Friends in my will.

❏ I want to name The Friends as a beneficiary of all or part of my life insurance or retirement plan.

❏ I wish to make a planned gift to honor a loved one.

❏ I'm interested in making a deferred gift such as a charitable trust or gift annuity.

❏ I would like to create an endowment fund.

❏ I have already included The Friends in my estate plan and would like more information on the Briggs Circle.

Once you decide to make a gift, you may use the following language in your will:

*I give to The Friends of the Saint Paul Public Library, 325 Cedar Street, Suite 555, Saint Paul, MN 55101, _____ percent of my residuary estate (or, the sum of $_____, or a description of the property, securities, etc.) for its endowment funds.*

# Count me in!

Have you already included The Friends in your estate plans? Let us know so that we may include you in **The John and Myrtle Briggs Circle.** The Briggs Circle is composed of individuals who have chosen to make a lasting commitment to The Friends with a provision in their will or estate plan.

For additional information, please contact Liz Boyd, Planned Giving Officer, at 651-222-3242 or email Liz@thefriends.org.

**THE FRIENDS OF THE SAINT PAUL PUBLIC LIBRARY**
325 Cedar Street, Suite 555 • Saint Paul, MN 55101
651-222-3242 • Fax: 651-222-1988 • www.thefriends.org

## Make a Planned Gift Today to Build the Library of Tomorrow!

THE
**FRIENDS**
OF THE **SAINT PAUL**
**PUBLIC LIBRARY**

## What is Planned Giving?

*Planned giving is any deferred gift intended to benefit the future of The Friends of the Saint Paul Public Library.  There are a variety of financial arrangements that will allow you to make a planned gift to The Friends.*

- **Bequest in Your Will**
  You may make a bequest of:
  - cash
  - stocks and bonds
  - real estate
  - personal property
  - a percentage of your estate.

- **Life Insurance**
  You may designate The Friends as beneficiary on your insurance policy or transfer the policy outright.

- **Individual Retirement Accounts**
  You may designate The Friends as beneficiary of all or a portion of your account.

- **Trusts**
  A trust may be established to benefit The Friends now or at a later time.

- **Annuities**
  You may make an outright gift to The Friends and receive annuity payments until a specified time in the future.

## Restricted or Unrestricted?

Unrestricted gifts allow The Friends to build endowment funds and respond to the changing needs of the Library. Restricted gifts may be accepted if they are consistent with the mission of The Friends of the Saint Paul Public Library.

**THE FRIENDS OF THE SAINT PAUL PUBLIC LIBRARY**

## Who can leave a legacy?

Contrary to popular belief, you do not have to be wealthy to leave a meaningful legacy.  Anyone can make a planned gift regardless of the dollar value of one's estate.

## How will *my* gift make a difference?

Throughout the years, the Saint Paul Public Library has benefited greatly from planned gifts established by individuals.  Through their generosity, The Friends has provided:

- funding for tens of thousands of library books and materials;
- free, award-winning literary and music programs;
- support for renovating and constructing new library buildings; and,
- community outreach programs.

Make a planned gift to The Friends today, and you will provide for the future of the Saint Paul Public Library.

*The Friends of the Saint Paul Public Library is a private, nonprofit, membership organization established in 1945 to support the Saint Paul Public Library.*

## Our Mission

The Friends expands the Library's capacity to serve Saint Paul's many communities.  Our mission is:

- To increase the use of the Library through public awareness and cultural programming;
- To advocate for strong public funding of the Library; and
- To provide private funding to enhance Library services.

**RBC Wealth Management™**
presents:

## Opus & Olives
### Mark your calendar: October 9, 2011.
### For email updates, visit us online at www.thefriends.org.

*Proceeds from the event benefit The Friends of the Saint Paul Public Library and literacy programs of the Pioneer Press. For tickets, visit us online or call 651-222-3242. To learn about sponsorship opportunities, please call 651-366-6492.*

Make a date with your friends to join us for an evening of great food and drinks and wonderful authors including this year's emcee, **Frank Delaney.** A guest author back in 2007, we enjoyed the charming and erudite Delaney so much that we asked him back as emcee. Two of four additional authors are signed, including National Book Award-finalist, **Erik Larson,** and international bestseller and library advocate, **Karin Slaughter!** Watch for updates in the *Pioneer Press,* on Twitter and Facebook, or sign up for email updates on The Friends' website: www.thefriends.org.

**THE FRIENDS OF THE SAINT PAUL PUBLIC LIBRARY**

325 Cedar Street, Suite 555
Saint Paul, MN 55101-1055
*www.thefriends.org*

PRESENTING SPONSOR

RBC Wealth Management™

**RBC**

HOST:

**THE FRIENDS** OF THE SAINT PAUL PUBLIC LIBRARY

CO-HOST & MEDIA SPONSOR:

**PIONEER PRESS** TwinCities•com

BESTSELLER PARTNERS:

**DELTA**

Hubbard Broadcasting, Inc., and the Hubbard Broadcasting Foundation

**TRAVELERS**

RECOMMENDED READ PARTNERS:

**HMS** HOST

**MAIRS AND POWER, INC.** INVESTMENT COUNSEL

**MGM** Wine & Spirits of East Saint Paul and Woodbury

**Vanguard Travel** Unlimited →

**Xcel Energy** RESPONSIBLE BY NATURE™

ADDITIONAL SPONSORS:

Guy Carpenter & Co., LLC
Legacy Wealth
Metropolitan State University Foundation
Moore, Costello & Hart, PLLP
Morgan Stanley Smith Barney – The Waterbury Group
Random House, Inc.

BankCherokee
Bearance Management Group
Bremer Bank
Cuningham Group
Ergodyne
Frauenshuh HealthCare Real Estate Solutions
Goff Public

Robins, Kaplan, Miller & Ciresi, LLP
St. Paul Radiology Foundation
UBS Financial Services, Inc.
Wellington Management, Inc.
Western Bank
Wilkerson Associates
Winthrop & Weinstine

A portion of book sales contributed by Common Good Books.

Printing support provided by Modern Press and Xcel Energy.

Opus & Olives 2011 – The Friends of the Saint Paul Public Library 651-222-3242 • www.thefriends.org

**OPUS & OLIVES**
Fine Print & Fine Food

RBC Wealth Management™ presents the eighth annual

## Opus & Olives
### Fine Print & Fine Food
### Sunday, October 9, 2011

**Crowne Plaza Hotel - Saint Paul Riverfront**
**11 East Kellogg Boulevard**

**5:00 p.m.   Autograph Reception and Book Sales**

**6:15 p.m.   Dinner & Author Program**

**9:00 p.m.   Delta Air Lines Raffle** – *With only 400 tickets to be sold, you'll need to act fast to get in on this year's exciting raffle! Winner need not be present.*

*Complimentary valet parking available.*
*Additional autographing and book sales will follow the*
*author program. Please reply by September 29, 2011.*
*Cocktail or business attire suggested.*

---

**Save time at the event and pre-order your book selections!**

**Opus & Olives bookseller, Common Good Books, will have them packaged and ready for you to pick up and get autographed. Call 651-225-8989 to place your order from the authors' latest titles and backlist.**

Opus & Olives is a fundraising event hosted by – and supporting the work of – The Friends of the Saint Paul Public Library and local literacy projects of the *Pioneer Press*.

The Friends is a 501(c)(3) nonprofit organization whose mission is to increase the use of the Library; to advocate for strong public funding of the Library; and to provide private funding to enhance Library services.

For income tax purposes, all but $50 per ticket is tax-deductible to the full extent of the law.

## Master of Ceremonies:
### Frank Delaney
*The Matchmaker of Kenmare*

## Featured Authors:
### Mitchell Zuckoff
*Lost in Shangri-La: A True Story of Survival, Adventure and the Most Incredible Rescue Mission of World War II*

### Karin Slaughter
*Fallen*

### Amy Waldman
*The Submission*

### Erik Larson
*In the Garden of Beasts: Love, Terror, and an American Family in Hitler's Berlin*

BookMarks™ — Book Art In Johnson County

# BookMarks Auction

## Thursday, November 10, 2011

5:30 pm–7:30 pm. Live auction at 6:30 pm.
Coralville Center for the Performing Arts, 1301 5th St., Coralville, Iowa

Bring this invitation for free admission with a guest! Enjoy drinks and light refreshments.

**RSVP by November 5, 2011, to info@cityofliterature.org or 319.887.6100**

## See them before they go!

Our twenty-eight delightful, bigger-than-life BookMarks statues will be on public display around the area until the week of October 24th. Statues that have not already been purchased by their sponsors will be offered to the highest bidders at the live and silent auctions. Proceeds will benefit the Iowa City UNESCO City of Literature, and the public libraries of Coralville, Iowa City, and North Liberty.

Auctioneer: Mark Sharpless, Sharpless Auctions, Iowa City.
**Please note: $1,000.00 is the starting bid for the live and silent auctions.**

## Purchase a BookMark and donate it!

If yours is not the best permanent home for one of these unique artworks, please consider purchasing a BookMark and donating it to a local school or non-profit organization.

**The following schools would be delighted by the donation:**
City High School, Regina Elementary & High School, South East Junior High, West High School, and Garner, Kirkwood, Lemme, Lincoln, Lucas, Mann, Penn, Shimek, Twain, Weber, and Wood Elementary Schools.

**BOOK**MARKS™
BOOK ART IN JOHNSON COUNTY
June–October 2011

**To see them before they go, visit www.bookmarksiowa.org and download the map to all 28 statues.**

# about the authors

So you think you can't write a book by committee? Think again! *Beyond Book Sales: The Complete Guide to Raising Real Money for Your Library* was written by a committee of six individuals, all of them experts with fifty collective years of experience in library fund-raising. Each author wrote chapters that focused on his or her areas of expertise, and every chapter was edited by the committee as a whole and finally by the book's editor.

Each author is a consultant with Library Strategies, a consulting group of the nationally recognized Friends of the Saint Paul Public Library. The lead author and primary editor is **Susan Dowd,** Capital Campaign Coordinator, Special Projects Coordinator, and a librarian. **Liz Boyd** is Director of Individual and Planned Giving. **Sue Hall** is the Coordinator of Library Strategies and "Opus & Olives," The Friends' major fund-raising event. **Ann McKinnon** is Director of Communications and Marketing. **Wendy Moylan** is Director of Institutional Relations. **Peter Pearson** is the President of The Friends of the Saint Paul Public Library and Lead Consultant for Library Strategies.

To learn more about Library Strategies go to: www.librarystrategiesconsulting .org, or visit The Friends of the Saint Paul Public Library website at: www.thefriends .org.

# index